April 17–19, 2012
Beijing, China

**Association for
Computing Machinery**

Advancing Computing as a Science & Profession

HiCoNS'12

Proceedings of the 1st ACM International Conference on

High Confidence Networked Systems

Sponsored by:
ACM SIGBED

Supported by:
TRUST

**Association for
Computing Machinery**

Advancing Computing as a Science & Profession

The Association for Computing Machinery
2 Penn Plaza, Suite 701
New York, New York 10121-0701

ISBN: 978-1-4503-1263-9

Additional copies may be ordered prepaid from:

ACM Order Department
PO Box 30777
New York, NY 10087-0777, USA

Phone: 1-800-342-6626 (USA and Canada)
+1-212-626-0500 (Global)
Fax: +1-212-944-1318
E-mail: acmhelp@acm.org
Hours of Operation: 8:30 am – 4:30 pm ET

ACM Order Number: 4771201

Printed in the USA

General Chairs' Welcome

It is our great pleasure to welcome you to the *2012 1ˢᵗ ACM International Conference on High Confidence Networked Systems (HiCoNS'12)* as part of CPSWeek 2012. HiCoNS aims to bring together novel concepts and theories that can help in the development of the science of high confidence networked systems, in particular those considered cyber-physical systems (CPS). The conference will focus on system theoretic approaches to address fundamental challenges to increase the confidence of networked CPS by making them more secure, dependable, and trustworthy. An emphasis will be the control and verification challenges arising as a result of complex interdependencies between networked systems, in particular those at the intersection of cyber and physical areas. In doing so, the conference aims to advance the development of principled approaches to high confidence networked CPS.

This year's inaugural conference establishes what we hope will be a premier venue for showcasing research focused on improving the confidence of cyber-physical systems, in particular modern control technologies based on embedded computers and networked systems that monitor and control large-scale physical processes.

The conference technical program is exceptionally strong and we were pleased with the interest from so many authors who submitted to the conference. We would like to thank the Program Committee Co-Chairs Saurabh Amin and Gabor Karsai for their efforts to produce the conference program and the entire Program Committee who worked very hard in reviewing papers and providing feedback to the authors.

We also received significant support and guidance from the CPSWeek 2012 Steering Committee and we would like to especially thank CPSWeek 2012 General Chair Prof. Wei Zhao and his staff for their assistance with the overall organization, coordination, and local arrangements.

Finally, we would like to thank conference sponsor the ACM Special Interest Group on Embedded Systems (ACM SIGBED) and conference organizer the Team for Research in Ubiquitous Secure Technology (TRUST), a National Science Foundation Science & Technology Center. Putting together *HiCoNS'12* was truly a team effort!

We hope that you will find this program interesting and thought-provoking and that the conference will provide you with a valuable opportunity to share ideas with other researchers and practitioners from institutions around the world.

S. Shankar Sastry
HiCoNS'12 General Chair
University of California, Berkeley, USA

Tamer Başar
HiCoNS'12 General Chair
University of Illinois at Urbana-Champaign, USA

Program Committee Chairs' Welcome

It is our great pleasure to welcome you to the *2012 1st ACM International Conference on High Confidence Networked Systems (HiCoNS'12)* as part of CPSWeek 2012. HiCoNS aims to foster collaborations between researchers from the fields of control and systems theory, embedded systems, game theory, software verification, formal methods, and computer security who are addressing various aspects of resilience of cyber-physical systems (CPS). HiCoNS was established after growing interest and enthusiasm that was created by the *First Workshop on Secure Control Systems (SCS)* at CPSWeek 2010 and the *Workshop on the Foundations of Dependable and Secure Cyber-Physical Systems (FDSCPS)* at CPSWeek 2011.

This year's conference aimed to present novel research, development, and experimentation addressing the security, robustness, and reliability of cyber-physical systems that govern the operation of critical infrastructures such as power transmission, water distribution, transportation, healthcare, building automation, and many more.

The use of Internet-connected devices and commodity IT solutions and the malicious intents of hackers and cybercriminals have made these technologies more vulnerable. Despite attempts to develop guidelines for the design and operation of systems via security policies, much remains to be done to achieve a principled, science-based approach to enhance security, trustworthiness, and dependability of networked cyber-physical systems. The technical program of HiCoNS'12 will present theories and methodologies from such areas as fault-tolerant and networked control systems, game theory for multi-agent dynamics in uncertain environments, and learning and verification theory for secure and trustworthy cyber-physical systems. The technical program includes sessions focused on Resilient Networks, Security Games, Attack Diagnosis, and Security Experimentation. During these sessions, oral presentations will cover both recent research results as well as new directions for future research and development. In addition, the program includes invited talks and panel discussions on emerging topics in resilience of CPS.

We would like to thank our colleagues on the Program Committee who both submitted papers and expended a significant amount of time and energy in reviewing papers and formulating constructive comments and suggestions to the authors.

We hope conference attendees find the program as informative and engaging as we do and that these proceedings will serve as a valuable reference for security researchers and developers.

Saurabh Amin
HiCoNS'12 Program Chair
Massachusetts Institute of Technology, USA

Gabor Karsai
HiCoNS'12 Program Chair
Vanderbilt University, USA

Table of Contents

HiCoNS 2012 Conference Organization vi

Session 1: Resilient Networks

- **Consensus of Multi-Agent Networks in the Presence of Adversaries Using Only Local Information** 1
  Heath J. LeBlanc, Haotian Zhang, Shreyas Sundaram *(University of Waterloo)*,
  Xenofon Koutsoukos *(Vanderbilt University)*

- **HMM-Based Characterization of Channel Behavior for Networked Control Systems** 11
  Jian Chang, Krishna K. Venkatasubramanian, Chinwendu Enyioha, Shreyas Sundaram,
  George J. Pappas, Insup Lee *(University of Pennsylvania)*

- **Coordinated Variable Structure Switching in Smart Power Systems: Attacks and Mitigation** 21
  Shan Liu, Deepa Kundur, Takis Zourntos, Karen Butler-Purry *(Texas A&M University)*

Session 2: Security Games

- **Leader Selection Games under Link Noise Injection Attacks** 31
  Andrew Clark, Linda Bushnell, Radha Poovendran *(University of Washington)*

- **A Dynamic Game-Theoretic Approach to Resilient Control System Design for Cascading Failures** 41
  Quanyan Zhu, Tamer Başar *(University of Illinois at Urbana-Champaign)*

Session 3: Attack Diagnosis

- **Integrity Attacks on Cyber-Physical Systems** 47
  Yilin Mo, Bruno Sinopoli *(Carnegie Mellon University)*

- **Attack Models and Scenarios for Networked Control Systems** 55
  André Teixeira, Daniel Pérez, Henrik Sandberg, Karl H. Johansson *(KTH Royal Institute of Technology)*

- **Distributed Detection and Isolation of Topology Attacks in Power Networks** 65
  James Weimer *(KTH Royal Institutute of Technology)*, Soummya Kar *(Carnegie Mellon University)*,
  Karl Henrik Johansson *(KTH Royal Institute of Technology)*

Session 4: Security Experimentation

- **NCS Security Experimentation using DETER** 73
  Alefiya Hussain *(University of Southern California)*, Saurabh Amin *(Massachusetts Institute of Technology)*

- **Integrated Simulation and Emulation Platform for Cyber-Physical System Security Experimentation** 81
  Wei Yan, Yuan Xue, Xiaowei Li, Jiannian Weng *(Vanderbilt University)*,
  Timothy Busch *(The State University of New York - Institute of Technology)*,
  Janos Sztipanovits *(Vanderbilt University)*

Author Index 89

HiCoNS 2012 Conference Organization

General Chairs: S. Shankar Sastry *(University of California, Berkeley, USA)*

Tamer Başar *(University of Illinois at Urbana-Champaign, USA)*

Program Chairs: Saurabh Amin *(Massachusetts Institute of Technology, USA)*

Gabor Karsai *(Vanderbilt University, USA)*

Publicity Chair: Larry Rohrbough *(University of California, Berkeley, USA)*

Program Committee: Tansu Alpcan *(University of Melbourne, Australia)*

John Baras *(University of Maryland, USA)*

Prabir Barooah *(University of Florida, USA)*

Alvaro Cárdenas *(Fujitsu Laboratories of America, USA)*

Emilio Frazzoli *(Massachusetts Institute of Technology, USA)*

Ian Hiskens *(University of Michigan, USA)*

Naira Hovakimyan *(University of Illinois at Urbana-Champaign, USA)*

Karl Henrik Johansson *(Royal Institute of Technology (KTH), Sweden)*

Xenofon Koutsoukos *(Vanderbilt University, USA)*

Deepa Kundur *(Texas A&M University, USA)*

Cedric Langbort *(University of Illinois at Urbana-Champaign, USA)*

Brad Martin *(National Security Agency, USA)*

George Pappas *(University of Pennsylvania, USA)*

Radha Poovendran *(University of Washington, USA)*

Henrik Sandberg *(Royal Institute of Technology (KTH), Sweden)*

William Sanders *(University of Illinois at Urbana-Champaign, USA)*

Galina Schwartz *(University of California, Berkeley, USA)*

Uday Shanbhag *(University of Illinois at Urbana-Champaign, USA)*

Bruno Sinopoli *(Carnegie Mellon University, USA)*

John Stankovic *(University of Virginia, USA)*

Shreyas Sundaram *(University of Waterloo, Canada)*

Janos Sztipanovits *(Vanderbilt University, USA)*

Paulo Tabuada *(University of California, Los Angeles, USA)*

Rahul Telang *(Carnegie Mellon University, USA)*

Stephen Wicker *(Cornell University, USA)*

Sponsor:

Supporter:

Consensus of Multi-Agent Networks in the Presence of Adversaries Using Only Local Information

Heath J. LeBlanc
Institute for Software
Integrated Systems
Dept. of Electrical Engineering
and Computer Science
Vanderbilt University
Nashville, TN, USA
heath.j.leblanc@vanderbilt.edu

Haotian Zhang
Department of Electrical and
Computer Engineering
University of Waterloo
Waterloo, ON, Canada
h223zhan@uwaterloo.ca

Shreyas Sundaram
Department of Electrical and
Computer Engineering
University of Waterloo
Waterloo, ON, Canada
ssundara@uwaterloo.ca

Xenofon Koutsoukos
Institute for Software
Integrated Systems
Dept. of Electrical Engineering
and Computer Science
Vanderbilt University
Nashville, TN, USA
xenofon.koutsoukos@vanderbilt.edu

ABSTRACT

This paper addresses the problem of resilient consensus in the presence of misbehaving nodes. Although it is typical to assume knowledge of at least some nonlocal information when studying secure and fault-tolerant consensus algorithms, this assumption is not suitable for large-scale dynamic networks. To remedy this, we emphasize the use of local strategies to deal with resilience to security breaches. We study a consensus protocol that uses only local information and we consider worst-case security breaches, where the compromised nodes have full knowledge of the network and the intentions of the other nodes. We provide necessary and sufficient conditions for the normal nodes to reach consensus despite the influence of the malicious nodes under different threat assumptions. These conditions are stated in terms of a novel graph-theoretic property referred to as *network robustness*.

Categories and Subject Descriptors

C.2.4 [**Computer-Communication Networks**]: Distributed Systems; H.1.1 [**Models and Principles**]: Systems and Information Theory—*General Systems Theory*

General Terms

Algorithms, Security, Theory

Keywords

Consensus, Multi-agent network, Resilience, Adversary

1. INTRODUCTION

The engineering community has witnessed a paradigm shift from centralized to distributed system design, propelled by advances in networking and low-cost, high performance embedded systems. In particular, this has led to significant interest in the design and analysis of *multi-agent networks*. A multi-agent network consists of a set of individuals called *agents*, or *nodes*, equipped with some means of sensing or communicating along with computational resources and possibly actuation. Through a medium, which is referred to as the *network*, the agents share information in order to achieve specific *group objectives*. Some examples of group objectives include consensus [22, 26], synchronization [6, 27], surveillance [5], and formation control [9]. In order for the group objectives to be achieved, *distributed algorithms* are used to coordinate the behavior of the agents.

There are several advantages to using multiple agents over a single one. First, the objective may be complex and challenging, or possibly even infeasible for a single agent to achieve. Second, employing many agents can provide robustness in the case of failures or faults. Third, networked multi-agent systems are flexible and can support reconfigurability. Finally, there are performance advantages that can be leveraged from multiple agents. For example, in surveillance and monitoring applications, a multi-agent network provides redundancy and increased fidelity of information [5, 14].

Along with the advantages come certain challenges. Perhaps the most fundamental challenge in the design of networked multi-agent systems is the restriction that the coordination algorithms use only *local information*, i.e., information obtained by the individual agent through sensor measurements, calculations, or communication with neighbors in the network. In this manner, the feedback control laws must be *distributed*.

A second challenge lies in the fact that not only is each agent typically a dynamical system, but the network itself is dynamic. This challenge arises because the agents may be mobile and the environment may be changing, thus giving rise to dynamic (or switching) networks. Since the distributed algorithms depend directly on the network, this additional source of dynamics can affect the stability and performance of the networked system.

An especially important challenge is that multi-agent networks, like all large-scale distributed systems, have many entry points for malicious attacks or intrusions. For the success of the group objective, it is important that the cooperative control algorithms are designed in such a way that they can withstand the compromise of a subset of the nodes and *still guarantee some notion of correct behavior at a minimum level of performance*. We refer to such a multi-agent network as being *resilient* to adversaries. Given the growing threat of malicious attacks in large-scale cyber-physical systems, this is an important and challenging problem [4].

One of the most fundamental group objectives is to reach consensus on a quantity of interest. This concept is deeply intuitive, yet imprecise. Hence, there are several variations on how consensus problems are defined. At one extreme, consensus may be *unconstrained*, and there is no restriction on the agreement quantity. In other cases, consensus may be *partially constrained* by some rule or prescribed to lie in a set of possible agreement values which are in some way reasonable to the problem at hand. At the other extreme, consensus may be *function constrained*, or χ-*constrained*, in which case the consensus value must satisfy a particular function of the initial values of the nodes [7, 28]. In all of these cases, it is important that consensus algorithms be *resilient* to various forms of uncertainty, whether the source of uncertainty is caused by implementation effects, faults, or security breaches.

The problem of reaching consensus resiliently in the presence of misbehaving nodes has been studied in distributed computing [15, 20], communication networks [11], and mobile robotics [1, 3, 8]. Among other things, it has been shown that given F Byzantine or malicious nodes, there exists a strategy for the misbehaving nodes to disrupt consensus if the network connectivity[1] is $2F$ or less. Conversely, if the network connectivity is at least $2F + 1$, then there exists strategies for the *normal* nodes to use that ensure consensus is reached [20, 23, 29]. However, these methods either require that normal nodes have at least some nonlocal information or assume that the network is *complete*, i.e., all-to-all communication or sensing [1, 3, 8, 15, 16]. Moreover, these algorithms tend to be computationally expensive. Therefore, there is a need for resilient consensus algorithms that are *low complexity* and *operate using only local information*.

Typically, an upper bound on the number of faults or threats in the network is assumed, i.e., at most F out of n nodes fail or are compromised. We refer to this *threat assumption*, or *scope of threat*, as the F-*total model*. In cases where it is preferable to make *no global assumptions*, we are interested in other threat assumptions that are strictly local. For example, whenever each node only assumes that at most F nodes in its *neighborhood* are compromised (but there is no other bound on the total number of compromised nodes), the scope of threat is F-*local*.

In addition to the *number* of misbehaving nodes, one can consider various *threat models* for the misbehaving nodes; examples include *non-colluding* [23], *malicious* [16, 23, 29], or *Byzantine* [1, 15, 17, 32] nodes. Non-colluding nodes are unaware of the network topology, which other nodes are misbehaving, or the states of non-neighboring nodes. On the other hand, malicious nodes have full

knowledge of the networked system and therefore, worst case behavior must be assumed. The only difference between malicious and Byzantine nodes lies in their capacity for deceit. Malicious nodes are unable to convey different information to different neighbors in the network, whereas Byzantine nodes can.

Recently, we have studied resilient algorithms in the presence of misbehaving nodes. In [16], we introduce the Adversarial Robust Consensus Protocol (ARC-P) for consensus in the presence of malicious agents under the F-total model in continuous-time complete networks, with the agents also modeled in continuous time. The results of [16] are extended to both malicious and Byzantine threat models in networks with constrained information flow and dynamic network topology in [17]. In [34], we study general distributed algorithms with F-local malicious adversaries, encompassing ARC-P. In [17, 34], we show that traditional graph theoretic properties such as connectivity and degree, which have played a vital role in characterizing the resilience of distributed algorithms (see [20, 29]), are no longer adequate when the agents make purely local decisions (i.e., without knowing nonlocal aspects of the network topology). Instead, in [34] we introduce a novel topological property, referred to as *network robustness*, and show that this concept is highly effective at characterizing the ability of purely local algorithms to succeed. Separate sufficient and necessary conditions are provided in [34] for ARC-P to achieve resilient consensus in discrete time, and it is shown that the preferential attachment mechanism for generating complex networks produces robust graphs.

In this paper, we continue our study of resilient consensus in the presence of malicious nodes while using only local information. We are interested in partially constrained, asymptotic consensus in dynamic networks. To allow for multiple interpretations of the results, we formulate the problem in a setting common to discrete and continuous time for node dynamics and time-invariant or time-varying network topologies. We extend the Adversarial Robust Consensus Protocol (ARC-P) introduced in [16] to weighted networks. We then describe robust network topologies that are rich enough to enable resilience to malicious nodes, but are not too restrictive in terms of communication cost (i.e., number of communication links); in particular, we generalize the robustness property of [34]. Given these topological properties, we fully characterize the consensus behavior of the normal nodes using ARC-P under the F-total model of malicious nodes, and provide, for the first time, a necessary and sufficient condition for the algorithm to succeed. Additionally, for the F-local threat model, we provide improved separate necessary and sufficient conditions for asymptotic agreement of the normal nodes in the presence of malicious nodes.

The rest of the paper is organized as follows. Section 2 introduces the problem in a framework common to discrete and continuous time. Section 3 presents ARC-P in the unified framework. Section 4 motivates the need for robust network topologies and introduces the formal definitions. The main results are given in Section 5. A simulation example is presented in Section 6. Finally, some discussion is given in Section 7.

2. PROBLEM FORMULATION

Consider a time-varying network modeled by the (finite, simple) *directed graph*, or *digraph*, $\mathcal{D}[t] = \{\mathcal{V}, \mathcal{E}[t]\}$, where $\mathcal{V} = \{1, ..., n\}$ is the *node set* and $\mathcal{E}[t] \subset \mathcal{V} \times \mathcal{V}$ is the *directed edge set* at time t. The node set is partitioned into a set of *normal nodes* $\mathcal{N}$ and a set of *adversary nodes* $\mathcal{M}$. Note that $t \in \mathbb{R}_{\geq 0}$ for continuous time and $t \in \mathbb{Z}_{\geq 0}$ for discrete time. When we refer to both cases, we generically say *at time t*.

The time-varying topology of the network is governed by a piecewise constant switching signal $\sigma(\cdot)$, which is defined on $\mathbb{Z}_{\geq 0}$ for

---

[1]The network connectivity is defined as the smaller of the two following values: (i) the size of a minimal vertex cut and (ii) $n - 1$, where n is the number of nodes in the network.

discrete time and $\mathbb{R}_{\geq 0}$ for continuous time, and takes values in the set of all digraphs on n nodes. Let $\{\tau_k\}$, $k \in \mathbb{Z}_{\geq 0}$ denote the set of switching instances. For continuous time, we assume that there exists some constant $\tau \in \mathbb{R}_{>0}$ such that $\tau_{k+1} - \tau_k \geq \tau$ for all $k \geq 0$. In other words, $\sigma(\cdot)$ is subject to the *dwell time* τ.

Each directed edge $(j, i) \in \mathcal{E}[t]$ models *information flow* and indicates that node i can be influenced by (or receive information from) node j at time t. The set of *in-neighbors*, or just *neighbors*, of node i at time t is defined as $\mathcal{V}_i[t] = \{j \in \mathcal{V} : (j, i) \in \mathcal{E}[t]\}$ and the (in-)degree of i is denoted $d_i^{\text{in}}[t] = |\mathcal{V}_i[t]|$. Likewise, the set of *out-neighbors* of node i at time t is defined as $\mathcal{V}_i^{\text{out}}[t] = \{j \in \mathcal{V} : (i, j) \in \mathcal{E}[t]\}$. Because each node has access to its own state at time t, we also consider the *inclusive neighbors* of node i, denoted $\mathcal{J}_i[t] = \mathcal{V}_i[t] \cup \{i\}$. Note that time-invariant networks are represented simply by dropping the dependence on time t.

2.1 Update Model

Suppose that each node $i \in \mathcal{N}$ begins with some private value $x_i[0] \in \mathbb{R}$ (which could represent an opinion, vote, measurement, etc.). The nodes interact synchronously by conveying their value to (out-)neighbors in the network. Each normal node updates its own value over time according to a prescribed rule, which is modeled as

$$D[x_i[t]] = f_{i,\sigma(t)}(\{x_j[t]\}), \quad j \in \mathcal{J}_i[t], i \in \mathcal{N},$$

where $D[x_i[t]] = \dot{x}_i[t]$ is the *derivative operator* for continuous time and $D[x_i[t]] = x_i[t+1] - x_i[t]$ is the *forward difference operator* for discrete time. Each function $f_{i,\sigma(t)}(\cdot)$ can be arbitrary,[2] and may be different for each node, depending on its role in the network. These functions are designed *a priori* so that the normal nodes reach consensus. However, some of the nodes may not follow the prescribed strategy if they are compromised by an adversary. Such misbehaving nodes threaten the group objective, and it is important to design the $f_{i,\sigma(t)}(\cdot)$'s in such a way that the influence of such nodes can be eliminated or reduced without prior knowledge about their identities.

2.2 Threat Model

DEFINITION 1. *A node $k \in \mathcal{M}$ is said to be **malicious** if*

- *it is not normal (i.e., it does not follow the prescribed update model either for at least one time-step in discrete time, or for some time interval of nonzero Lebesgue measure in continuous time);*

- *it conveys the same value, $x_k[t]$, to each out-neighbor;*

- *(for continuous-time systems) its value trajectory, $x_k[t]$ $\forall t$, is a uniformly continuous function of time.*

A few remarks are in order concerning malicious nodes. First, each malicious node is allowed to be omniscient (i.e., it knows all other values and the full network topology; it is aware of the update rules $f_{i,\sigma(t)}(\cdot)$, $\forall i \in \mathcal{N}$; it knows which other nodes are adversaries; and it knows the plans of the other adversaries). The statement in the definition that the malicious nodes are not normal is intended to capture the idea that they do not apply the prescribed update rule for all time. The second assumption is intended as an assertion on the network realization. That is, if the network is realized through sensing or broadcast communication, it is assumed that the out-neighbors receive the same information. The third point is a technical assumption that applies only to malicious

---
[2]In continuous time, $f_{i,\sigma(t)}(\cdot)$ must satisfy appropriate assumptions to ensure existence of solutions.

nodes modeled in continuous time. Limited only by these assumptions, the malicious nodes are otherwise allowed to operate in an arbitrary (potentially worst case) manner.

2.3 Scope of Threats

To be more precise, we formally define the scope of the threats. While there are various stochastic models that could be used to formalize the threat assumptions, here we use a deterministic approach and consider upper bounds on the number of compromised nodes either in the network (F-total) or in each node's neighborhood (F-local).

DEFINITION 2 (F-TOTAL SET). *A set $\mathcal{S} \subset \mathcal{V}$ is F-**total** if it contains at most F nodes in the network, i.e., $|\mathcal{S}| \leq F$, $F \in \mathbb{Z}_{\geq 0}$.*

DEFINITION 3 (F-LOCAL SET). *A set $\mathcal{S} \subset \mathcal{V}$ is F-**local** if it contains at most F nodes in the neighborhood of the other nodes for all t, i.e., $|\mathcal{V}_i[t] \bigcap \mathcal{S}| \leq F$, $\forall i \in \mathcal{V} \setminus \mathcal{S}$, $F \in \mathbb{Z}_{\geq 0}$.*

It should be noted that because the network topology may be time-varying, the local properties defining an F-local set must hold at all time instances. These definitions facilitate the definitions of the scope of threat models.

DEFINITION 4. *A set of adversary nodes is F-**totally bounded** or F-**locally bounded** if it is an F-total set or F-local set, respectively. We refer to these threat scopes as the F-**total** and F-**local** models, respectively.*

F-totally bounded faults have been studied in distributed computing [15, 20, 32] and mobile robotics [1, 3, 8] for both stopping (or crash) failures and Byzantine failures. The F-locally bounded fault model has been studied in the context of fault-tolerant broadcasting [12, 24].

2.4 Resilient Asymptotic Consensus

Given the threat model and scope of threats, we formally define resilient asymptotic consensus. Let $M_{\mathcal{N}}[t]$ and $m_{\mathcal{N}}[t]$ be the *maximum* and *minimum* values of the normal nodes at time t, respectively.

DEFINITION 5 (RESILIENT ASYMPTOTIC CONSENSUS). *The normal nodes are said to achieve **resilient asymptotic consensus** in the presence of (a) F-totally bounded, or (b) F-locally bounded misbehaving nodes if $|x_i[t] - x_j[t]| \rightarrow 0$ as $t \rightarrow \infty$, for all $i, j \in \mathcal{N}$, the normal values converge to a point (i.e., the consensus value) for any choice of initial values, and the normal values remain in the interval $[m_{\mathcal{N}}[0], M_{\mathcal{N}}[0]]$ for all t,. Whenever the scope of threat is understood, we simply say that the normal nodes reach **asymptotic consensus**.*

The resilient asymptotic consensus problem has two important conditions. First, the normal nodes must reach asymptotic consensus in the presence of misbehaving nodes given a particular threat model (e.g., malicious node) and scope of threat (e.g., F-total). This is a condition on agreement. Additionally, it is required that the interval containing the initial values of the normal nodes is an invariant set for the normal nodes, and that the consensus value to which the consensus process converges lies within this interval. This condition is a validity or safety condition that constrains the consensus quantity.

3. CONSENSUS ALGORITHM

Linear consensus algorithms have attracted significant interest in recent years [22, 26], due to their applicability in a variety of contexts. In such strategies, at time t, each node senses or receives information from its neighbors, and changes its value according to

$$D[x_i[t]] = \sum_{j \in \mathcal{J}_i[t]} w_{ij}[t] x_j[t], \qquad (1)$$

where $w_{ij}[t]$ is the weight assigned to node j's value by node i at time t.

Different conditions have been reported in the literature to ensure asymptotic consensus is reached [13, 21, 25, 31, 33]. In discrete time, it is common to assume that there exists a constant $\alpha \in \mathbb{R}$, $0 < \alpha < 1$ such that all of the following conditions hold:[3]

- $w_{ij}[t] = 0$ whenever $j \notin \mathcal{J}_i[t], i \in \mathcal{N}, t \in \mathbb{Z}_{\geq 0}$;

- $w_{ij}[t] \geq \alpha, \forall j \in \mathcal{V}_i[t], i \in \mathcal{N}, t \in \mathbb{Z}_{\geq 0}$;

- $w_{ii}[t] \geq \alpha - 1, \forall i \in \mathcal{N}, t \in \mathbb{Z}_{\geq 0}$;

- $\sum_{j=1}^{n} w_{ij}[t] = 0, \forall i \in \mathcal{N}, t \in \mathbb{Z}_{\geq 0}$.

In continuous time there are similar conditions, except in this case the self-weights are given by

$$w_{ii}[t] = - \sum_{j \in \mathcal{V}_i[t]} w_{ij}[t], \quad \forall i \in \mathcal{N}, \forall t \in \mathbb{R}_{\geq 0}.$$

In this case, to make sure the weights are uniformly bounded, we additionally assume $\exists \beta \in \mathbb{R}_{>0}, \beta \geq \alpha$, such that $w_{ij}[t] \leq \beta$, for all $i, j \in \mathcal{N}$ and $t \in \mathbb{R}_{\geq 0}$. Similar to the discrete time case, the weights $w_{ij}[t]$ are zero precisely whenever $j \notin \mathcal{J}_i[t]$, and bounded below by α otherwise. Together, these conditions imply the analogue of the fourth condition above.

Given these conditions, a necessary and sufficient condition for reaching asymptotic consensus in time-invariant networks is that the digraph has a *rooted out-branching*, also called a *rooted directed spanning tree* [26]. The case of dynamic networks is not quite as straightforward. In this case, under the conditions stated above, a sufficient condition for reaching asymptotic consensus is that there exists a uniformly bounded sequence of contiguous time intervals such that the union of digraphs across each interval has a rooted out-branching [25]. Recently, a more general condition referred to as the *infinite flow property* has been shown to be both necessary and sufficient for asymptotic consensus for a class of discrete-time stochastic models [30]. Finally, the lower bound on the weights is needed because there are examples of asymptotically vanishing weights in which consensus is not reached [19].

In general, the problem of selecting the best weights in the linear update rule (1) is nontrivial, and the choice affects the rate of consensus. The problem of selecting the optimal weights (with respect to the speed of the consensus process) in time-invariant, discrete-time, bidirectional networks is addressed in [33] by formulating a semidefinite program (SDP). However, this SDP is solved at design time with global knowledge of the network topology. A simple choice of weights for discrete time systems that requires only local information is to let $w_{ij}[t] = 1/(1 + d_i^{\text{in}}[t])$ for $j \in \mathcal{V}_i[t]$ and $w_{ii}[t] = -d_i^{\text{in}}[t]/(1 + d_i^{\text{in}}[t])$. In continuous time, a simple choice is to let $w_{ij} \equiv 1$ for $j \in \mathcal{V}_i[t]$ and $w_{ii}[t] = -d_i^{\text{in}}[t]$.

One problem with the linear update given in (1) is that it is not resilient to misbehaving nodes. In fact, it was shown in [10,13] that a single 'leader' node can cause all agents to reach consensus on an arbitrary value of its choosing (potentially resulting in a dangerous situation in physical systems).

The Adversarial Robust Consensus Protocol (ARC-P) addresses this vulnerability of the linear update of (1) by a simple modification. Instead of trusting every neighbor by using every value in the update, the normal node first removes the extreme values from consideration in the update by effectively setting their weights (temporarily) to zero. It is shown in subsequent sections that this simple strategy provides resilience against malicious nodes in robust networks.

3.1 Description of ARC-P

At time t, each normal node i obtains the values of other nodes in its neighborhood. At most F of node i's neighbors may be malicious; however, node i is unsure of which neighbors may be compromised. To ensure that node i updates its value in a safe manner, it removes the extreme values with respect to its own value according to the following protocol.

1. At time t, each normal node i obtains the values of its neighbors, and forms a sorted list.

2. If there are less than F values strictly larger than its own value, $x_i[t]$, then normal node i removes all values that are strictly larger than its own. Otherwise, it removes precisely the largest F values in the sorted list (breaking ties arbitrarily). Likewise, if there are less than F values strictly smaller than its own value, then node i removes all values that are strictly smaller than its own. Otherwise, it removes precisely the smallest F values.

3. Let $\mathcal{R}_i[t]$ denote the set of nodes whose values were removed by normal node i in step 2 at time t. Each normal node i applies the update

$$D[x_i[t]] = \sum_{j \in \mathcal{J}_i[t] \setminus \mathcal{R}_i[t]} w_{ij}[t] x_j[t], \qquad (2)$$

where the weights $w_{ij}[t]$ satisfy the conditions stated above, but with $\mathcal{J}_i[t]$ replaced by $\mathcal{J}_i[t] \setminus \mathcal{R}_i[t]$.[4]

As a matter of terminology, we refer to the largest number of values that a node could throw away as the *parameter* of the algorithm. Above, the parameter of ARC-P with the F-local and F-total models is $2F$.

Observe that the set of nodes removed by normal node i, $\mathcal{R}_i[t]$, is possibly time-varying. Hence, even though the underlying network topology may be fixed, ARC-P effectively induces switching behavior, and can be viewed as the linear update of (1) with a specific rule for state-dependent switching (the rule given in step 2).

4. ROBUST NETWORK TOPOLOGIES

4.1 Network Robustness

In this section, we introduce *robust network topologies* that satisfy certain graph theoretic properties, which we refer to generically as *network robustness*. Network robustness formalizes the notion of sufficient redundancy of information flow to subsets of a network in a single hop. Therefore, this property holds promise to be effective for the study of resilient distributed algorithms that use

---

[3]The conditions on the weights are modified from what is reported in the literature to account for the forward difference operator. Accounting for this, the updated value of each node is formed as a convex combination of the neighboring values and its own value.

[4]In this case, a simple choice for the weights in discrete time is to let $w_{ij}[t] = 1/(1 + d_i^{\text{in}}[t] - |\mathcal{R}_i[t]|)$ for $j \in \mathcal{V}_i[t]$ and $w_{ii}[t] = (|\mathcal{R}_i[t]| - d_i^{\text{in}}[t])/(1 + d_i^{\text{in}}[t] - |\mathcal{R}_i[t]|)$. In continuous time, let $w_{ij} \equiv 1$ for $j \in \mathcal{V}_i[t]$ and $w_{ii}[t] = |\mathcal{R}_i[t]| - d_i^{\text{in}}[t]$.

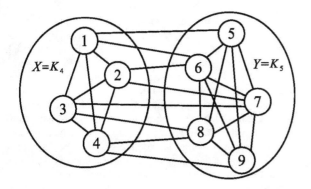

Figure 1: Example of a 5-connected graph satisfying Prop. 1 whenever $F = 2$.

only local information. In contrast, network connectivity formalizes the notion of sufficient redundancy of information flow across the network through independent paths. Due to the fact that each independent path may include multiple intermediate nodes, network connectivity is well-suited for studying resilient distributed algorithms that assume such nonlocal information is available (for example, by explicitly relaying information across multiple hops in the network [20], or by 'inverting' the dynamics on the network to recover the needed information [23, 29]). However, network connectivity is no longer an appropriate metric for an algorithm that uses purely local information, such as ARC-P. This is demonstrated by the following proposition [34].

PROPOSITION 1. *There exists a graph with connectivity $\kappa = \lfloor \frac{n}{2} \rfloor + F - 1$ in which ARC-P does not ensure asymptotic consensus.*

Figure 1 illustrates an example of this kind of graph with $n = 9$, $F = 2$, and $\kappa = 5$. In this graph, there are two cliques (complete subgraphs), $X = K_4$ and $Y = K_5$, where K_n is the complete graph on n nodes. Each node in X has exactly $F = 2$ neighbors in Y, and all but two nodes in Y have $F = 2$ neighbors in X (nodes 5 and 9 have only one neighbor in X, because otherwise a node in X would have more than $F = 2$ neighbors in Y). One can see that if the initial values of nodes in X and Y are $a \in \mathbb{R}$ and $b \in \mathbb{R}$, respectively, with $a \neq b$, then asymptotic consensus is not achieved whenever ARC-P is used with parameter $2F$ – even in the absence of misbehaving nodes. This is because each node views the values of its F neighbors from the opposing set as extreme, and removes all of these values from its list. The only remaining values for each node are from its own set, and thus no node ever changes its value.

The situation can be even worse in the more general case of digraphs. Examples of digraphs are illustrated in [17] that are $(n-1)$-connected and have minimum out-degree $n - 2$, yet ARC-P still cannot guarantee asymptotic consensus. Thus, even digraphs with a relatively large connectivity (or minimum out-degree) are not sufficient to guarantee consensus of the normal nodes, indicating the inadequacy of these traditional metrics to analyze the convergence properties of ARC-P. Taking a closer look at the graph in Fig. 1, we see that the reason for the failure of consensus is that no node has enough neighbors in the opposite set; this causes every node to throw away all useful information from outside of its set, and prevents consensus. Based on this intuition, the following properties, i.e., r-reachable sets and r-robustness, were introduced in [34].

DEFINITION 6 (r-REACHABLE SET). *Given a digraph $\mathcal{D}$ and a subset S of nodes of $\mathcal{D}$, we say S is an r-reachable set if $\exists i \in S$ such that $|\mathcal{V}_i \setminus S| \geq r$, where $r \in \mathbb{Z}_{\geq 0}$.*

A set S is r-reachable if it contains a node that has at least r neighbors outside of S. The parameter r quantifies the redundancy of information flow from nodes outside of S to *some* node inside S. Intuitively, the r-reachability property captures the idea that some node inside the set is influenced by a sufficiently large number of nodes from outside the set. The above reachability property pertains to a given set S; in order to generalize this notion of redundancy to the entire network, we introduce the following definition of r-robustness.

DEFINITION 7 (r-ROBUSTNESS). *A digraph $\mathcal{D} = \{\mathcal{V}, \mathcal{E}\}$ is r-robust if for every pair of nonempty, disjoint subsets of $\mathcal{V}$, at least one of the subsets is r-reachable.*

The reason that pairs of nonempty, disjoint subsets of nodes are considered in the definition of r-robustness can be seen in the example of Fig. 1. If either X or Y were 3-reachable ($r = F + 1 = 3$), then at least one node would be sufficiently influenced by a node outside of its set in order to drive it away from the values of its group, and thereby lead its group to the values of the other set. However, if there are misbehaving nodes in the network, then the situation becomes more complex. For example, consider the F-total model of malicious nodes, and consider two sets X and Y in the graph. Let s be the total number of nodes in these two sets that each have at least $F + 1$ neighbors outside their own set. If $s \leq F$, then simply by choosing these nodes to be malicious, the sets X and Y contain no normal nodes that bring in enough information from outside, and thus the system can be prevented from reaching consensus. This reasoning suggests a need to specify a minimum number of nodes that are sufficiently influenced from outside of their set (in this example, at least $F + 1$ nodes). This intuition leads to the following generalizations of r-reachability and r-robustness.

DEFINITION 8 ((r, s)-REACHABLE SET). *Given a digraph $\mathcal{D}$ and a subset of nodes S, we say that S is an (r, s)-reachable set if there are at least s nodes in S with at least r neighbors outside of S, where $r, s \in \mathbb{Z}_{\geq 0}$; i.e., given $\mathcal{X}_S = \{i \in S : |\mathcal{V}_i \setminus S| \geq r\}$, then $|\mathcal{X}_S| \geq s$.*

Observe that r-reachability is equivalent to $(r, 1)$-reachability; hence, (r, s)-reachability is a strict generalization of r-reachability. If a set S is (r, s)-reachable, we know there are at least s nodes in S with at least r neighbors outside of S. Thus, if S is (r, s)-reachable, then it is (r, s')-reachable, for $s' \leq s$. Also, it is clear that $s \leq |S|$ and all subsets of nodes of any digraph are $(r, 0)$-reachable. The additional specificity on the number of nodes with redundant information flow from outside of their set is useful for defining a more general notion of robustness.

DEFINITION 9 ((r, s)-ROBUSTNESS). *A digraph $\mathcal{D} = \{\mathcal{V}, \mathcal{E}\}$ is (r, s)-robust if for every pair of nonempty, disjoint subsets S_1 and S_2 of $\mathcal{V}$ such that S_1 is $(r, s_{r,1})$-reachable and S_2 is $(r, s_{r,2})$-reachable with $s_{r,1}$ and $s_{r,2}$ maximal (i.e., $s_{r,k} = |\mathcal{X}_{S_k}|$ where $\mathcal{X}_{S_k} = \{i \in S_k : |\mathcal{V}_i \setminus S_k| \geq r\}$ for $k \in \{1, 2\}$), then at least one of the following hold:*

(i) $s_{r,1} = |S_1|$;

(ii) $s_{r,2} = |S_2|$;

(iii) $s_{r,1} + s_{r,2} \geq s$.

A few remarks are in order with respect to this definition. The (r, s)-robustness property generally aims to capture the idea that "enough" nodes in the sets S_1 and S_2 have at least r neighbors outside of their respective sets, for all nonempty and disjoint $S_1, S_2 \subset$

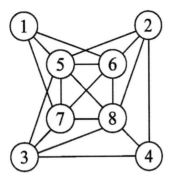

Figure 2: A 3-robust graph that is *not* (3,2)-robust.

$\mathcal{V}$. In order to specify what is meant by "enough" nodes, it is necessary to take the maximal $s_{r,k}$ for which $\mathcal{S}_k$ is $(r, s_{r,k})$-reachable with $k \in \{1, 2\}$ (since $\mathcal{S}_k$ is $(r, s'_{r,k})$-reachable for $s'_{r,k} \leq s_{r,k}$). Clearly, if $s_{r,k} = |\mathcal{S}_k|$ for either $k \in \{1, 2\}$, then *all* nodes in $\mathcal{S}_k$ have at least r neighbors outside of $\mathcal{S}_k$, in which case at least one of conditions (i) or (ii) is satisfied, and we say there are "enough" nodes. Alternatively, if there are at least s nodes with at least r neighbors outside of their respective sets in the union $\mathcal{S}_1 \cup \mathcal{S}_2$, then condition (iii) is satisfied, and we say there are "enough" nodes. The reason to have multiple interpretations of what constitutes "enough" nodes is to be able to state the property uniformly over all nonempty and disjoint pairs of subsets of nodes. Clearly, if $|\mathcal{S}_1 \cup \mathcal{S}_2| < s$, then condition (iii) cannot be satisfied. More generally, in many cases where $\min\{|\mathcal{S}_1|, |\mathcal{S}_2|\} < s$, it is also not possible to satisfy condition (iii); e.g., whenever $\mathcal{S}_1 \cup \mathcal{S}_2 = \mathcal{V}$ and $r \geq s$. On the other hand, for relatively large sets (i.e., $\min\{|\mathcal{S}_1|, |\mathcal{S}_2|\} \geq s$), conditions (i) and (ii) do imply condition (iii).

An important observation is that $(r, 1)$-robustness is equivalent to r-robustness. This holds because conditions $(i) - (iii)$ for $(r, 1)$-robustness collapse to the condition that at least one of $\mathcal{S}_1$ and $\mathcal{S}_2$ is r-reachable. In general, a digraph is (r, s')-robust if it is (r, s)-robust for $s' \leq s$; therefore, a digraph is r-robust whenever it is (r, s)-robust, for $s \geq 1$. The converse, however, is not true. Consider the graph in Fig. 2. This graph is 3-robust, but is not $(3, 2)$-robust. For example, let $\mathcal{S}_1 = \{1, 3, 5, 6, 7\}$ and $\mathcal{S}_2 = \{2, 4\}$. Thus, only node 2 has at least 3 nodes outside of its set, so all of the conditions $(i) - (iii)$ fail. Therefore, (r, s)-robustness is a strict generalization of r-robustness.

Next, consider again the example of Fig. 1. It can be shown that this graph is $(2, s)$-robust, for all $s \in \mathbb{Z}_{\geq 0}$. This follows because *all* nodes in at least one of the sets $\mathcal{S}_1$ and $\mathcal{S}_2$ have at least 2 neighbors outside of their set, for any nonempty and disjoint $\mathcal{S}_1, \mathcal{S}_2 \subset \mathcal{V}$. Therefore, condition (iii) in the definition *never* needs to hold true, and the definition is satisfied with $r = 2$ for all $s \in \mathbb{Z}_{\geq 0}$. It is rather atypical, in general, for digraphs to satisfy (r, s)-robustness for all $s \in \mathbb{Z}_{\geq 0}$; however, it can be the case for graphs with high connectivity and small diameter.

On the other hand, the graph in Fig. 1 is *not* 3-robust. This can be shown by selecting $\mathcal{S}_1 = X$ and $\mathcal{S}_2 = Y$. Note that an (r, s)-robust digraph is (r', s)-robust for $r' \leq r$. The question then arises, how does one compare relative robustness between digraphs? Clearly, if digraph $\mathcal{D}_1$ is (r_1, s_1)-robust and digraph $\mathcal{D}_2$ is (r_2, s_2)-robust with maximal r_k and s_k[5] for $k \in \{1, 2\}$, where $r_1 > r_2$ and $s_1 > s_2$, then one can conclude that $\mathcal{D}_1$ is more

robust than $\mathcal{D}_2$. However, in cases where $r_1 > r_2$ but $s_1 < s_2$, which digraph is more robust? For example, the graph of Fig. 1 is $(2, s)$-robust for all $s \in \mathbb{Z}_{\geq 0}$, but is not 3-robust, whereas the graph in Fig. 2 is 3-robust, but is not $(2,5)$-robust (e.g., let $\mathcal{S}_1 = \{1, 5, 6\}$ and $\mathcal{S}_2 = \{2, 3, 4\}$). In general, the r-robustness property takes precedence in the partial order that determines relative robustness, and the maximal s in (r, s)-robustness is used for finer grain partial ordering (i.e., ordering the robustness of two r-robust digraphs with the same value of r). Therefore, the graph in Fig. 2 is more robust than the graph of Fig. 1. Yet, the graph of Fig. 2 is only 3-connected, whereas the graph of Fig. 1 is 5-connected. Hence, it is possible that a digraph with *less* connectivity is *more* robust.

We demonstrate in Section 5 that the r-robustness property is useful for analyzing ARC-P with parameter $2F$ under the F-local model, and show that (r, s)-robustness is the key property for analyzing ARC-P with parameter $2F$ under the F-total model. More specifically, we show that $(F+1, F+1)$-robustness of the network is both necessary and sufficient for normal nodes using ARC-P with parameter $2F$ to achieve resilient asymptotic consensus whenever the scope of threat is F-total, the threat model is malicious, and the network is time-invariant. Likewise, we show that $(2F+1)$-robustness of the network is sufficient for ARC-P with parameter $2F$ to achieve resilient asymptotic consensus whenever the scope of threat is F-local.

4.2 Construction of Robust Digraphs

Note that robustness requires checking every possible nonempty disjoint pair of subsets of nodes in the digraph for certain conditions. Currently, we do not have a computationally efficient method to check whether these properties hold in arbitrary digraphs. However, in [34] it is shown that the common *preferential-attachment* model for complex networks (e.g., [2]) produces r-robust graphs, provided that a sufficient number of links are added to the network as new nodes are attached. In this subsection, we extend this construction to show that preferential attachment also leads to (r, s)-robust graphs.

THEOREM 1. *Let* $\mathcal{D} = \{\mathcal{V}, \mathcal{E}\}$ *be an* (r, s)-*robust digraph (with* $s \geq 1$*). Then the digraph* $\mathcal{D}' = \{\mathcal{V} \cup \{v_{new}\}, \mathcal{E} \cup \mathcal{E}_{new}\}$*, where* v_{new} *is a new vertex added to* $\mathcal{D}$ *and* $\mathcal{E}_{new}$ *is the directed edge set related to* v_{new}*, is* (r, s)-*robust if* $d^{in}_{v_{new}} \geq r + s - 1$*.*

The above result indicates that to construct an (r, s)-robust digraph with n nodes (where $n > r$), we can start with an (r, s)-robust digraph with relatively smaller order (such as a complete graph), and continually add new nodes with incoming edges from at least $r + s - 1$ nodes in the existing digraph. Note that this method does not specify *which* existing nodes should be chosen. The preferential-attachment model corresponds to the case when the nodes are selected with a probability proportional to the number of edges that they already have. This leads to the formation of so-called *scale-free* networks [2], and is cited as a plausible mechanism for the formation of many real-world complex networks. Theorem 1 indicates that a large class of scale-free networks are resilient to the threat models studied in this paper (provided the number of edges added in each round is sufficiently large when the network is forming).

For example, Fig. 3 illustrates a $(3, 2)$-robust graph constructed using the preferential attachment model starting with the complete graph on 5 nodes, K_5 (which is also $(3,3)$-robust and is the only $(3,2)$-robust digraph on 5 nodes), and with 4 new edges added to each new node. Note that this graph is also 4-robust, which could *not* be predicted from Theorem 1 since K_5 is not 4-robust. Therefore, it is actually possible (but not guaranteed) to end up with

---

[5]We adopt the convention that given a digraph that is (r, s)-robust for all $s \in \mathbb{Z}_{\geq 0}$, its maximal s is ∞.

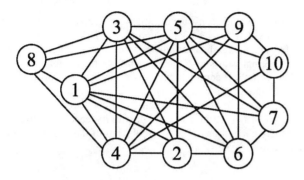

Figure 3: A $(3, 2)$-robust graph constructed from K_5 using preferential attachment.

a *more* robust digraph than the initial one using the preferential-attachment growth model.

5. RESILIENT CONSENSUS RESULTS

In this section, we provide the key results showing that sufficiently robust digraphs guarantee resilient consensus. Due to space limitations, the proofs are omitted here; instead, we provide a brief outline of the arguments. The full proofs are given in [18].

5.1 F-Total Model

THEOREM 2. *Consider a time-invariant network modeled by a directed graph $\mathcal{D} = \{\mathcal{V}, \mathcal{E}\}$. In the presence of malicious nodes under the F-total model, ARC-P with parameter $2F$ achieves resilient asymptotic consensus if and only if the network topology is $(F + 1, F + 1)$-robust.*

Outline of proof:
(*Sufficiency*) Recall that $M_{\mathcal{N}}[t]$ and $m_{\mathcal{N}}[t]$ are the *maximum* and *minimum* values of the normal nodes at time t, respectively. Define $\Phi[t] = M_{\mathcal{N}}[t] - m_{\mathcal{N}}[t]$ and note that $\Phi[t] \to 0$ as $t \to \infty$ if and only if the normal nodes reach asymptotic consensus. Since Φ is a non-increasing function of t, the main idea of the proof is to show that after some bounded time t_c, $\Phi[t]$ will shrink by a certain nontrivial fraction $0 < c_t < 1$, i.e. $\Phi[t + t_c] \le c_t \Phi[t], \forall t$. To show this, the $(F + 1, F + 1)$-robustness property is used to show that there exists a chain of subsets of nodes in either the subset of normal nodes with maximum value, or the subset of normal nodes with minimum value such that the nodes in the first subset in the chain have enough neighbors with values smaller (or larger) than their own in order to drive their values away from the extreme value. Then, all nodes in the next subset in the chain are guaranteed to have enough neighbors to drive their values away from the extreme value, and so on, until the last of the extreme values are shifted by a nontrivial amount. The uniform continuity of the malicious nodes' value trajectories and the bounds on the weights are used in order to formalize the argument.

(*Necessity*) If $\mathcal{D}$ is not $(F + 1, F + 1)$-robust, then there are nonempty, disjoint $\mathcal{S}_1, \mathcal{S}_2 \subset \mathcal{V}$ such that none of the conditions $(i) - (iii)$ hold. Suppose the initial value of each node in $\mathcal{S}_1$ is a and each node in $\mathcal{S}_2$ is b, with $a < b$. Let all other nodes have initial values taken from the interval (a, b). Since $s_{F+1,1} + s_{F+1,2} \le F$, suppose all nodes in $\mathcal{X}_{\mathcal{S}_1}$ and $\mathcal{X}_{\mathcal{S}_2}$ are malicious and keep their values constant. With this assignment of adversaries, there is still at least one normal node in both $\mathcal{S}_1$ and $\mathcal{S}_2$ since $s_{F+1,1} < |\mathcal{S}_1|$ and $s_{F+1,2} < |\mathcal{S}_2|$, respectively. Since these normal nodes remove the F or less values of in-neighbors outside of their respective sets, no consensus among normal nodes is reached. □

When the network is time-varying, one can state the following corollary of the above theorem.

COROLLARY 1. *Consider a time-varying network modeled by a directed graph $\mathcal{D}[t] = \{\mathcal{V}, \mathcal{E}[t]\}$. In the presence of malicious nodes under the F-total model, ARC-P with parameter $2F$ achieves resilient asymptotic consensus if there exists $t_0 \ge 0$ such that $\mathcal{D}[t]$ is $(F + 1, F + 1)$-robust, $\forall t \ge t_0$.*

Outline of proof: The proof is similar to the proof of sufficiency of Theorem 2. In continuous time, the dwell time assumption is used by constructing the bounded time horizon t_c over which we are guaranteed that $\Phi[t]$ will shrink by a nontrivial fraction so that $t_c < \tau/2$. But, at any time t, the digraph may switch before time $t + t_c$, which may disrupt the chain argument made in the time-invariant case. But, since $t_c < \tau/2$, we may reconstruct a new chain at the switching instance, and are then assured that by time $t + 2t_c$, $\Phi[t]$ will shrink by a certain nontrivial fraction. □

To illustrate these results on the examples of Section 4, the graphs in Figs. 1, 2, and 3 can withstand the compromise of at most 1 malicious node in the network using ARC-P with parameter $2F = 2$ (each graph is (2,2)-robust but not (3,3)-robust). This is not to say that it is impossible for the normal nodes to reach consensus if there are, for example, two nodes that are compromised. Instead, these results say that it is not possible that *any* two nodes can be compromised and still guarantee resilient asymptotic consensus using ARC-P with parameter $2F = 4$.

5.2 F-Local Model

THEOREM 3. *Consider a time-invariant network modeled by a directed graph $\mathcal{D} = \{\mathcal{V}, \mathcal{E}\}$. In the presence of malicious nodes under the F-local model, ARC-P with parameter $2F$ achieves resilient asymptotic consensus if the topology of the network is $(2F + 1)$-robust; furthermore, a necessary condition is for the topology of the network to be $(F + 1)$-robust.*

Outline of proof: The sufficiency proof in this case is similar to the proof of Theorem 2. The necessity proof is given in [34]. □

COROLLARY 2. *Consider a time-varying network modeled by a directed graph $\mathcal{D}[t] = \{\mathcal{V}, \mathcal{E}[t]\}$. In the presence of malicious nodes under the F-local model, ARC-P with parameter $2F$ achieves resilient asymptotic consensus if there exists $t_0 \ge 0$ such that the topology of the network $\mathcal{D}[t]$ is $(2F + 1)$-robust, $\forall t \ge t_0$.*

To illustrate these results, consider the 3-robust graph of Fig. 2. Recall that this graph cannot generally sustain 2 malicious nodes as specified by the 2-total model; it is not (3,3)-robust. However, under the 1-local model, it can sustain two malicious nodes if the *right* nodes are compromised. For example, nodes 1 and 4 may be compromised under the 1-local model and the normal nodes will still reach consensus. This example illustrates the advantage of the F-local model, where there is no concern about global assumptions. If a digraph is $(2F + 1)$-robust, then up to F nodes may be compromised in any node's neighborhood, possibly resulting in more than F malicious nodes in the network (as in the previous example).

6. SIMULATIONS

This section presents a numerical example to illustrate our results. In this example, the network is given by the (2,2)-robust graph shown in Fig. 4. Since the network is (2,2)-robust, it can sustain a single malicious node in the network under the 1-total model. Suppose that the node with the largest degree, node 14, is compromised and turns malicious. The nodes have continuous dynamics and the normal nodes use either the Linear Consensus Protocol (LCP) given in (1) or ARC-P for their control input. In either case, the weights are selected to be unity for all neighboring nodes that are kept, with the self-weights selected as $-d_i^{in}$ for LCP and $|\mathcal{R}_i[t]| - d_i^{in}$ for ARC-P for each normal node $i \in \mathcal{N}$. The initial values of the nodes are shown in Fig. 4 beneath the label of the node's value. The goal of the malicious agent is to drive the values of the normal nodes to a value of 2.

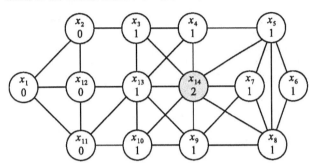

Figure 4: (2,2)-Robust Network topology.

The results for this example are shown in Fig. 5. It is clear in Fig. 5(a) that the malicious node is able to drive the values of the normal nodes to its value of 2 whenever LCP is used. On the other hand, the malicious node is unable to achieve its goal whenever ARC-P is used. Note that due to the large degree of the malicious node, it has the potential to drive the consensus process to any value in the interval $[0, 1]$ by choosing the desired value as its initial value and remaining constant. However, this is allowed with resilient asymptotic consensus (because the consensus value is within the range of the initial values held by normal nodes). Another observation is that the consensus process in the case of ARC-P is slower than LCP; this is to be expected, due to the fact that ARC-P effectively removes certain edges from the network at each time-step. Finally, we remark that the chain argument sketched in the outline of the proof of Theorem 2 is demonstrated in Fig. 5(b). To see this, denote the set of normal nodes with initial value 0 as $\mathcal{S}_0$ and the set of normal nodes with initial value 1 as $\mathcal{S}_1$. Then, $\mathcal{S}_0 = \{1, 2, 11, 12\}$ and $\mathcal{S}_1 = \{3, 4, 5, 6, 7, 8, 9, 10, 11, 12, 13\}$. Construct the following chain of subsets of $\mathcal{S}_0$: $\mathcal{T}_0^1 = \{11\}$, $\mathcal{T}_0^2 = \{12\}$, $\mathcal{T}_0^3 = \{1, 2\}$. These subsets of $\mathcal{S}_0$ are defined recursively by the following steps:

1. Let $\mathcal{T}_0^1$ include all nodes in $\mathcal{S}_0$ that have at least $F + 1 = 2$ neighbors outside of $\mathcal{S}_0$ (in this case, node 11).

2. Form $\mathcal{S}_0^1 = \mathcal{S}_0 \setminus \mathcal{T}_0^1$.

3. Let $\mathcal{T}_0^2$ include all nodes in $\mathcal{S}_0^1$ that have at least $F + 1 = 2$ neighbors outside of $\mathcal{S}_0^1$ (in this case, node 12).

4. Form $\mathcal{S}_0^2 = \mathcal{S}_0^1 \setminus \mathcal{T}_0^2$.

5. Let $\mathcal{T}_0^3$ include all nodes in $\mathcal{S}_0^2$ that have at least $F + 1 = 2$ neighbors outside of $\mathcal{S}_0^2$ (in this case, nodes 1 and 2).

6. Form $\mathcal{S}_0^3 = \mathcal{S}_0^2 \setminus \mathcal{T}_0^3$.

7. Quit whenever $\mathcal{S}_0^k = \emptyset$ or $\mathcal{T}_0^k = \emptyset$ (in this case $\mathcal{S}_0^3 = \emptyset$ and $k = 3$).

In a similar manner, construct the following chain of subsets of $\mathcal{S}_1$: $\mathcal{T}_1^1 = \{13\}$, $\mathcal{T}_1^2 = \{3, 10\}$, $\mathcal{T}_1^3 = \{4, 9\}$, $\mathcal{T}_1^4 = \emptyset$. Unlike the previous chain, this chain terminates with $\mathcal{S}_1^k \neq \emptyset$. For this reason, not all normal values in $\mathcal{S}_1$ are driven from their initial value of 1. Now, with these constructions, we can see the trajectories of the values of nodes in each subset in Fig. 5(b). For example, node 11 in $\mathcal{T}_0^1$ corresponds to the value trajectory that immediately increases at $t = 0$. Node 12 in $\mathcal{T}_0^2$ is the next to increase away from 0, and finally nodes 1 and 2 in $\mathcal{T}_0^3$ are the last of the nodes of $\mathcal{S}_0$ to increase from 0.

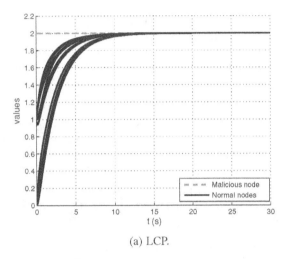

(a) LCP.

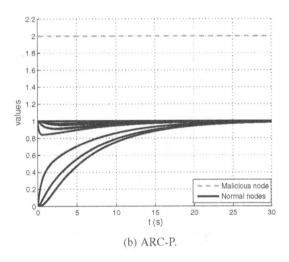

(b) ARC-P.

Figure 5: Malicious node attempts to drive the values of the normal nodes to a value of 2. The malicious node succeeds whenever LCP is used, but fails whenever ARC-P is used.

7. DISCUSSION

The notion of graph connectivity has long been the backbone of investigations into fault tolerant and secure distributed algorithms. Indeed, under the assumption of full knowledge of the network topology, connectivity is *the key* metric in determining whether a fixed number of malicious adversaries can be overcome. However, in large scale systems and complex networks, it is not practical for the various nodes to obtain knowledge of the global network topology. This necessitates the development of algorithms that allow the

Table 1: Related work for resilient consensus in synchronous networks using only local information (no nonlocal information, no relays, and the network is *not* complete).

Scope \ Threat Model	Byzantine	Malicious
F-total	[17,32]	[17], this paper
F-local	–	[34], this paper

nodes to operate on purely local information. This paper continues and extends the work started in [16, 17, 34], and represents a step in this direction for the particular application of distributed consensus. Using the ARC-P algorithm developed in [16], the notion of robust graphs introduced in [34], and the extensions of each presented here, we characterize necessary/sufficient conditions for the normal nodes in large-scale networks to mitigate the influence of adversaries. We show that the notions of robust digraphs are the appropriate analogues to graph connectivity when considering purely local filtering rules at each node in the network. Just as the notion of connectivity has played a central role in the existing analysis of reliable distributed algorithms with global topological knowledge, we believe that robust digraphs (and its variants) will play an important role in the investigation of purely local algorithms.

In a recent paper, developed independently of our work, Vaidya *et al.* have characterized the tight conditions for resilient consensus using only local information whenever the threat model is Byzantine and the scope of threat is F-total [32]. The network constructions used in [32] are very similar to the robust digraphs presented here. In particular, the networks in [32] also require redundancy of information flow between subsets of nodes in the network in a single hop.

Finally we summarize the main works related to resilient consensus using only local information in Table 1. In this table, we include only works on resilient consensus (also referred to as Byzantine approximate consensus, or just approximate consensus in the literature) in synchronous networks that use only local information, with no relaying of information across the network and with networks that are *not* complete (since complete networks provide global information and have high communication cost). Further discussion about the relationship of the results in this paper (and in [16, 17, 32, 34]) to approximate consensus can be found in [34] and [32].

8. ACKNOWLEDGMENTS

H. J. LeBlanc and X. Koutsoukos are supported in part by the National Science Foundation (CNS-1035655, CCF-0820088), the U.S. Army Research Office (ARO W911NF-10-1-0005), and Lockheed Martin. The views and conclusions contained herein are those of the authors and should not be interpreted as necessarily representing the official policies or endorsements, either expressed or implied, of the U.S. Government. H. Zhang and S. Sundaram are supported in part by a grant from the Natural Sciences and Engineering Research Council of Canada (NSERC), and by a grant from the Waterloo Institute for Complexity and Innovation (WICI).

9. REFERENCES

[1] N. Agmon and D. Peleg. Fault-tolerant gathering algorithms for autonomous mobile robots. *SIAM J. Comput.*, 36(1):56–82, 2006.

[2] R. Albert and A.-L. Barabási. Statistical mechanics of complex networks. *Rev. Mod. Phys.*, 74(1):47–97, Jan 2002.

[3] Z. Bouzid, M. G. Potop-Butucaru, and S. Tixeuil. Optimal byzantine-resilient convergence in uni-dimensional robot networks. *Theoretical Computer Science*, 411(34-36):3154–3168, 2010.

[4] A. A. Cárdenas, S. Amin, and S. Sastry. Research challenges for the security of control systems. In *Proceedings of the 3rd conference on Hot topics in security*, July 2008.

[5] D. W. Casbeer, D. B. Kingston, R. W. Beard, T. W. Mclain, S.-M. Li, and R. Mehra. Cooperative forest fire surveillance using a team of small unmanned air vehicles. *International Journal of Systems Sciences*, 37(6):351–360, May 2006.

[6] N. Chopra and M. W. Spong. Passivity-based control of multi-agent systems. In *Advances in Robot Control, From Everyday Physics to Human-Like Movements*, Sadao Kawamura and Mikhail Svinin (Eds), pages 107 – 134. Springer Verlag, Berlin, 2006.

[7] J. Cortés. Distributed algorithms for reaching consensus on general functions. *Automatica*, 44(3):726 – 737, 2008.

[8] X. Défago, M. Gradinariu, S. Messika, and P. Raipin-Parvédy. Fault-tolerant and self-stabilizing mobile robots gathering. In S. Dolev, editor, *Distributed Computing*, volume 4167 of *Lecture Notes in Computer Science*, pages 46–60. Springer Berlin, Heidelberg, 2006.

[9] J. A. Fax and R. M. Murray. Information flow and cooperative control of vehicle formations. *IEEE Transactions on Automatic Control*, 49(9):1465–1476, 2004.

[10] V. Gupta, C. Langbort, and R. Murray. On the robustness of distributed algorithms. In *IEEE Conf. on Decision and Control*, pages 3473 –3478, San Diego, California, December 2006.

[11] J. Hromkovic, R. Klasing, A. Pelc, P. Ruzicka, and W. Unger. *Dissemination of Information in Communication Networks*. Springer-Verlag, 2005.

[12] A. Ichimura and M. Shigeno. A new parameter for a broadcast algorithm with locally bounded Byzantine faults. *Information Processing Letters*, 110:514–517, 2010.

[13] A. Jadbabaie, J. Lin, and A. Morse. Coordination of groups of mobile autonomous agents using nearest neighbor rules. *IEEE Transactions on Aut. Control*, 48(6):988 – 1001, jun. 2003.

[14] D. Kingston, R. Beard, and R. Holt. Decentralized perimeter surveillance using a team of UAVs. *IEEE Transactions on Robotics*, 24(6):1394 –1404, Dec. 2008.

[15] L. Lamport, R. Shostak, and M. Pease. The Byzantine generals problem. *ACM Trans. Program. Lang. Syst.*, 4(2):382–401, 1982.

[16] H. J. LeBlanc and X. D. Koutsoukos. Consensus in networked multi-agent systems with adversaries. In *Proceedings of the 14th international conference on Hybrid systems: computation and control*, (HSCC '11), pages 281–290, Chicago, IL, 2011.

[17] H. J. LeBlanc and X. D. Koutsoukos. Low complexity resilient consensus in networked multi-agent systems with adversaries. In *Proceedings of the 15th international conference on Hybrid systems: computation and control*, (HSCC '12), Beijing, China, 2012. to appear.

[18] H. J. LeBlanc, H. Zhang, S. Sundaram, and X. D. Koutsoukos. Consensus of multi-agent networks in the presence of adversaries using only local information. *CoRR, arxiv*, 2012.

[19] J. Lorenz and D. Lorenz. On conditions for convergence to

consensus. *IEEE Transactions on Automatic Control*, 55(7):1651–1656, July 2010.

[20] N. A. Lynch. *Distributed Algorithms*. Morgan Kaufmann Publishers Inc., San Francisco, California, 1997.

[21] L. Moreau. Stability of multiagent systems with time-dependent communication links. *IEEE Trans. on Aut. Control*, 50(2):169 – 182, Feb. 2005.

[22] R. Olfati-Saber, J. A. Fax, and R. M. Murray. Consensus and cooperation in networked multi-agent systems. *Proceedings of the IEEE*, 95(1):215–233, 2007.

[23] F. Pasqualetti, A. Bicchi, and F. Bullo. Consensus computation in unreliable networks: A system theoretic approach. *IEEE Trans. on Aut. Control*, 57(1):90–104, Jan. 2012.

[24] A. Pelc and D. Peleg. Broadcasting with locally bounded Byzantine faults. In *Information Processing Letters*, pages 109–115, 2005.

[25] W. Ren and R. Beard. Consensus seeking in multiagent systems under dynamically changing interaction topologies. *IEEE Transactions on Automatic Control*, 50(5):655 – 661, May 2005.

[26] W. Ren, R. Beard, and E. Atkins. Information consensus in multivehicle cooperative control. *IEEE Control Systems Magazine*, 27(2):71–82, April 2007.

[27] L. Scardovi and R. Sepulchre. Synchronization in networks of identical linear systems. *Automatica*, 45(11):2557–2562, 2009.

[28] S. Sundaram and C. Hadjicostis. Distributed function calculation and consensus using linear iterative strategies. *IEEE Journal on Selected Areas in Communications*, 26(4):650–660, May 2008.

[29] S. Sundaram and C. Hadjicostis. Distributed function calculation via linear iterative strategies in the presence of malicious agents. *IEEE Trans. on Aut. Control*, 56(7):1495 –1508, July 2011.

[30] B. Touri and A. Nedić. On ergodicity, infinite flow, and consensus in random models. *IEEE Transactions on Automatic Control*, 56(7):1593–1605, July 2011.

[31] J. N. Tsitsiklis. *Problems in Decentralized Decision Making and Computation*. PhD thesis, Department of EECS, MIT, 1984.

[32] N. Vaidya, L. Tseng, and G. Liang. Iterative approximate Byzantine consensus in arbitrary directed graphs. *CoRR*, abs/1201.4183, 2012.

[33] L. Xiao and S. Boyd. Fast linear iterations for distributed averaging. *Systems and Control Letters*, 53:65–78, 2004.

[34] H. Zhang and S. Sundaram. Robustness of information diffusion algorithms to locally bounded adversaries. In *Proceedings of the American Control Conf.*, June 2012. to appear.

HMM-Based Characterization of Channel Behavior for Networked Control Systems

Jian Chang
Computer and Information
Science Department
University of Pennsylvania
Philadelphia, PA
jianchan@cis.upenn.edu

Krishna K. Venkatasubramanian
Computer and Information
Science Department
University of Pennsylvania
Philadelphia, PA
vkris@cis.upenn.edu

Chinwendu Enyioha
Department of Electrical and
Systems Engineering
University of Pennsylvania
Philadelphia, PA
cenyioha@ee.upenn.edu

Shreyas Sundaram
Department of Electrical and
Computer Engineering
University of Waterloo
Waterloo, ON, Canada
ssundara@uwaterloo.ca

George J. Pappas
Department of Electrical and
Systems Engineering
University of Pennsylvania
Philadelphia, PA
pappasg@ee.upenn.edu

Insup Lee
Computer and Information
Science Department
University of Pennsylvania
Philadelphia, PA
lee@cis.upenn.edu

ABSTRACT

We study the problem of characterizing the behavior of lossy and data corrupting communication channels in a networked control setting, where the channel's behavior exhibits temporal correlation. We propose a behavior characterization mechanism based on a *hidden Markov model* (HMM). The use of a HMM in this regard presents multiple challenges including dealing with incomplete observation sequences (due to data losses and corruptions) and the lack of *a priori* information about the model complexity (number of states in the model). We address the first challenges by using the plant state information and history of received/applied control inputs to fill in the gaps in the observation sequences, and by enhancing the HMM learning algorithm to deal with missing observations . Further, we adopt two model quality criteria for determining behavior model complexity. The contributions of this paper include: (1) an enhanced learning algorithm for refining the HMM model parameters to handle missing observations, and (2) simultaneous use of two well-defined model quality criteria to determine the model complexity. Simulation results demonstrate over 90% accuracy in predicting the output of a channel at a given time step, when compared to a traditional HMM based model that requires complete knowledge of the model complexity and observation sequence.

Categories and Subject Descriptors

B.4.5 [**Reliability, Testing, and Fault-Tolerance**]: Redundant Design; G.3 [**Probability AND Statistics**]: Markov Process; K.6.m [**Miscellaneous**]: Security

General Terms

Algorithms, Design, Reliability, Security

Keywords

Networked Control System, Majority Voting, Hidden Markov Model

1. INTRODUCTION

Networked control systems (NCS) are spatially distributed control systems where the communication between the plant sensors, plant actuators, and controllers takes place through a network [9]. However, the presence of a network within the control loop can adversely affect the performance of the system due to the inherent unreliability (*e.g.*, packet drops or transmission latency) of the communication channel. Such anomalies have direct consequences on the stability of the plant, as shown in previous studies [1, 2, 7, 8, 11, 17, 19].

As NCS have become more pervasive in large-scale industrial networks [22], the potential for data corruption due to unmitigated faults or malicious attacks increases considerably. However, an investigation of the combined effects of packet drops and data corruptions in the network in NCS has received limited attention. Our previous paper [24] studied a NCS with lossy and faulty (*i.e.*, data-corrupting) communication channels, and examined the use of a triple-modular-redundant channels. We use a majority voting scheme augmented with a simple channel behavior model to determine which channel inputs to apply to a plant within a given time-step. The goal is to tolerate a single data-corrupting channel and achieve mean square stability, assuming that the behavior of each communication channel can be modeled as an independent and identically distributed (i.i.d.) random variable.

This assumption of channel behavior being modeled as an i.i.d. random variable may not often hold in practice, especially in the case of wireless channels where burst errors or faults often persist over multiple time-steps [16]. Consequently, in this paper we focus on studying the scenarios where the behavior of each channel at the current time-step is *correlated* with its behavior in the previous t time-steps (for some unknown t). To this end, we adopt a hidden Markov model (HMM) framework to design a channel behavior characterization mechanism. The idea is to construct an HMM-based behavior model for each communication channel in the NCS. Given a channel's observed behavior sequence over time, the parameters of the corresponding HMM are computed and progressively refined. This HMM-based approach provides a probabilistic characterization of the channel's tendency to correctly or incorrectly transmit data at a given time-step. Using this behavior model, for an input received over a specific communication channel, one can make well-informed decisions about whether it should be applied to stabilize the plant. This is particularly useful in the event majority voting fails in a time-step due to the lossy and data corrupting nature of the channels (resulting in insufficient information to make a decision). Previous studies have focused on using HMMs as the reasoning engine to identify root causes of faults or erroneous states of the system [6, 10, 14, 21, 26–28]. In contrast, we adopt a black-box view that only focuses on identifying the correlation between a channel's current behavior and its behavior history. This allows us to propose a more general solution to the problem of dealing with unreliable channels in an NCS setting.

Designing an effective channel behavior characterization mechanism using HMMs (in the context of NCS) presents two important challenges: (1) *Incomplete and Uncertain Observations:* Due to the presence of data loss and corruption, existing majority voting schemes cannot always accurately discern the behavior of the communication channels at every time step. This introduces considerable incompleteness and uncertainty in the observation sequence and the channel's behavior model. (2) *Unknown Model Complexity:* It is critical to identify the number of states of the HMM behavior model (henceforth referred to as *model complexity*), which accurately captures a channel's behavior pattern. However, such information is often unknown *a priori*.

In addressing these challenges, we make two main *contributions*: (1) We design an enhanced learning algorithm for refining the HMM model parameters, which can handle missing observations. Additionally, we simultaneously reduce the missing observations by using the history of received and applied control inputs and the knowledge of the current plant state to fill the gaps in the observation sequences, with the benefit of hindsight. (2) We adopt two well-defined model quality criteria to determine the HMM complexity.

The rest of the paper is organized as follows. In Section 2 we discuss the system model and problem statement. In Section 3 we present the HMM-based channel behavior characterization mechanism followed by Section 4 where we present the enhanced HMM learning algorithm that can deal with missing data. In Section 5 we present our approach to

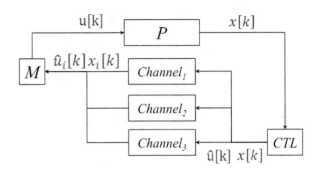

Figure 1: System Model

determine the model complexity. In Section 6 we present the evaluation results and in Section 7, we conclude the paper.

2. SYSTEM MODEL AND PROBLEM STATEMENT

Consider the networked control system shown in Figure 1. The plant P is given by the dynamical system

$$\mathbf{x}[k+1] = \mathbf{A}\mathbf{x}[k] + \mathbf{B}\mathbf{u}[k] \ , \qquad (1)$$

where the matrices $\mathbf{A}$ and $\mathbf{B}$ are real-valued matrices of appropriate dimensions. $\mathbf{x} \in \mathbb{R}^n$ is the system state vector, $\mathbf{u} \in \mathbb{R}^m$ is the system input vector, and k denotes the time-step of the system.

To obtain the desired behavior from the plant, the state $\mathbf{x}[k]$ is sent to a controller CTL. Based on $\mathbf{x}[k]$ (or perhaps the entire history of past states), the controller computes an input $\hat{\mathbf{u}}[k]$ to apply to the plant. This value is then sent through an imperfect communication channel. In this paper, we consider three types of behaviors that a channel can exhibit at any given time-step: (1) *correct behavior (denoted as C):* the data is faithfully transmitted; (2) *faulty (data-corrupting) behavior (denoted as I):* the data being transmitted is modified due to unmitigated faults or malicious attacks; (3) *lossy (data-dropping) behavior (denoted as D):* the data is lost during the transmission.

To compensate for the faulty and lossy nature of the channels, we consider a triple-modular redundant scheme (see Figure 1). This scheme consists of three disjoint communication channels between the controller and the plant. The channels are used to send the control input $\hat{\mathbf{u}}[k]$ along with system state measurement $\mathbf{x}[k]$ to keep track of the plant dynamics based on the inputs applied over time. A *manager* component M receives values $\hat{\mathbf{u}}_i[k]$ ($i \in \{1, 2, 3\}$) sent through the three different channels and makes a decision on what input $\hat{\mathbf{u}}_i[k]$ to apply. To apply correct control inputs to the plant and to avoid corrupted ones, the manager M needs to properly discern a channel's behavior. By default, the manager implements a *majority voting* scheme for this purpose. With triple-modular redundancy, majority voting can be effective in the identification of the faulty channel when only one channel exhibits such behavior in a given time-step, and there are no packet losses. On the other hand, majority voting with lossy and faulty channels works as follows:

- The reception of at least two matching inputs at the manager in a given time-step results in its acceptance as a correct input (C) and its consequent application to the plant. Any channel whose value does not match this correct input is deemed as producing an incorrect input (I). Similarly, channels that drop the control input in a time-step are classified as dropped (D).

- If in a given time-step, two inputs are received and they do not match, or only one input is received then majority voting fails to find an appropriate input. In this case we use X to denote the behavior of such channels in that time-step (Example 1).

Example 1 *The true behaviors of the three input channels and the behavior types discerned using the majority voting scheme (X denotes the unknown behavior) is demonstrated.*

- *True behavior sequences:*

Channel 1	C C C C C C I D
Channel 2	C I C I I D I D
Channel 3	C C D D I D I D

- *Discerned behavior sequences using majority voting:*

Channel 1	C C C X X X X D
Channel 2	C I C X X D X D
Channel 3	C C D D X D X D

Due to the ambiguity introduced by packet drops and corruptions, we showed in [24] that a simple majority voting scheme may actually not provide stability if the channels drop packets with a sufficiently high probability (even when a single fault-free channel with the same probability of packet drop would be able to provide stability). We went on to demonstrate the use of a simple Bayesian estimator to improve the performance of majority voting by assuming that the behavior (both correct and incorrect) of each channel can be modeled as an i.i.d. random variable. We relax this assumption in this paper, since it is restrictive and may not hold in many practical situations.

Example 2 *For the Bernoulli packet-drop behavior model studied in previous works [8, 9, 20, 24], the probability distribution of possible behavior types is given below, where p is the data drop probability.*

$$\begin{cases} D & with\ probability\ p \\ C & with\ probability\ 1-p \\ I & with\ probability\ 0 \end{cases}$$

This model represents a case where the behavior at the current time-step is independent from the behavior type of the previous time-steps. In other words, its current behavior is correlated with behavior over the previous *zero* time-steps.

Example 3 *Consider a scenario where a channel alternatively exhibits the three types of behaviors described above. The observed behavior sequence Ω_S of this channel is:*

$$\Omega_S = C\ I\ D\ C\ I\ D\ C\ I\ D\ C\ I\ \dots$$

In the above example, it is clear that the behavior type at the current time-step is correlated with (and actually completely specified by) the behavior in the previous *one* time-step. This behavior model is more general than the i.i.d. assumption made by previous works studying NCS [8, 9, 20, 24].

Problem 1 *In this paper, we study the problem of developing a robust and effective behavior characterization mechanism in the context of NCS, which focuses on the scenarios where a channel's behavior at the current time-step is correlated with its behavior in the previous t time-steps, for some unknown integer t.*

Remark: Note that we do not focus on the issue of *stability* in this paper. We assume that the system is designed in such a way that stability (in an appropriate sense) is attained despite the presence of packet drops (*e.g.,* if the conditions provided in works such as [7, 9, 15, 24], *etc.* are satisfied). Instead, our main goal is to design a *monitoring* mechanism to characterize the behavior and quality of the various channels, which can then be used by the plant operator to take appropriate actions, such as shutting down a severely malfunctioning channel. We will show how the hidden Markov model and its standard learning algorithms can be adapted and modified for effective channel behavior modeling, and to handle the particular complexities in the networked control context.

3. CHANNEL BEHAVIOR CHARACTERIZATION

In this section, we present the design of an effective behavior characterization mechanism for NCS using the hidden Markov model (HMM). Before delving into the details, we make the following important assumptions regarding the channels in our system model :

1. We consider a setup with *three* channels and assume each channel operates independently of the others; that is, there is no correlation between their behaviors at any time-step. Each of the channels can exhibit correct, faulty and lossy behavior.

2. We assume I inputs received from two or more channels at the same time-step will not agree under the majority voting scheme; only C (correct) inputs will match with each other.

3. There exists an appropriate Lyapunov function for the system that decreases whenever correct (C) inputs are applied; we assume that incorrect (I) inputs will not decrease this function.

3.1 Hidden Markov Model

To formally represent the class of behavior patterns discussed in Section 2, we adopt a hidden Markov model (HMM) framework [18]. A HMM consists of N states, denoted by

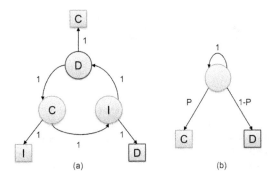

Figure 2: Examples of HMM Fault Model

the set $\Omega_X = \{q_1, \ldots, q_N\}$, and M outputs, denoted by the set $\Omega_O = \{v_1, \ldots, v_M\}$. The relationships between a fixed set of states and set of outputs is specified by two stochastic processes $\Lambda = \{E, F\}$. The first stochastic process describes the transition between states, whose parameters are encoded in the transition probability matrix $E = \{e_{ij}\}$, where $e_{ij} = P(\Omega_X(t+1) = q_j | \Omega_X(t) = q_i)$. The second stochastic process describes the relationship between each state and all the possible outputs, whose parameters are encoded in the emission probability matrix $F = \{f_i\}$, where $f_i = \{P(\Omega_O = v_1 | \Omega_X = q_i), \ldots, P(\Omega_O = v_M | \Omega_X = q_i)\}$. In a HMM, only the outputs (which are dependent on the states) are visible; the states and transitions between them are not directly observable, and are therefore *hidden*.

The HMM is an ideal modeling choice in our setting, since the temporal correlation between a channel's current behavior and its behavior history can be considered to be Markovian. As a result, we model the three possible behavior types of the channels as the output of the HMM. Furthermore, the behavior sequences with length t can be modeled using N states in the HMM, where $N = 3^t$ (this corresponds to the combination of all possible behavior sequences with length t). For instance, as illustrated in Figure 2(a),[1] the HMM of Example 3 has $3^1 = 3$ states, to model the correlation between its current behavior and its behavior in the previous $t = 1$ time-step. Similarly, for Example 2, the corresponding HMM has $3^0 = 1$ state to model the correlation between its current behavior and behavior of the previous $t = 0$ time-steps, as shown in Figure 2(b).

HMMs have traditionally been used to answer two main questions: (1) given the observed sequence, estimate the most likely model parameters of the hidden model Λ; and (2) given the model parameters Λ and the observed sequence, find the most likely state sequence up to the current time-step and the most likely output at a given time-step. The Baum-Welch algorithm [25] is used as a means to achieve the former, efficiently estimating the model parameters in two passes, iteratively. The first pass goes forward in time and computes a conditional probability $P(q_i | \Omega_{1:k}^S)$ of ending up in any particular state q_i given the first k outputs in the observation sequence Ω_S; while the second goes backward in time and computes the conditional probability $P(\Omega_{k:t}^S | q_i)$ of seeing the remaining observations in the sequence given any state q_i as the starting point. These two types of conditional probabilities can then be combined to obtain the dis-

---

[1]The state transitions and output emissions with 0 probability are omitted.

Algorithm 1 Behavior Characterization Scheme

1: Set value of the variable $Model_C$ for each channel, based on a priori over-estimation of the number of states in the HMM
2: **if** The majority voting scheme finds matching inputs **then**
3:   Correctly identify the behavior type for each channel
4:   Append the observed behavior to the behavior history of channels
5:   Refine missing observations in the behavior history with hindsight
6:   **if** Sufficient observations are accumulated for a channel **then**
7:     Execute the model complexity estimation algorithm to update the value of variable $Model_C$ for that channel
8:   **end if**
9:   Update each channel's behavior model based on the $Model_C$ value and apply traditional HMM learning algorithm
10: **else**
11:   Use each channel's behavior model to predict its behavior type at this time-step
12:   Update each channel's behavior model using an enhanced HMM learning algorithm
13: **end if**

---

tribution over states at any specific point in time given the entire observation sequence. Similarly, the latter question, studied in [12], is addressed by computing the conditional probability $P(q_i | \Omega_{1:k}^S)$ to find the most likely state sequence. By combining this conditional probability with the emission probability matrix, one can further obtain the most likely output at a given time-step.

3.2 Overview of Behavior Characterization

In this paper, we use hidden Markov Model as the basis for characterizing the channel's behavior, given the observation sequence. Applying this established technique in our setting is, however, non-trivial. There are two major challenges: (1) the behavior history may contain missing entries (which are denoted as X) due to the limitation of the majority voting scheme. Since this unknown behavior type X is not contained in the output set $\Omega_O = \{C, I, D\}$ of the HMM, the classic learning algorithm for HMMs cannot properly learn the channel behavior; and (2) the number of the HMM states is also not known *a priori* in our setting.

A skeletal picture of our channel behavior characterization mechanism is shown in Algorithm 1. The behavior characterization is implemented as a part of the manager block M in the NCS and operates in six steps:

- **Line 1**: Start with an estimate of the complexity of each channel's behavior model (*i.e.*, the number of states in the HMM required to describe the channel's behavior pattern) as its input. Such an estimate can be obtained based on application-specific knowledge, or from experience[2]. During the early phase of our be-

---

[2]It is important to note that an accurate estimation of such model complexity may not be easy to obtain in some applications, so one would prefer to have an over-estimated the value, trading-off computational expense for model expressiveness.

havior characterization mechanism (when only limited observations of channel behavior are available), this model complexity estimate will be used as the basis for constructing the behavior model for each channel.

- **Lines 2-4**: Observe the data received from the channels at the current time-step k and discern the corresponding behavior types (*i.e.*, C, I, or D) using majority voting.

- **Line 5**: If majority voting succeeds at time-step k, then for all time-steps j, $0 < j \leq k-1$, where majority voting was not successful in assessing the channels' behavior (*i.e.*, due to incomplete information), use the current state information (which has been correctly inferred via majority voting), and the history of received and applied control inputs to infer the behavior of the channels up to time-step j. (see Section 4)

- **Lines 6-8**: Once sufficient observations of channel behaviors are accumulated, use the model complexity estimation algorithm to update the estimate of the model complexity ($Model_C$) (see Section 5).

- **Line 9**: Use the observed channels' behavior sequence to refine the correspond HMM-based behavior model using the estimated $Model_C$ value as its parameter.

- **Lines 11-12**: If the majority voting scheme fails to make a decision at time-step k, we use the behavior model of each channel to predict its behavior in that time-step. An enhanced HMM learning algorithm is used, which considers the true behavior types of the corresponding channels as unknown at this time step, and updates the corresponding behavior models appropriately, as we shall see in the Section 4. This continues until a future time-step $k+l$, when the majority voting scheme succeeds (restart at Line 2)

4. HANDLING INCOMPLETE OBSERVATION SEQUENCE

We propose two countermeasures to address the limitations of majority voting in providing a complete observation sequence: (1) We design a scheme to reduce the number of time-steps in which the behavior is unknown. (2) We adopt a modified version of the Baum-Welch algorithm as our enhanced HMM learning algorithm, similar to the approach proposed in [29], for handling the missing data in the observation sequence.

4.1 Reducing Incompleteness of Observation Sequence

The reducing of incomplete observation sequence is a five step process. They include: (1) the controller C sends both the control input $\hat{\mathbf{u}}[k]$ and the system state measurement $\mathbf{x}[k]$ over the network ; (2) the manager keeps the history of all the control inputs received from the channels and the ones applied to the plant; (3) if the majority voting scheme has matching data at time-step k, we obtain the correct system state $\mathbf{x}[k]$; (4) the dynamical model shown in Equation (1) is then used to recover the state of the plant at the previous points in time when the state was unknown due to lack of information for majority voting; and (5) for every X before time k, the manager uses the recovered state to determine

whether the inputs provided by the channels at that time step would have decreased the Lyapunov function — if so, the input will be labeled as C (under the assumption that I inputs won't drive the plant state towards stability).

Step (5) in the above sequence can be accomplished if the plant dynamics satisfy certain conditions. For instance, since

$$\mathbf{x}[k] = \mathbf{A}^T \mathbf{x}[k-T] + \begin{bmatrix} \mathbf{B} & \mathbf{AB} & \cdots & \mathbf{A}^{T-1}\mathbf{B} \end{bmatrix} \begin{bmatrix} \mathbf{u}[k-1] \\ \mathbf{u}[k-2] \\ \vdots \\ \mathbf{u}[k-T] \end{bmatrix}$$

for any nonnegative integer T, one can recover $\mathbf{x}[k-T]$ from the above expression if $\mathbf{A}^T$ is invertible (or equivalently, if $\mathbf{A}$ is invertible).

Remark: The aforementioned improved mechanism can also be applied to a system with nonlinear dynamics

$$\mathbf{x}[k+1] = f(\mathbf{x}[k], \mathbf{u}[k]) \qquad (2)$$

as well, where the goal is to determine the state $\mathbf{x}[k-T]$ given $\mathbf{x}[k]$. Inspired by [13, 23], the extraction of a previous state given the current state can be done by simultaneously solving a set of nonlinear equations, provided that the nonlinear dynamics (2) satisfy certain properties.

4.2 Learning with Incomplete Observation Sequence

In the absence of a successful majority voting in a time-step, it is possible that observation sequence from a channel has missing elements. In [29], the authors propose an enhanced model parameter learning algorithm for hidden semi-Markov models with missing data in the observation sequence, and use it for mobility tracking applications. In this paper, we adopt a similar approach and design an algorithm that handles missing observations for HMM by modifying the Baum-Welch algorithm. In the original Baum-Welch algorithm, the iterative computation of the forward and backward probabilities require the use of the emission probability matrix. However, the emission probability for unknown behavior type X is not defined. To mitigate this issue, the idea is to consider all possible behaviors that can be exhibited while updating the model parameters when the unknown feedback X is encountered. In this paper, we consider X to be either C or I with equivalent probability values.[3] Therefore, the emission probability for X can be interpreted as the combination of the emission probability of C and I. The rest of the Baum-Welch algorithm remains unchanged.

5. MODEL COMPLEXITY ESTIMATION

Initially, we use an over-estimation of the number of states in the HMM for modeling a channel's behavior pattern. We then use a model complexity estimation algorithm to accurately determine the actual number of states with limited observation of channel behavior. In the algorithm, we adopt two model quality criterion: (1) *Condition number* γ, which is defined as $\gamma = \sigma_{min}(E|F)/\sigma_{max}(E|F)$, where σ_{min} and σ_{max} are the smallest and largest singular values of the HMM parameter concatenation matrix $E|F$, respectively [3]; and (2) *Observation probability*, which is defined

---

[3] Since feedback type D can always be confidently discerned, we do not need to consider it as a possibility.

15

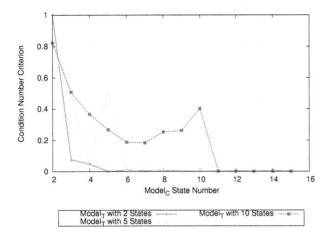

Figure 3: Condition Number Variability

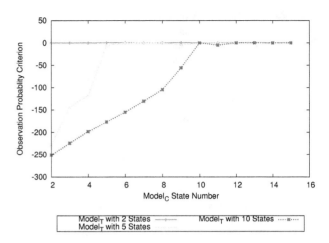

Figure 4: Observation Probability Variability

as the probability for the learned HMM model to generate the observed behavior sequence.

5.1 Condition Number

The condition number criterion determines whether certain states in the model are redundant or unnecessary. Figure 3 shows the variation in the condition number with respect to candidate model complexity (referred to as $Model_C$). The figure shows the results for three scenarios where the ground truth for actual number of states in the model (referred to as $Model_T$) are 2, 5 and 10 respectively. Irrespective of the $Model_T$ value, the pattern observed hold consistently:

- When the $Model_C \leq Model_T$, the condition number of the candidate model first decreases and then increases, with a local maxima at $Model_C = Model_T$. However, the condition number values are still relatively high, even at local minimas. The reason here is that when the model is not expressive enough, it can only capture certain sub-patterns within the entire underlying behavior pattern, until $Model_C = Model_T$.

- When $Model_C > Model_T$, the condition number of the candidate model drastically decreases and tends toward 0. This reflects the fact that certain states in the candidate model are redundant (*i.e.*, unnecessary for capturing the ground truth behavior pattern).

5.2 Observation Probability

The observation probability criterion indicates how well the learned HMM model captures the observed behavior sequence. We illustrate this criterion in Figure 4. Similar to the condition number criterion, Figure 4 shows variation in the observation probability with respect to $Model_C$. The figure shows the results for three scenarios where $Model_T$ is set to 2, 5, and 10, respectively. Irrespective of the $Model_T$ value, again the patterns we observed hold consistently:

- When the $Model_C \leq Model_T$, the observation probability of the candidate model monotonically increases, and reach its maximum value when $Model_C = Model_T$.

- When $Model_C > Model_T$, the observation probability value remains mostly unchanged. The reason here is

that as the value $Model_C$ increases, the behavior pattern captured by the candidate behavior model is increasingly closer to the ground truth, until $Model_C = Model_T$ when the observation probability criterion reach its maximum value. And when $Model_C > Model_T$, the candidate model complexity is an over-kill for modeling the ground truth behavior pattern, and the observation probability value cannot increase further.

In other words, using a candidate model with $Model_C > Model_T$ (*i.e.*, an over-estimation of the behavior model complexity), the expressiveness of candidate model is good enough to capture the underlying behavior pattern, the only drawback is that it requires additional computational resources and potentially more observation data to train the candidate model, compared to the ideal ground truth.

5.3 Combined Criterion

By combining these two criterion, we can design a model complexity estimation algorithm that achieves two goals: (1) output an accurate estimation for $Model_T$; (2) achieve the first goal with "limited" tries of different candidate models. A pseudocode description of our model complexity estimation algorithm is shown in Algorithm 2. The overall algorithm consists of two stages. In the first stage, we attempt to identify a proper lower and upper bound of candidate model complexity by utilizing the condition number criterion (line 2 - 13). The idea is to exponentially increase the lower and upper bound for every iteration (line 4 and line 11), until we successful detect the drastic change of the condition number value between the two bounds (line 7). As we discussed previously, such a pattern indicates that the true model complexity lies between the lower bound and upper bound value. We record these bounds, as well as the observation probability value of the upper bound model to be used in the later stage (line 8-9). In the second stage, we attempt to find the smallest value for $Model_C$ that can achieve the highest observation probability value (*i.e.*, as the upper bound model) using a binary search scheme [4] (line 16-30). Let the range between the two bounds be n, then the best, worst and average time complexity of the algorithm is $O(1)$, $O(logn)$, and $O(logn)$, respectively.

Algorithm 2 Model Complexity Estimation Algorithm
1: Initialize variable i to be 1
2: **while** TRUE **do**
3:    Set the lower bound (LB) and upper bound (UB) of candidate model state number to be 2^i and $2^{(i+1)}$, respectively
4:    Learn two HMM models with state number to be the lower bound and upper bound, respectively
5:    Compute the condition number and observation probability criterion for the two models, denote these values as CN_{LB}, OP_{LB}, and CN_{UB}, OP_{UB}, respectively
6:    **if** $CN_{LB} >> CN_{UB}$ **then**
7:       Record the observation probability value OP_{UB}
8:       Output LB, UB
9:       Break
10:    **else**
11:       $i = i + 1$
12:       Continue
13:    **end if**
14: **end while**
15:
16: Set variable $s = \lfloor((LB + UB)/2)\rfloor$, that is the largest integer value smaller than or equal to $(LB + UB)/2$
17: **while** TRUE **do**
18:    Learn a candidate HMM model with state number s, and compute observation probability of it, denote as OP_S
19:    **if** $OP_S \simeq OP_{UB}$ **then**
20:       Set $LB = s$;
21:       Set $s = \lceil((LB + UB)/2)\rceil$, that is the smallest integer value larger than or equal to $(LB + UB)/2$
22:    **else**
23:       Set $UB = s$;
24:       Set $s = \lfloor((LB + UB)/2)\rfloor$;
25:    **end if**
26:    **if** $LB \equiv UB$ **then**
27:       Output s
28:       Break
29:    **else**
30:       Continue
31:    **end if**
32: **end while**

6. EVALUATION

It has been proved in the literature that the HMM learning algorithm will converge to the ground truth with infinite observations of the behavior sequence [5]. In practice, one needs to train the model with "sufficient" observation data to achieve good convergence. Similarly, one requires sufficient data for our model complexity estimation algorithm to work effectively. The sufficiency of observation data is highly dependent on the model complexity and often needs to be determined empirically. In Figure 5, we present our results from numerical experiments. We run the HMM learning algorithm 20 times for different $Model_T$ values (i.e., as shown by the x-axis in Figure 5). For each run, we gradually increase the length of the observation sequence and record the length when the candidate model complexity converges to $Model_T$. The median, minimum and maximum value of the training sequence length for different model complexity values are illustrated in Figure 5. As a result, to ob-

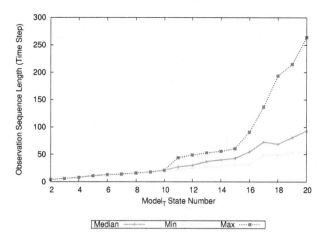

Figure 5: **Amount of Observation Data Sufficient for various** $Model_T$

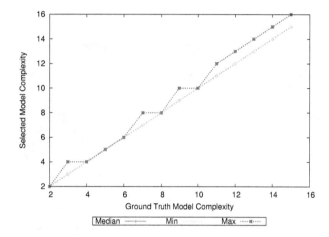

Figure 6: **Effectiveness of Model Complexity Estimation**

tain an accurate model complexity estimation (line 6-8 in Algorithm 1), the observation sequence length should be greater than some minimum threshold value of the training sequence length required for the chosen candidate model complexity. In practice, to obtain such threshold values for different model complexities requires conducting empirical experiments as we discuss above.

In Figure 6, we show the effectiveness of our model complexity estimation algorithm. We ran the algorithm 20 times for different $Model_T$ values (as shown as the x-axis in Figure 6) with sufficient data (i.e., more than the minimum value for each complexity level, as shown in Figure 5). The Median, Min, and Max value of the model complexity estimation results are reported. We can see that the algorithm never under-estimates the model complexity, which is desirable for maintaining the accuracy of the overall behavior characterization scheme. Further, the algorithm only occasionally over-estimates the model complexity, and the difference between the over-estimated model and the ground truth model is acceptably small (often only one state more for the over-estimated model).

We then evaluated the effectiveness of our proposed scheme

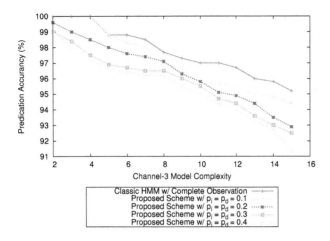

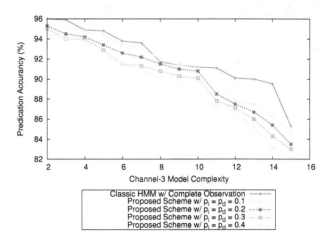

Figure 7: Proposed Approach Effectiveness (Median Value)

Figure 8: Proposed Approach Effectiveness (Minimum Value)

(as described in Algorithm 1) using simulation. In the experiment, we have two communication channels with their behavior modeled with a Bernoulli distribution with packet drop rate p_d and data-corruption rate p_i. Additionally, we have a third channel whose behavior model is temporally correlated. We set the steady-state probability of packet-drop and data-corruption rates for the third channel to be 33%, respectively. The goal is to vary the values p_d and p_i of the two Bernoulli channels (from 10% to 40% as shown by different curves in Figure 7 and Figure 8), and control the percentage of unknown observations in the behavior sequence when applying the majority voting scheme. Then, we vary the model complexity of the third channel (from 2 to 15 states as shown by the x-axis in Figure 7 and Figure 8) and apply our model complexity estimation algorithm, after accumulating enough observations (as discussed in Section 5). By running the simulation 20 times with 1000 time-steps each, we measured the predication accuracy of the learned behavior model for the third channel at each time-step the majority voting scheme failed. For comparison purposes, we run a classic HMM learning algorithm in parallel. The algorithm is aware of the true model complexity value and has access to complete channel behavior observations (without unknown observations).

Figure 7 and 8 show the results of this experiment. Overall, our proposed scheme can achieve very high predication accuracy when compared to the classic HMM algorithm with complete observation sequence. We observe median prediction accuracy to be greater than 90% for most cases (see Figure 7), and minimum values greater than 80% (see Figure 8). The overall downward trend of the graph is because as the model complexity increases, the differences between the learned model and the true model increases as well.

7. CONCLUSION

We studied the problem of characterizing the behavior of communication channels in a networked control system, where the channel's behavior exhibits temporal correlation. We proposed a behavior characterization mechanism based on the hidden Markov model. We showed that there are many challenges in adopting this approach due to incomplete observations and the lack of *a priori* information about the model complexity. Further, we demonstrated that these challenges can be addressed by: 1) designing an enhanced learning algorithm for refining the HMM model parameters, which can handle missing observations. Additionally, we simultaneously reduce the missing observations by using the history of received and applied control inputs and the knowledge of the current plant state to fill the gaps in the observation sequences, with the benefit of hindsight; and (2) using two well-defined model quality criteria simultaneously to determine the HMM complexity. In the future, we intend to study and characterize stability of the system as the manager M in Fig. 1 switches between different (correct and incorrect) channels to apply a control input to the plant, as it learns their behavior model.

References

[1] Saurabh Amin, Alvaro Cardenas, and S. Sastry. Safe and secure networked control systems under denial-of-service attacks. In Rupak Majumdar and Paulo Tabuada, editors, *Hybrid Systems: Computation and Control*, volume 5469 of *Lecture Notes in Computer Science*, pages 31–45. 2009.

[2] A. Bemporad, W.P.M.H. Heemels, and M. Johansson (eds). *Networked Control Systems*, volume 406. Lecture Notes in Control and Information Sciences, Springer-Verlag, 2010.

[3] Terry Caelli and Brendan McCane. Component analysis of hidden markov models in computer vision. In *Proceedings of the 12th International Conference on Image Analysis and Processing*, pages 510–, Washington, DC, USA, 2003. IEEE Computer Society.

[4] Thomas H. Cormen, Clifford Stein, Ronald L. Rivest, and Charles E. Leiserson. *Introduction to Algorithms*. McGraw-Hill Higher Education, 2nd edition, 2001.

[5] Brian G. and Leroux. Maximum-likelihood estimation for hidden markov models. *Stochastic Processes and their Applications*, 40(1):127 – 143, 1992.

[6] M Ge. Hidden markov model based fault diagnosis for stamping processes. *Mechanical Systems and Signal Processing*, 18(2):391–408, 2004.

[7] V. Gupta, A. F. Dana, J. Hespanha, R. M. Murray, and B. Hassibi. Data transmission over networks for estimation and control. *IEEE Transactions on Automatic Control*, 54(8):1807–1819, Aug. 2009.

[8] C. N. Hadjicostis and R. Touri. Feedback control utilizing packet dropping network links. In *Proc. of the 41st IEEE Conference on Decision and Control*, pages 1205–1210, 2002.

[9] J. P. Hespanha, P. Naghshtabrizi, and Y. Xu. A survey of recent results in networked control systems. *Proc. of the IEEE*, 95(1):138–162, Jan. 2007.

[10] J Huang and P Zhang. Fault diagnosis for diesel engines based on discrete hidden markov model. *2009 Second International Conference on Intelligent Computation Technology and Automation*, pages 513–516, 2009.

[11] O. C. Imer, S. Yuksel, and T. Basar. Optimal control of LTI systems over unreliable communication links. *Automatica*, 42(9):1429–1439, Sep. 2006.

[12] G. D. Forney Jr. The Viterbi algorithm. *Proceedings of the IEEE*, 61(3):268 – 278, March 1973.

[13] M. Krstic, I. Kanellakopoulos, and PV Kokotovic. Nonlinear design of adaptive controllers for linear systems. *Automatic Control, IEEE Transactions on*, 39(4):738–752, 1994.

[14] J Lee, S Kim, Y Hwang, and C Song. Diagnosis of mechanical fault signals using continuous hidden markov model. *Journal of Sound and Vibration*, 276(3-5):1065–1080, 2004.

[15] Michael D. Lemmon and Xiaobo Sharon Hu. Almost sure stability of networked control systems under exponentially bounded bursts of dropouts. In *HSCC*, pages 301–310, 2011.

[16] A.S. Matveev and A.V. Savkin. Comments on control over noisy channels and relevant negative results. *Automatic Control, IEEE Transactions on*, 50(12):2105 – 2110, Dec. 2005.

[17] A.R. Mesquita, J.P. Hespanha, and G. Nair. Redundant data transmission in control/estimation over wireless networks. In *Proc. of the 2009 American Control Conference*, pages 3378–3383, 2009.

[18] L. Rabiner and B. Juang. An introduction to hidden markov models. *ASSP Magazine, IEEE*, 3(1):4 –16, Jan 1986.

[19] L. Schenato, B. Sinopoli, M. Franceschetti, K. Poolla, and S. S. Sastry. Foundations of control and estimation over lossy networks. *Proc. of the IEEE*, 95(1):163–187, Jan. 2007.

[20] P. Seiler and R. Sengupta. Analysis of communication losses in vehicle control problems. In *Proc. of the 2001 American Control Conference*, pages 1491–1496, 2001.

[21] P. J. Smyth. Hidden Markov models for fault detection in dynamic systems. *NASA STI/Recon Technical Report N*, 933:30413, April 1993.

[22] K. Stouffer, J. Falco, and K. Scarfone. Guide to industrial control systems (ICS) security. Technical Report 800-82, National Institute of Standards and Technology, Sep. 2008.

[23] J. Stumper and R. Kennel. Inversion of linear and nonlinear observable systems with series-defined output trajectories. In *Computer-Aided Control System Design (CACSD), 2010 IEEE International Symposium on*, pages 1993–1998. IEEE, 2010.

[24] Shreyas Sundaram, Jian Chang, Krishna K. Venkatasubramanian, Chinwendu Enyioha, Insup Lee, and George J. Pappas. Reputation-based networked control with data-corrupting channels. In *Proceedings of the 14th international conference on Hybrid systems: computation and control*, HSCC '11, pages 291–300, 2011.

[25] Lloyd R. Welch. Hidden Markov Models and the Baum-Welch Algorithm. *IEEE Information Theory Society Newsletter*, 53(4), December 2003.

[26] Wee Chin Wong and Jay H. Lee. Fault detection and diagnosis using hidden markov disturbance models. *Industrial & Engineering Chemistry Research*, 49(17):7901–7908, 2010.

[27] Ren-Wu Yan and Jin-Ding Cai. Application of hidden markov model to fault diagnosis of power electronic circuit. *2009 IEEE Circuits and Systems International Conference on Testing and Diagnosis*, pages 1–4, 2009.

[28] Jie Yu. Multiway discrete hidden markov model-based approach for dynamic batch process monitoring and fault classification. *AIChE Journal*, 2011.

[29] Shun-Zheng Yu and Hisashi Kobayashi. A hidden semi-markov model with missing data and multiple observation sequences for mobility tracking. *Signal Process.*, 83:235–250, February 2003.

Coordinated Variable Structure Switching in Smart Power Systems: Attacks and Mitigation

Shan Liu, Deepa Kundur, Takis Zourntos and Karen Butler-Purry
Department of Electrical and Computer Engineering
Texas A&M University
College Station, Texas 77843-3128, USA
{liu2712, dkundur, takis, klbutler}@tamu.edu

ABSTRACT

Recently, a class of cyber-physical attacks termed coordinated variable structure switching attacks has been identified for future smart grid systems. Here, an attacker who has remotely gained access to a circuit breaker or switch is able to disrupt power system operation by applying a state-dependent switching sequence. The sequence can be effectively designed employing variable structure systems theory. In this work, we extend this research to demonstrate an approach to mitigation within this variable structure system framework. Specifically, we study strategies employed by a power system operator in the face of a switching attack to steer the system to a stable equilibrium through persistent co-switching and by leveraging the existence of a stable sliding mode. We demonstrate how such co-switching can be designed for a variant of the WECC 3-machine, 9-bus system using linearized models and then employ simulations in MATLAB/Simulink and PSCAD to demonstrate its potential in practice.

Categories and Subject Descriptors

C.4 [**Computer Systems Organization**]: Performance of Systems—*Modeling techniques*; G.1.7 [**Mathematics of Computing**]: Ordinary Differential Equations—*Convergence and stability*; I.6.5 [**Computing Methodologies**]: Model Development—*Modeling methodologies*

General Terms

Performance, security, theory

Keywords

cyber-physical system security, coordinated variable structure switching, smart grid attack mitigation

1. INTRODUCTION

It is well known that future smart grid systems aim to enable greater reliability, efficiency, economics, sustainability and security. This is achieved through the marriage of information technology with the power generation and delivery network. Within such a cyber-physical system increased autonomy and functionality is enabled, in part, through situational awareness and distributed control. A physical-to-cyber bridge manifests at measurement devices such as phasor measurement units (PMUs) and intelligent electronic devices (IEDs) to enable the acquisition of highly granular data for use in decision-making. A cyber-to-physical bridge arises at actuators including circuit breakers and switches which can be remotely controlled by system operators and distributed control devices.

Recently, the authors have demonstrated how an opponent can leverage the future connectivity of these breakers and switches to disrupt power delivery. Specifically, we have identified the existence of a class of cyber-physical system attacks entitled *coordinated variable structure switching attacks* in which an opponent can employ local state information to design a switching sequence that can destabilize synchronous generators leading to various forms of instability and power loss [2,3].

In this work, we extend our research to demonstrate an approach to mitigation within this variable structure system framework. Specifically, we study strategies employed by a power system operator in the face of a switching attack to steer the system to a stable equilibrium through persistent co-switching and by leveraging a stable *sliding mode*. In the next section, we provide a necessary background to variable structure systems and the sliding mode. We highlight the conditions for the existence of a sliding mode and demonstrate how the concept can be employed by either an attacker or system operator to achieve diverse objectives. In Section 3 we detail a mathematical approach to design a mitigation technique against the class of switching attacks and apply it to the Western Electricity Coordinating Council (WECC) 3-machine, 9-bus system. Simulations are employed to verify our design results in Section 4. The paper concludes with final remarks in Section 5.

2. COORDINATED VARIABLE STRUCTURE SWITCHING

2.1 Variable Structure Systems and the Sliding Mode

Variable structure systems are a class of hybrid dynamical systems that consist of a family of subsystems and one or more rules that govern the switching among them [6]. Such systems exhibit both continuous and discrete states of behavior important for modeling some underlying characteristics of cyber-physical systems. For example, the switching behavior represents an important analogy for discrete-time decision-making especially involving power network reconfiguration as determined by the state of associated circuit breakers and switches. Moreover, the subsystem dynamics represent a convenient structure from which to model power system physics under a static switch condition. The natural scalability of variable structure systems enables the modeling of complex interdependencies in cyber-enabled power systems.

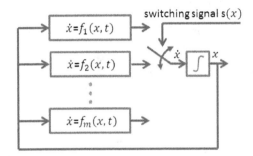

Figure 1: State-dependent variable structure system.

Fig. 1 is a pictorial representation of a variable structure system with *state-dependent* switching. Here, the subsystem dynamics are described as:

$$\dot{x} = f_i(x,t) \qquad (1)$$

where $i \in \{1, \ldots, m\}$ is the subsystem index (also known as the switch position), $x \in \mathbb{R}^{n \times 1}$ is the state vector, $f_i(x,t) \in \mathbb{R}^{n \times 1}$ is the subsystem dynamics corresponding to switch position i and $s(x) \in \mathbb{R}^{1 \times n}$ is the switching signal where $s(x) = 0$ is called the *switching surface*. For certain system parameters and selection of $s(x)$ it can be shown that Eq. 1 exhibits a form of behavior known as a *sliding mode* [1,6]. Here, the trajectory of x is attracted and subsequently confined to the n-dimensional surface $s(x) = 0$, which in the case of a sliding mode is also termed the *sliding surface*.

The necessary and sufficient conditions for the existence of a sliding mode are given by:

$$\lim_{s(x) \to 0^+} \dot{s}(x) < 0 \quad \text{and} \quad \lim_{s(x) \to 0^-} \dot{s}(x) > 0. \qquad (2)$$

For $m = n = 2$ and

$$\dot{x}(t) = \begin{cases} f_1(x,t), & s(x) > 0 \\ f_2(x,t), & s(x) \le 0 \end{cases}, \qquad (3)$$

Fig. 2 pictorially describes how the sliding surface partitions two distinct regions in state-space given by $s(x) > 0$ and $s(x) < 0$. When in either one of these regions local to the

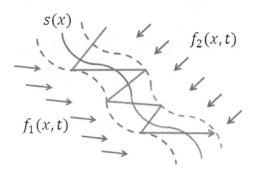

Figure 2: Under the conditions of Eq. 2 a state x is (locally) attracted to the sliding surface $s(x) = 0$, and once on this surface it will stay on the surface.

sliding surface, the state is attracted back to it as governed by the complementary sign of $\dot{s}(x)$ in Eq. 2.

Recently we have demonstrated how variable structure system theory can be applied to the modeling of power system reconfiguration and its subsequent attack. Through judicious selection of a sliding surface, an attacker can construct switching attacks on select breakers to destabilize power system components [2,3].

2.2 Cyber-Physical Attack via Variable Structure Theory

As power systems become increasingly cyber-enabled, cyber attack will become a possible method of wrongly gaining control of networked electromechanical switches. Forms of cyber attack may include intrusion into the communications infrastructure that networks the switch or the operating system of a device that controls it. Coordinated variable structure switching attacks are facilitated through cyber attack, but are designed to have a specific goal of physical disruption. They require that the opponent have control over the electromechanical switching actions of one or more relay(s) and/or circuit breaker(s) of the target power system as well as knowledge of the local state dynamics and partial state values.

An approach to construct a coordinated variable structure switching attack involves modeling the power system under consideration as a variable structure system and then identifying an appropriate sliding surface $s(x)$ that when applied as state-dependent switching, will destabilize the system; details are found in [2,3].

We illustrate attack construction through the elementary example of Fig. 3, which represents a load shedding scenario. The (blue) dashed lines and hexagons represent (cyber) communication channels, sensors, breaker actuators and the system control center. The (black) solid lines correspond to physical power system devices such as generators, loads, switches and transmission lines. In this example, the generator G can serve one of two possible loads $Z1$ or $Z2$ controlled through load switch $S2$. Employing information from sensors $S1$ and $S2$, the control center makes decisions on the position of $S2$ and hence the serviced load. The overall, switched system of Fig. 3 can be modeled as:

$$\dot{x} = \begin{cases} f_1(x,t), & s(x) > 0 \\ f_2(x,t), & s(x) \le 0 \end{cases} \qquad (4)$$

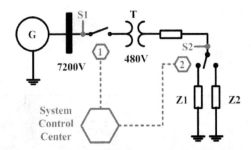

Figure 3: Elementary variable structure system example. Two different dynamics describe behavior of the power system depending on the status of switch $S2$.

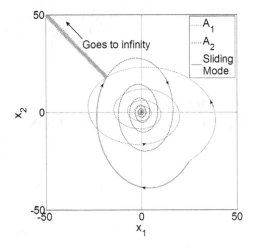

Figure 4: Phase portraits of switched system with $s = x_1 + x_2$.

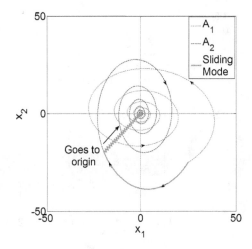

Figure 5: Phase portraits of switched system with $s = -x_1 + x_2$.

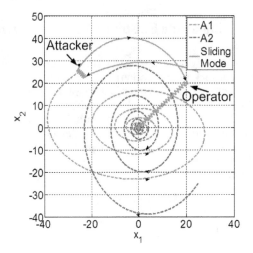

Figure 6: State trajectory for attack (at $t = 0$) using $s(x) = x_1 + x_2$ and attacker lockout and operator control (at $t = 1$s) using $s(x) = -x_1 + x_2$.

where $x \in \mathbb{R}^{n \times 1}$ is the state vector, $f_i(x,t) \in \mathbb{R}^{n \times 1}$, $i \in \{1, 2\}$ is the subsystem dynamics when $S2$ connects Z_i, and $s(x) \in \mathbb{R}^{1 \times n}$ where $s(x) = 0$ is the switching surface.

Consider a specific case of Fig. 3 in which we assume linear models and $n = 2$; where $x = [x_1, x_2]^T$. Suppose,

$$\dot{x} = \begin{cases} A_1 x, & s(x) > 0, \text{ where } A_1 = \begin{bmatrix} -1 & -10 \\ 5 & -0.5 \end{bmatrix} \\ A_2 x, & s(x) \leq 0, \text{ where } A_2 = \begin{bmatrix} -0.5 & 5 \\ -10 & -1 \end{bmatrix} \end{cases} \quad (5)$$

for some $s(x)$. It can be shown that both subsystems (i.e., in a static switch position) are globally asymptotically stable. However, under the following switching rules

$$s(x) = x_1 + x_2 \quad \text{and} \quad s(x) = -x_1 + x_2$$

the switched system trajectories of Fig. 4 and Fig. 5 are exhibited. The first switching rule exhibits unstable sliding mode behavior and would be appropriate to be employed by an attacker for system destabilization. The second switching rule enables the system to converge to the stable equilibrium point.

We have shown in [2, 3] how variable structure system theory can be used to design switching rules for attack to destabilize the system through the selection of an appropriate sliding surface $s(x)$. In this work, we focus on the properties of *stable* sliding modes and leverage their existence to equip operators with a means of mitigation against such attacks once detected.

To illustrate our idea, consider the situation whereby a switching attack is remotely applied to a system described by Eq. 5 using $s(x) = x_1 + x_2$ at time $t = 0$ seconds. Suppose through cyber and physical means of intrusion detection, an operator is able to identify the the attack and remove remote access capability of the opponent. In order to steer the system back to a stable equilibrium point, the operator can exploit the stable sliding mode of $s(x) = -x_1 + x_2$ at say time $t = 1$ second. The resulting state trajectory of the limited-time attack and operator control is shown in Fig. 6 with corresponding switch status in Fig. 7. We observe that the system travels along the unstable sliding mode until the attacker lockout and subsequent trajectory steering back to the equilibrium by the operator.

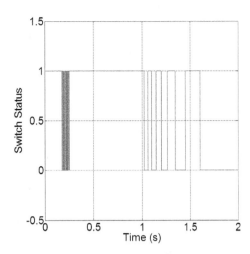

Figure 7: Switch status during attack and mitigation.

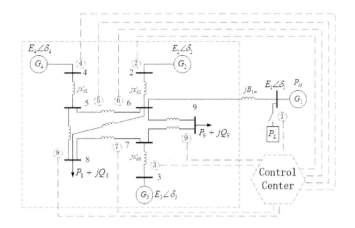

Figure 8: One line diagram of revised Western Electricity Coordinating Council (WECC) 3-machine, 9-bus system. The (red) dashed rectangle is approximated as a SMIB system.

2.3 Sliding Mode Existence for Linear Dynamics

Mathematically determining the existence of a sliding mode (for either attack or mitigation) for a general class of variable structure systems is equivalent to establishing that the conditions of Eq. 2 hold. Analytic results are difficult to determine for general subsystem dynamics, functions $s(x)$ and problem dimensionality. However, assuming linear models of dynamics and the switching surface and for a single switch case, the following theorem has been derived by the authors in [4] regarding the existence of such sliding modes.

THEOREM 1 (EXISTENCE OF A SLIDING MODE). *Given the variable structure system:*

$$\dot{x} = \begin{cases} A_1 x + b_1, & s(x) > 0 \\ A_2 x + b_2, & s(x) \leq 0 \end{cases} \quad (6)$$

where $x \in \mathbb{R}^{n \times 1}$, $A_i \in \mathbb{R}^{n \times n}$, $b_1 \in \mathbb{R}^{n \times 1}$ *and*

$$s(x) = Cx \in \mathbb{R} \quad (7)$$

for constant row vector $C = [c_1 \ c_2 \ \cdots \ c_n] \in \mathbb{R}^{1 \times n}$ *the necessary and sufficient conditions for the existence of a sliding mode are:*

$$\begin{cases} C(A_1 x + b_1) < 0, & s(x) > 0 \\ C(A_2 x + b_2) > 0, & s(x) < 0 \end{cases}. \quad (8)$$

We assert that this theorem is useful for identifying the parameters C to construct coordinating variable structure switching attacks or mitigation strategies because many power system configurations can be approximated as tractable low-order linear models within a local range of operating conditions. Specifically, an opponent or operator would have to determine the vector C for a given $A_i, b_i, i \in \{1, 2\}$ such that Eq. 8 holds. It can be shown that stable and unstable sliding modes exist and the operator can leverage such stable modes of behavior.

3. COORDINATED VARIABLE STRUCTURE SWITCHING FOR MITIGATION

In this section, we demonstrate the utility of Theorem 1 in determining a strategy for switching-based operator mitigation through study of a variant of the well known Western Electricity Coordinating Council (WECC) 3-machine, 9-bus system.

3.1 System Modeling and Variable Structure Representation

Fig. 8 shows both cyber and physical components of the WECC 3-machine, 9-bus system. The (blue) dashed lines represent the cyber components which correspond to communication channels, sensors, breaker actuators and the control center. The (black) solid lines illustrate physical power system elements including generators, loads, switches, transmission lines.

We approximate this system using the following second order nonlinear single-machine infinite bus (SMIB) model:

$$\begin{cases} \dot{\delta}_1 & = \omega_1 \\ M_1 \dot{\omega}_1 & = P_{M1} - E_1^2 G_{11} - s_L P_L \\ & \quad -E_1 E_\infty B_{1\infty} \sin \delta_1 - D_1 \omega_1 \end{cases} \quad (9)$$

where δ_1 and ω_1 are the rotor angle and rotor speed deviation of Generator G_1, respectively, and collectively form the system state vector $x = [\delta_1 \ \omega_1]^T$. The parameters M_1, D_1 and E_1 represent the moment of inertia, damping coefficient, and internal voltage of Generator G_1, respectively, E_∞ is the voltage magnitude at the infinite bus, P_L is the local load at Bus 1, s_L is the load switch status ($s_L = 1$, if the load is connected; $s_L = 0$, otherwise), and $B_{1\infty}$ is the transfer susceptance of the line between Bus 1 and infinite bus.

For simplicity, we may rewrite Eq. 9 as:

$$\begin{cases} \dot{\delta}_1 = \omega_1 \\ M_1 \dot{\omega}_1 = P_1 - C_{1\infty} \sin \delta_1 - D_1 \omega_1 \end{cases} \quad (10)$$

where $P_1 = P_{M1} - E_1^2 G_{11} - s_L P_L$ and $C_{1\infty} = E_1 E_\infty B_{1\infty}$. Assuming that $C_{1\infty} = 1, D_1 = 0.1, M_1 = 0.1, P_{M1} - E_1^2 G_{11} - P_L = 0, P_{M1} - E_1^2 G_{11} = 0.9$, the overall variable structure system can be represented as:

$$A_1 : \begin{cases} \dot{\delta}_1 = \omega_1 \\ \dot{\omega}_1 = -10 \sin \delta_1 - \omega_1 \end{cases} \quad \text{if } P_L \text{ connected}$$

$$A_2 : \begin{cases} \dot{\delta}_1 = \omega_1 \\ \dot{\omega}_1 = 9 - 10 \sin \delta_1 - \omega_1 \end{cases} \quad \text{if } P_L \text{ not connected}$$

$$(11)$$

where the system state $[\delta_1 \ \omega_1]^T$ represents the phase angle and frequency of Generator G_1.

3.2 Sliding Mode Existence

To apply Theorem 1 to our WECC system model of Eq. 11, we must linearize its representation. We make the simple approximation that $\sin \delta_1 \approx \delta_1$ when δ_1 is small. Assuming $s > 0$ and $s \leq 0$ corresponds to the load switch being closed (subsystem A_1) and open (subsystem A_2), respectively, we therefore obtain:

$$\dot{\delta}_1 = \omega_1$$
$$\dot{\omega}_1 = \begin{cases} -10\delta_1 - \omega_1, & s > 0 \\ 9 - 10\delta_1 - \omega_1, & s \leq 0 \end{cases}, \quad (12)$$

which corresponds to:

$$A_1 = A_2 = \begin{bmatrix} 0 & -1 \\ -10 & -1 \end{bmatrix},$$

$$b_1 = \begin{bmatrix} 0 \\ 0 \end{bmatrix}$$

and

$$b_2 = \begin{bmatrix} 0 \\ 9 \end{bmatrix}$$

in Eq. 6.

We may use Theorem 1 and leverage the linearity of the inequality boundaries to analytically determine the existence and parameter range of a linear sliding surface of the form $s(x) = Cx$. Specifically, we determine the range of C that guarantees the equilibrium point x^* is in the region of attraction given by:

$$\begin{cases} C(A_1 x^* + b_1) < 0, & s(x^*) > 0 \\ C(A_2 x^* + b_2) > 0, & s(x^*) < 0 \end{cases}.$$

For the linearized system of Eq. 12, the following existence conditions for the sliding mode $s = c_1 \delta_1 + c_2 \omega_1$ are determined:

$$\begin{cases} \begin{cases} c_1 \omega_1 - 10c_2\delta_1 - c_2\omega_1 < 0 \\ c_1\delta_1 + c_2\omega_1 > 0 \end{cases} \\ \begin{cases} c_1\omega_1 - 10c_2\delta_1 - c_2\omega_1 + 9c_2 > 0 \\ c_1\delta_1 + c_2\omega_1 < 0 \end{cases} \end{cases}. \quad (13)$$

The results for $x^* = [\delta_1^* \ \omega_1^*]^T = [1.1198 \ 0]^T$ (at the equilibrium of system A_2) are presented in Fig. 9.

As discussed in our previous work [2,3], a sliding mode can also be selected through visual inspection of the overlapping phase portraits of A_1 and A_2. Specifically, an attacker must identify a line whereby the trajectories of the active switched subsystem are pointing towards $s(x) = 0$. Fig. 10 shows the individual and overlapping phase portraits of the linearized subsystems of Eq. 12. Using both techniques (Theorem 1 and visual inspection) we, for example, can determine that the following sliding modes exist: an unstable sliding mode

at $s = \delta_1 + 0.5\omega_1$ appropriate for an attacker and a stable sliding mode at $s = \delta_1 + 10\omega_1$ appropriate for an operator trying to stabilize the system.

In the next section employing the attack and mitigation parameters identified here using linearized models, we execute our operator co-switching in the face of a coordinated variable structure switching attack on the lower order nonlinear model of Eq. 11 using MATLAB/Simulink and on a higher order model implemented in PSCAD®. We demonstrate how the identified parameters prove to result in an effective approach for operator restabilization.

4. SIMULATION RESULTS

4.1 SMIB Swing Equation Model

4.1.1 Phase Portraits

The nonlinear second order system model of Eq. 11 is characterized in Fig. 11, which presents the individual phase portraits for the switch in the closed and open position, and the overlapping phase portraits useful in identify a feasible sliding surface $s(x) = 0$. To determine the individual phase portraits, the equilibrium and saddle points are identified by setting the left hand side of the corresponding subsystem dynamics to zero. The system Jacobian matrix is employed to distinguish between the two.

The Jacobin matrix of subsystem A_1 can be expressed as:

$$J_1 = \begin{bmatrix} 0 & 1 \\ -10 \cos \delta_1 & -1 \end{bmatrix}. \quad (14)$$

Based on the Jacobian matrix, we identify that the equilibrium points $(2n\pi, 0)$ are stable focus (as all of the resulting eigenvalues of J_1 are all in the left hand plane) and $(2n\pi + \pi, 0)$ are saddle points (one or more eigenvalues of J_1 is in the right hand plane). The stability boundary of the system can be obtained based on the saddle points and inverse time system dynamics. The stability boundary partitions the 2-dimensional space into "smaller" periodically repeating spaces. Each such space includes one stable focus. If the initial state of the system lies in this space, the system will converge to the stable focus within this more compact space shown in the left graph of Fig. 11.

Similarly, we can identify that the equilibrium points of subsystem A_2 are $(2n\pi + 1.1198, 0)$ and $(2n\pi + 2.0218, 0)$, where n is an integer. The Jacobin matrix can be expressed as:

$$J_2 = \begin{bmatrix} 0 & 1 \\ -10 \cos \delta_1 & -1 \end{bmatrix}. \quad (15)$$

Thus, we identify that the equilibrium points $(2n\pi + 1.1198, 0)$ are stable focus and $(2n\pi + 2.0218, 0)$ are saddle points. The stability boundary of the system is obtained similarly to the case of A_1 above.

Using the overlapping phase portrait of Fig. 11, visual inspection can be employed to determine that $s = \delta_1 + 0.5\omega_1$ and $s = \delta_1 + 10\omega_1$ are indeed sliding modes of the system.

4.1.2 Empirical Results

In order to determine the validity of our proposed approach for mitigation, we simulate the nonlinear swing equation model of Eq. 11 in MATLAB/Simulnk. We first assume that the load is disconnected from the system (i.e., the variable structure system is switched initially to A_2). Therefore,

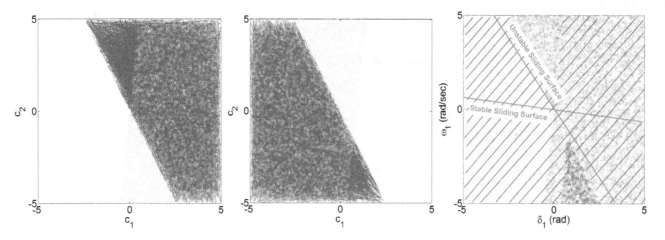

Figure 9: [left] Range of C for $s > 0$. [middle] Range of C for $s < 0$. [right] Overall range of C for existence of sliding mode; $s = \delta_1 + 0.5\omega_1$ (unstable) and $s = \delta_1 + 10\omega_1$ (stable) are highlighted.

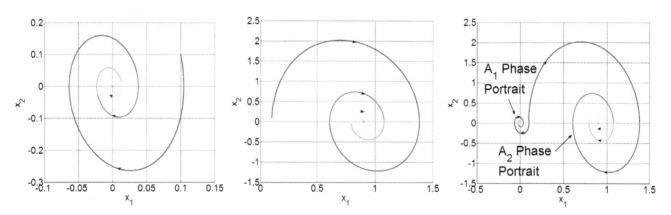

Figure 10: [left] Linearized phase portrait of system A_1. [middle] Linearized phase portrait of system A_2. [right] Overlapping linearized phase portraits.

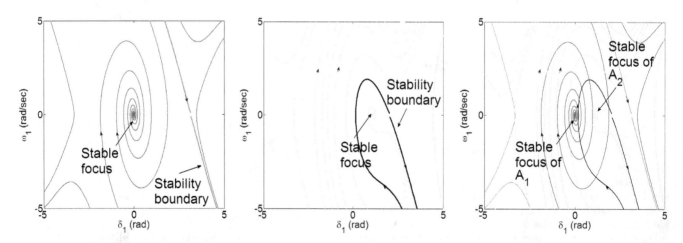

Figure 11: Phase portraits of Eq. 11 subsystems [left] for switch in closed position (A_1), [middle] for switch in open position (A_2), [right] shown overlapping.

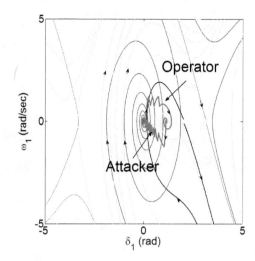

Figure 12: State trajectory employing the SMIB swing equation model in the presence of an attack (0-2.5 s) and operator co-switching (starting at 2.5s) for re-stabilization.

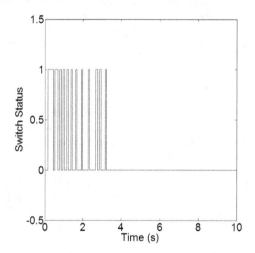

Figure 13: Load switch status during attack and mitigation.

the initial state of the system is chosen as the stable focus of A_2 given by $(1.1198, 0)$. If $s > 0$, the system dynamics switch to system A_1; otherwise, the system dynamics switch to system A_2. Due to the chattering effects, as detailed in [3] we employ a hysteresis effect to make the switching frequency finite.

We assume that an attacker applies a switching attack from 0 to 2.5 seconds employing the unstable sliding mode $s = \delta_1 + 0.5\omega_1$, which aims to drive the system trajectory across the stability boundary of the system A_2, to cause power system instability. Assuming that the operator is notified through intrusion detection systems of the attack, he/she can employs means to disconnect the attacker's remote access and re-steer the system trajectory back to the equilibrium point using the sliding surface $s = \delta_1 + 10\omega_1$ at 2.5 seconds. As can be seen in Fig. 12, the attacker is able to move the state over the stability boundary, but the operator successfully restabilizes the system. The corresponding load switch status is shown in Fig. 13.

4.2 PSCAD® Model

To further demonstrate the potential of our sliding mode design approach, we study applying the attack and mitigation switching strategies to a high order nonlinear PSCAD® model of the WECC 3-machine, 9-bus system of Fig. 8 [5]. Here, the base MVA is 100, the system normal frequency is 60 Hz and the generator parameters are detailed in Table 1. The transmission line connecting Generator G_1 and the infinite bus are modeled using an inductor of 0.014 H. The local load P_L is chosen to be 32.4 MW modeled using a constant resistor. The PSCAD® step size was chosen to be 50 μs. As in the former studies, the P_L load switch is used to attack the system.

Table 1: Generator parameters for WECC system

Name	Parameter	Gen 1	Gen 2
Rated RMS Line-Line Volatge	V_{gl-l}	13.8 kV	16.5 kV
Active Power	P_g	36 MW	100 MW
Power Factor	p_{fg}	0.8	0.8
Frequency	f	60 Hz	60 Hz
Direct axis unsaturated reactance	Xd	1.55	0.146
D axis unsaturated transient reactance	Xd'	0.22	0.0608
D axis open circuit unsaturated transient time constant	Tdo'	8.95 sec	8.96 sec
Q axis unsaturated reactance	Xq	0.76	0.0969
Q axis unsaturated transient reactance	Xq'	N.A	0.0969
Q axis open circuit unsaturated transient time constant	Tqo'	N.A	0.31
Inertia Constant	H	0.5 sec	23.64
Name	Parameter	Gen 3	Gen 4
Rated RMS Line-Line Volatge	V_{gl-l}	18.0 kV	13.8 kV
Active Power	P_g	163 MW	85MW
Power Factor	p_{fg}	0.8	0.8
Frequency	f	60 Hz	60 Hz
Direct axis unsaturated reactance	Xd	0.8958	1.3125
D axis unsaturated transient reactance	Xd'	0.1198	0.1813
D axis open circuit unsaturated transient time constant	Tdo'	6.0 sec	5.89 sec
Q axis unsaturated reactance	Xq	0.8645	1.2578
Q axis unsaturated transient reactance	Xq'	0.1969	0.25
Q axis open circuit unsaturated transient time constant	Tqo'	0.539	0.6
Inertia Constant	H	6.4	3.01

For consistent comparison, the initial state of the WECC

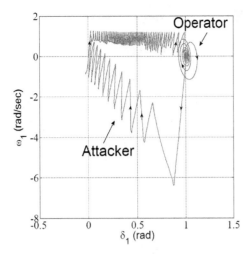

Figure 14: State trajectory employing the PSCAD® model in the presence of an attack (0-0.7s) and operator co-switching (starting at 0.7s) for re-stabilization.

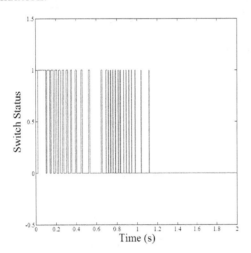

Figure 15: Load switch status during attack and mitigation.

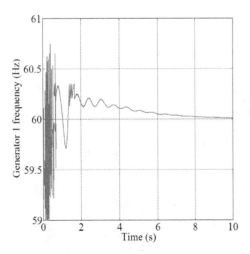

Figure 16: Generator G_1 frequency during attack and mitigation.

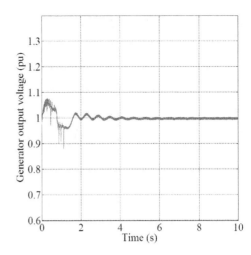

Figure 17: Generator G_1 output voltage during attack and mitigation.

system is set to to the stable focus of $(1.1198, 0)$ and the same sliding modes are employed by the attacker and operator. If $s > 0$, the system dynamics switch to system A_1 and if $s < 0$, they switch to A_2. The attacker applies the sliding mode attack from 0 to 0.7 seconds, which aims to drive the system trajectory across the stability boundary of A_2 at which point the switch is permanently set to A_2 making the system unstable. At 0.7 seconds, we assume the operator is notified of the attack the thus locks out the attacker by removing other forms of remote access to the switch and then applies switching to the load switch employing the stable sliding mode to drive the system trajectory back to the stable focus of system A_2.

Fig. 14 illustrates how the attacker moves the system over the stability boundary and the operator is subsequently able to redirect the state back to the stable equilibrium. The specific load switch status during both attack and mitigation is shown in Fig. 15. The Generator G_1 frequency and output voltage are displayed in Figs. 16 and 17 to show how operator co-switching enables transient, frequency and voltage stability in the power system.

5. CONCLUSIONS

This paper has extended our recent research identifying a class of power system reconfiguration vulnerabilities termed coordinated variable structure switching attacks by providing strategies for operators to re-stabilize the system (also through switching) once switch control is re-gained from the attacker. We propose a co-switching approach that exploits the existence of *stable* sliding modes that are then used to redirect the system trajectory back to an appropriate stable equilibrium point. Both analytic and empirical results are used to design and verify the potential of coordinated variable structure switching for mitigation.

6. ACKNOWLEDGMENTS

Funding for this work was provided through the Norman Hackerman Advanced Research Program Project 000512-0111-2009 and NSF grants EECS-1028246 and EEC-1062603. The authors also would like to thank Xianyong Feng for providing a preliminary version of the files for the PSCAD® simulations.

7. REFERENCES

[1] R. A. Decarlo, S. H. Zak, and G. P. Matthews. Variable structure control of nonlinear multivariable systems: A tutorial. *Proceedings of the IEEE*, 76(3):212–232, 1988.

[2] S. Liu, X. Feng, D. Kundur, T. Zourntos, and K. Butler-Purry. A class of cyber-physical switching attacks for power system disruption. In *Proc. 7th Cyber Security and Information Intelligence Research Workshop*, Oak Ridge National Laboratory, October 2011.

[3] S. Liu, X. Feng, D. Kundur, T. Zourntos, and K. L. Butler-Purry. Switched system models for coordinated cyber-physical attack construction and simulation. In *Proc. Second IEEE International Conference on Smart Grid Communications (SmartGridComm)*, Brussels, Belgium, October 2011.

[4] S. Liu, S. Mashayekh, D. Kundur, T. Zourntos, and K. Butler-Purry. A smart grid vulnerability analysis framework for coordinated variable structure switching attacks. In *Proc. IEEE Power Engineering Society General Meeting*, page under review, 2012.

[5] P. W. Sauer and M. A. Pai. *Power System Dynamics and Stability*. Stipes Publishing Co., 2007.

[6] Z. Sun and S. S. Ge. *Switched Linear Systems: Control and Design*. Springer-Verlag, London, 2005.

Leader Selection Games under Link Noise Injection Attacks

Andrew Clark, Linda Bushnell, and Radha Poovendran
Dept. of Electrical Engineering, University of Washington
Seattle, WA, USA
awclark@uw.edu, lb2@uw.edu, rp3@uw.edu

ABSTRACT

In a leader-follower multi-agent system, the states of a set of leader agents are controlled directly by the system owner and used to influence the behavior of the remaining follower agents. When deployed in hostile environments, leader-follower systems may be disrupted by adversaries introducing noise in the communication links between agents through interference or false packet insertion, thus corrupting the states of the follower agents. In this paper, we study the problem of mitigating the effect of noise injection attacks by selecting leader agents. We address two cases within a supermodular game-theoretic framework. In the first case, a fixed set of leaders is chosen when the system is initialized. We model this case as a Stackelberg game, in which the system moves first by choosing leaders in order to minimize the worst-case error and the adversary responds by introducing noise. In the second case, the set of leaders varies over time. We study the second case as a simultaneous-move game between the system and an adversary. We show that the game formulations for both cases have equilibria that can be approximated up to a provable bound using supermodular optimization techniques. We illustrate our approach via simulations.

Categories and Subject Descriptors

J.2 [**Computer Applications**]: Engineering

General Terms

Theory

Keywords

Submodular optimization, multi-agent systems, game theory

1. INTRODUCTION

Networked multi-agent systems (MAS) are prevalent in a variety of settings, such as formation control of unmanned vehicles [7]. In such systems, each agents receives inputs from its neighbors, performs computations to update its state, and then broadcast its updated state information to its neighbors. An important sub-class of MAS consists of leader-follower systems, in which a set of leader agents are controlled directly by the system owner and influence the remaining agents [8].

In a hostile environment, an adversary can disrupt the performance of a leader-follower system by injecting noise into the communication links between agents. The injected noise corrupts the inputs broadcast from leaders to followers, or between follower agents, causing agents to update their states based on incorrect information. These incorrectly updated states are then broadcast and used as inputs by other agents, causing noise-induced errors to propagate through the system. This noise injection attack can be performed, for example, by broadcasting an interfering signal in the vicinity of the communicating agents.

The effect of noise on a leader-follower system can be mitigated by selecting leader agents to minimize errors due to noise [4]. Leaders that are selected in order to minimize error due to benign, environmental noise, however, may leave the network vulnerable to an attack because an intelligent adversary can observe the set of leaders and inject link noise accordingly. There are two cases for leader selection in MAS in hostile environments. In the first case, a fixed set of leaders is used for the lifetime of the MAS, and hence must be chosen to minimize the worst-case error [8]. In the second case, the agents may be equipped with sensing hardware that allows them to monitor their environment, observe increased noise levels, and update the set of leaders accordingly [9]. Currently, however, there is no analytical approach for selecting leaders in either of these cases.

In this paper, we study the problem of leader selection to mitigate the effects of noise injection attacks. We develop our approach within a two-player game framework, in which the MAS owner selects a set of leaders in order to minimize the mean-square error in the agent states, while the adversary injects noise on a set of communication links in order to maximize this error. We make the following specific contributions:

- We study the problem of leader selection in MAS in the presence of an adversary mounting a link noise injection attack. We study two classes of the leader selection problem: (a) the problem of selecting a fixed set of leaders, and (b) the problem of adaptively choosing leaders in response to an attack.

- We model the selection of a fixed set of leaders as a

supermodular Stackelberg game, leading to efficient algorithms for approximating the optimal leader set up to a provable bound. As an intermediate step, we prove that the limit of a sequence of supermodular functions and the integral of a collection of supermodular functions are supermodular.

- We formulate a repeated, simultaneous-move game modeling the interaction between the adversary and the MAS for the case where the leader set may change over time. We develop efficient algorithms for approximating a mixed-strategy Nash equilibrium for the game, and provide bounds on its optimality for each player.

- We evaluate the performance of MAS under both models via simulation study. We compare our leader selection methods to other approaches, including random and degree-based leader selection, and show that our scheme leads to lower overall mean-square error in the agent states under link noise injection attacks. We further observe that allowing the leader set to vary over time improves the resilience of the MAS to noise injection.

2. RELATED WORK

Current approaches to mitigating link noise injection attacks on leader-follower systems focus on securing the communication protocol used by the agents, or designing the agent state dynamics to be robust to noise. Protocol-based methods, such as frequency hopping, attempt to hide the communication channel used for inter-agent communication and thereby prevent the adversary from injecting noise into the channel [11]. From a control-theoretic standpoint, the state dynamics of the agents can be designed to be robust to noise. In [14], a convex optimization approach to deriving the agent state dynamics in order to minimize the mean-square error due to link noise was proposed. While both protocol-based and control-theoretic methods can be used to improve the resilience of a MAS with given leaders to link noise injection, neither of these methods specifies which leaders should be chosen.

Choosing leader agents to act as control inputs to MAS has been examined in [4,8]. These approaches are based on MAS operating in the absence of adversaries, and hence may lead to a suboptimal leader set when an intelligent adversary attempts to disrupt the MAS.

The rest of this paper is organized as follows. In Section 3, the system model is presented, along with background on game theory and supermodular functions. In Section 4, we introduce a game-theoretic model for selection of a fixed set of leaders in the presence of adversaries. In Section 5, we formulate a game for the case where the set of leader agents changes in response to adversarial actions. Section 6 presents our simulation results. Section 7 concludes the paper.

3. SYSTEM MODEL AND PRELIMINARIES

In this section, the system and adversary models are presented. Needed background information on game theory and the theory of supermodular functions is also given.

3.1 System Model

An MAS consisting of n agents, indexed in the set $V = \{1, \ldots, n\}$, is considered. Each agent i is assumed to have a time-varying state $x_i(t) \in \mathbb{R}$. The state variable may represent heading or velocity (in the case where the MAS is a vehicle formation) or sensor measurements. Let $\mathbf{x}(t) \in \mathbb{R}^n$ denote the vector of agent states at time t.

A subset $S \subseteq V$, consisting of the leader agents, receives state values directly from the MAS owner. Let $\mathbf{x}_f(t) \in \mathbb{R}^{n-|S|}$ and $\mathbf{x}_l(t) \in \mathbb{R}^{|S|}$ denote the vectors of follower and leader states, respectively. Assume, without loss of generality that the indices are chosen such that $\mathbf{x}(t) = [x_f(t) \quad x_l(t)]^T$. The leader agent states $\mathbf{x}_l(t)$ are input by the MAS owner, while the follower agents update their state values.

Each follower agent $i \in V \setminus S$ receives a relative state value r_{ij} from each neighboring agent j, where $r_{ij} = x_i(t) - x_j(t) + \epsilon_{ij}(t)$. $\epsilon_{ij}(t)$ is a white noise process with mean 0 and variance ν_{ij}. The set of neighbors of agent i is denoted $N(i)$. If $j \in N(i)$, then we say a link (i, j) exists. Let E denote the link set. It is assumed that if $(i, j) \in E$, then $(j, i) \in E$ and $\nu_{ij} = \nu_{ji}$. The degree of agent i is defined to be the number of neighbors of i, $|N(i)|$.

In order to estimate its correct state value relative to the leader set, agent $i \in V \setminus S$ updates its state according to a best linear unbiased estimator of x_i, defined by [2]

$$\dot{x}_i(t) = -D_i^{-1} \sum_{j \in N(i)} \nu_{ij}^{-1} r_{ij}(t) \qquad (1)$$

where $D_i = \sum_{j \in N(i)} \nu_{ij}^{-1}$. It is assumed that each agent i has a mechanism to estimate the noise characteristics of each link (i, j) and choose the weights in (1) accordingly.

Define the $n \times n$ matrix L by

$$L = (L_{ij}) = \begin{cases} -\nu_{ij}^{-1}, & (i, j) \in E \\ D_i, & i = j \\ 0, & \text{else} \end{cases} \qquad (2)$$

L can be written in the form

$$L = \left(\begin{array}{c|c} L_{ff} & L_{fl} \\ \hline L_{lf} & L_{ll} \end{array} \right) \qquad (3)$$

so that the overall dynamics of the follower agents can be written in vector form as

$$\dot{\mathbf{x}}_f(t) = -D^{-1}(L_{ff} x_f(t) + L_{fl} x_l(t)) + W(t) \qquad (4)$$

where $W(t)$ is a white process. The following theorem, first proved in [2], describes the mean-squared error of each follower agent's state when the dynamics of (1) are used.

THEOREM 1. *Let* $\mathbf{x}^* \in \mathbb{R}^n$ *denote the target state of the MAS, defined by* $\mathbf{x}^* = \mathbf{x}_r + x_0 \mathbf{1}$, *where* $\mathbf{x}_r$ *is a known constant and* x_0 *is an unknown reference point. Suppose that* $\mathbf{x}_s(t) \equiv \mathbf{x}_s^*$ *for all* $s \in S$. *Then for each* $u \in V \setminus S$,

$$\lim_{t \to \infty} \mathbf{E}[(\mathbf{x}_u(t) - \mathbf{x}_u^*)^2] = (L_{ff}^{-1})_{uu} \qquad (5)$$

The total mean-square error due to noise is given by the function

$$\chi(S, \nu) = \sum_{u \in V \setminus S} (L_{ff}^{-1})_{uu}. \qquad (6)$$

We will analyze two cases of the leader set S. In the first case, the leader set S is fixed throughout the system lifetime [8]. In the second case, the leader set S may change over time [9].

3.2 Adversary Model

The MAS is assumed to be deployed in the presence of an adversary who is capable of injecting noise on the links between agents by broadcasting an interfering signal in the vicinity of the agents. This noise injection leads to an overall error variance $\nu_{ij} = \nu_{ij}^0 + \nu_{ij}^A$, where ν_{ij}^0 and ν_{ij}^A are the variances of the error on link (i, j) due to ambient noise and adversarial noise, respectively.

The variance ν_{ij}^A is equal to the received strength of the interfering signal broadcast by the adversary. The received strength depends on the position of the receiver, denoted $y_j \in \mathbb{R}^3$, the position of the adversary, denoted $z \in \mathbb{R}^3$, the transmit power of the adversary for link (i, j), denoted P_{ij}, and the path-loss constant of the propagation medium, denoted α. We assume that, in order to avoid detection, the adversary does not choose its position to coincide with any agents, so that $z \neq y_j$ for all j. The resulting error variance is given by $\nu_{ij}^A = P_{ij}\|y_j - z\|_2^{-\alpha}$. It is assumed that the adversary has a constraint P_A on the total power available, so that

$$\sum_{(i,j) \in E} P_{ij} = \sum_{(i,j) \in E} \nu_{ij}^A \|z - y_j\|_2^\alpha \leq P_A \qquad (7)$$

The adversary is assumed to know the network topology and the environmental noise characteristics ν_{ij}^0 for all $(i, j) \in E$. Furthermore, since the leader agents do not follow the dynamics (1), the adversary can determine the leader set S by eavesdropping on the agents' state values and observing which agents do not update their states according to (1).

3.3 Background – Game Theory

A game is defined by a set of players $\{\mathcal{P}_1, \ldots, \mathcal{P}_m\}$. Each player $\mathcal{P}_i$ has a set of strategies $\mathcal{S}_i$ and a utility function $U_i : \mathcal{S}_1 \times \cdots \times \mathcal{S}_m \to \mathbf{R}$. The utility function U_i represents $\mathcal{P}_i$'s benefit from its action $s_i \in \mathcal{S}_i$ and the actions of the remaining players. The goal of each player $\mathcal{P}_i$ is to maximize its utility U_i.

For simplicity, we restrict ourselves to two-player games ($m = 2$). It is assumed that each player knows the strategy space and utility function of the other player. In addition, in a *Stackelberg* game, player $\mathcal{P}_2$ observes the strategy $s_1 \in \mathcal{S}_1$ chosen by $\mathcal{P}_1$ before choosing a strategy $s_2 \in \mathcal{S}_2$. In order to maximize its utility, $\mathcal{P}_2$ will therefore choose strategy $s_2^* \in \mathcal{S}_2$ that satisfies[1]

$$s_2^* \in \arg \max_{s_2 \in \mathcal{S}_2} U_2(s_1, s_2) \qquad (8)$$

Let $s_2^*(s_1)$ denote $\mathcal{P}_2$'s optimal strategy when $\mathcal{P}_1$ chooses strategy s_1. $\mathcal{P}_1$ will therefore choose strategy s_1^* that maximizes its utility given $\mathcal{P}_2$'s response:

$$s_1^* \in \arg \max_{s_1 \in \mathcal{S}_1} U_1(s_1, s_2^*(s_1)) \qquad (9)$$

By contrast, in a *simultaneous-move game*, the two players choose their strategies at the same time, so that neither player observes the strategy of the other player. In this case, when the players are rational, they will choose their strategies according to a *Nash equilibrium*, defined as follows [1].

DEFINITION 1. *A pair of strategies* $(s_1^*, s_2^*) \in \mathcal{S}_1 \times \mathcal{S}_2$ *is a* Nash equilibrium *if and only if*

$$s_1^* = \arg \max_{s_1 \in \mathcal{S}_1} U_1(s_1, s_2^*) \qquad (10)$$

$$s_2^* = \arg \max_{s_2 \in \mathcal{S}_2} U_2(s_1^*, s_2) \qquad (11)$$

In words, if (s_1^*, s_2^*) is a Nash equilibrium, then $\mathcal{P}_i$ cannot change its strategy s_i^* without decreasing his utility. Any strategy s_1^* (resp. s_2^*) satisfying (10) (resp. (11)) is a *best response* for player $\mathcal{P}_1$ (resp. $\mathcal{P}_2$).

Each player may attempt to improve its performance by randomizing over a set of strategies. This concept is defined as follows.

DEFINITION 2. *A mixed strategy for player* $\mathcal{P}_i$ *consists of a set of ordered pairs* $\{(s_i^{(1)}, p_1), \ldots, (s_i^{(r)}, p_r)\}$, *where* $s_i^{(j)} \in \mathcal{S}_i$ *for all* j *and the* p_j's *are nonnegative real numbers that sum to 1. Under this strategy, player* $\mathcal{P}_i$ *chooses strategy* $s_i^{(j)}$ *with probability* p_j. *A mixed strategy equilibrium is a Nash equilibrium in which one or more players uses a mixed strategy.*

3.4 Background – Supermodular Functions

Let V be a finite set, and let 2^V denote the set of subsets of V. A supermodular function is defined as follows.

DEFINITION 3. *A function* $f : 2^V \to \mathbf{R}$ *is defined to be supermodular if, for any subsets* $S, T \subseteq V$ *with* $S \subseteq T$ *and* $v \in V \setminus T$,

$$f(S) - f(S \cup \{v\}) \geq f(T) - f(T \cup \{v\}) \qquad (12)$$

Definition 3 can be interpreted as a diminishing returns property of f as a function of S. The following two lemmas give methods for constructing supermodular functions [10].

LEMMA 1. *If* $f_1(S), \ldots, f_r(S)$ *is a set of supermodular functions of* S *and* $\alpha_1, \ldots, \alpha_r$ *are nonnegative constants, then* $f(S) = \sum_{i=1}^r \alpha_i f_i(S)$ *is a supermodular function.*

LEMMA 2. *If* $f(S)$ *is a supermodular function and* $r \geq 0$ *is constant, then the function* $\hat{f}(S) = \max\{f(S), r\}$ *is supermodular.*

The following theorem concerns limits of sequences of supermodular functions, and to the best of our knowledge has not appeared elsewhere in the literature.

THEOREM 2. *Suppose* $\{f_k(S)\}_{k=1}^\infty$ *is a collection of supermodular functions in* S, *and suppose that there exists a function* $f : 2^V \to \mathbb{R}$ *such that, for every* $S \subseteq V$ *and every* $\epsilon > 0$, *there exists* K *such that* $k > K$ *implies*

$$|f_k(S) - f(S)| < \epsilon. \qquad (13)$$

Then $f(S)$ *is supermodular.*

A proof of Theorem 2 can be found in the appendix.

4. PROBLEM FORMULATION – STATIC GAME

In this section, we consider the problem of choosing a fixed set of leaders in the presence of an adversary injecting noise.

---

[1]When more than one strategy s_2^* satisfies (8), we assume that $\mathcal{P}_2$ chooses the strategy satisfying (8) that minimizes U_1.

4.1 Game Definition

In this setting, the MAS owner first chooses a set of up to k leaders. The adversary then observes the set of leaders and chooses a set of error variances ν_{ij}^A satisfying the adversary's power constraint, given by (7). The goal of the adversary is to choose the vector ν^A such that the total system error $\chi(S, \nu^0 + \nu^A)$ of (6) is maximized, while the MAS owner's goal is to choose a set of leaders S such that the total error in the worst case is minimized.

We formulate this problem as a Stackelberg game, in which the first player, $\mathcal{P}_1$, is the MAS owner and the second player, $\mathcal{P}_2$, is the adversary. The strategy space $\mathcal{S}_1$ of the MAS owner is given by the set of possible leader sets, $\mathcal{S}_1 = \{S \subseteq V : |S| \leq k\}$. The adversary's strategy space, $\mathcal{S}_2$, consists of the set of feasible error variances (7).

The MAS utility is given by $U_{MAS}(S, \nu^A) = -\chi(S, \nu^0 + \nu^A)$, while the adversary's utility is given by $U_A(S, \nu^A) = \chi(S, \nu^0 + \nu^A)$, so that the MAS owner's goal is to minimize the total error variance, while the adversary's goal is to maximize it. In what follows, we explore the optimal pure strategies for each player in detail, leaving the analysis of possible mixed strategies as future work.

4.2 Solution Algorithms for Adversary

For a given leader set, the adversary's goal is to choose the error variances ν^A such that the total system error $\chi(S, \nu)$ is maximized. Hence the adversary's optimal strategy is given by the solution to the optimization problem

$$
\begin{aligned}
\underset{\nu_{ij}^A}{\text{maximize}} \quad & \chi(S, \nu^0 + \nu^A) \\
\text{s.t.} \quad & \nu_{ij}^A \geq 0 \quad \forall (i,j) \in E \\
& \sum_{(i,j) \in E} \nu_{ij}^A \|z - y_j\|_2^\alpha \leq P_A
\end{aligned} \tag{14}
$$

The following theorem leads to efficient solution algorithms for (14).

THEOREM 3. *The function $\chi(S, \nu)$ is a concave function of $\{\nu_{ij} : (i,j) \in E\}$.*

The proof of this theorem can be found in the appendix.

COROLLARY 1. *Problem (14) is a concave optimization problem.*

PROOF. The proof follows from Theorem 3 and the fact that the constraints of (14) are convex in ν_{ij}^A. □

As a result, the optimal strategy for the adversary can be computed in polynomial time using interior point algorithms [3].

4.3 Solution Algorithms for the MAS Owner

Since the adversary will choose the noise injection strategy that maximizes the error due to link noise, the goal of the MAS owner is to select leaders such that this worst-case error is minimized. The optimal strategy is therefore given as the solution to the optimization problem

$$
\begin{aligned}
\underset{S}{\text{minimize}} \quad & \max_{\nu^A} \chi(S, \nu^0 + \nu^A) \\
\text{s.t.} \quad & |S| \leq k
\end{aligned} \tag{15}
$$

Define $\chi(S) \triangleq \max_{\nu^A} \chi(S, \nu)$. Problem (15) involves optimizing over $\binom{n}{k}$ possible leader sets, which is infeasible when n or k is large. Moreover, functions of the form $g(S) = \max_i f_i(S)$, where $f_i(S)$ is supermodular, are not supermodular in general. We instead introduce an equivalent, supermodular formulation and derive a solution algorithm for (15) as a result.

As a preliminary, define $F_\zeta(S)$ by

$$
F_\zeta(S) \triangleq \frac{1}{|\mathcal{S}_2|} \int_{\mathcal{S}_2} \max\{\chi(S, \nu^0 + \nu^A), \zeta\} \, d\nu^A \tag{16}
$$

where $|\cdot|$ denotes the Lebesgue measure of a set. The function $F_\zeta(S)$ is supermodular as a function of S (see Appendix, Lemma 6). An algorithm for solving (15), based on the supermodularity of $F_\zeta(S)$, is as follows.

First, select parameters $\beta \geq 1$ and $\delta > 0$. The algorithm finds a set S satisfying $\chi(S) \leq \chi^*$, where χ^* is the optimal value of (15), and $|S| \leq \beta k$.

Define $\zeta_{min}^0 = 0$ and $\zeta_{max}^0 = \chi(\{1\})$, the error χ corresponding to leader set $S = \{1\}$. At the j-th iteration, let $\zeta^j = \frac{\zeta_{max}^{j-1} + \zeta_{min}^{j-1}}{2}$. The goal of the j-th iteration is to determine if there is a set S^j satisfying $\chi(S^j) \leq \zeta^j$ with $|S| \leq \beta k$. This is accomplished by solving the optimization problem

$$
\begin{aligned}
\text{minimize} \quad & |S| \\
\text{s.t.} \quad & F_\zeta(S) \leq \zeta^j
\end{aligned} \tag{17}
$$

noting that $\chi(S) \leq \zeta^j$ if and only if $F_\zeta(S) \leq \zeta^j$.

Problem (17) is solved as follows. Initialize $S^j = \emptyset$. At each iteration, choose v^* as

$$
v^* = \arg\max\{F_\zeta(S^j) - F_\zeta(S^j \cup \{v\}) : v \in V \setminus S\} \tag{18}
$$

Set $S^j = S^j \cup \{v\}$. The process continues until $F_\zeta(S^j) \leq \zeta^j$.

If S^j satisfies $|S^j| \leq \beta k$, then set $\zeta_{max}^j = \zeta^j$ and $\zeta_{min}^j = \zeta_{min}^{j-1}$. Otherwise, set $\zeta_{min}^j = \zeta^j$ and $\zeta_{max}^j = \zeta_{max}^{j-1}$. The algorithm terminates when $\zeta_{max}^j - \zeta_{min}^j < \delta$ and returns the set S^j. A pseudocode description of this approach is given as algorithm **Fixed-k**.

Fixed-k: Algorithm for selecting a fixed set of up to k leaders under worst-case noise injection attack

Input: Maximum number of leaders, k
Topology $G = (V, E)$, error variances $\nu^0(i,j)$
Parameters β and δ
Node positions y_j, $j \in V$, adversary position p
Output: Set of leaders S

$\zeta_{min} \leftarrow 0$, $\zeta_{max} \leftarrow \max_{\nu^A} \chi(\{1\}, \nu^0 + \nu^A)$	1
$j \leftarrow 0$	2
while $\zeta_{max} - \zeta_{min} \geq \delta$	3
$\quad \zeta \leftarrow (\zeta_{min} + \zeta_{max})/2$	4
$\quad S^j \leftarrow \emptyset$	5
$\quad$ **while** $F_\zeta(S^j) \geq \zeta$	6
$\quad\quad v^* \leftarrow \arg\max_{v \in V \setminus S^j}\{F_\zeta(S^j) - F_\zeta(S^j \cup \{v\})\}$	7
$\quad\quad S^j \leftarrow S^j \cup \{v^*\}$	8
$\quad$ **end while**	9
$\quad$ **if** $|S^j| > \beta k$	10
$\quad\quad \zeta_{min} \leftarrow \zeta$	11
$\quad$ **else**	12
$\quad\quad \zeta_{max} \leftarrow \zeta$	13
$\quad$ **end if**; $j \leftarrow j + 1$	14
end while	15
$S \leftarrow S^j$, return S	16

THEOREM 4. *If β satisfies*

$$\beta \geq 1 + \log \left\{ \frac{\max_{v \in V} F_\zeta(\{v\})}{\zeta^*} \right\} \quad (19)$$

*then **Fixed**-k returns a set S satisfying $\chi(S) \leq \chi(S^*)$ and $|S| \leq \beta k$.*

The proof can be found in the appendix. Corollary 1 implies that the adversary can compute the best-response to the chosen leader set S, while Theorem 4 proves that the strategy chosen by the MAS is within a provable bound of the optimum. These strategies, when taken together, therefore form an approximate Stackelberg equilibrium.

5. PROBLEM FORMULATION – REPEATED GAME

We now consider the case where the set of leaders can change over time.

5.1 Game Definition

Under this model, the MAS owner periodically updates the leader set S in order to minimize the overall system error $\chi(S, \nu)$, based on the observed noise characteristics ν. The adversary, upon observing a change in S, chooses a new noise injection strategy in order to maximize the error experienced by the MAS. This leads to a repeated game model for the interaction between the MAS and the adversary.

Formally, the MAS owner is the first player, $\mathcal{P}_1$, while the adversary is the second player, $\mathcal{P}_2$. At the t-th iteration of the game, the MAS owner selects a leader set S_t satisfying $|S_t| \leq k$. The adversary is unaware of the leader set for a time T, and hence chooses a vector of link error variances $\nu_t^A \in \mathcal{S}_2$ without knowledge of S_t, where $\mathcal{S}_2$ is defined as in Section 4. After time T elapses, the adversary discovers S_t and chooses a new vector of link error variances, $\tilde{\nu}_t^A \in \mathcal{S}_2$. An additional time T' elapses until the next iteration.

The penalty of the MAS at the t-th iteration is given by the average system error experienced, so that

$$U_{MAS}(S_t, \nu_t^A, \tilde{\nu}_t^A) = -\left(\frac{T}{T+T'} \chi(S, \nu^0 + \nu_t^A) + \frac{T'}{T+T'} \chi(S, \nu^0 + \tilde{\nu}_t^A) \right) \quad (20)$$

Similarly, the utility of the adversary is equal to the average system error:

$$U_A(S_t, \nu_t^A, \nu_t^{A\prime}) = \frac{T}{T+T'} \chi(S, \nu^0 + \nu_t^A) + \frac{T'}{T+T'} \chi(S, \nu^0 + \tilde{\nu}_t^A) \quad (21)$$

In what follows, it is assumed that it takes more time for the adversary to determine the leader set than for the MAS to detect the increase in error due to the noise injection attack, so that $T \gg T'$. Since the adversary and MAS are not aware of each other's strategies during this interval, this is a repeated simultaneous game with $U_{MAS}(S_t, \nu_t^A) \approx -\chi(S, \nu^0 + \nu_t^A)$ and $U_A(S_t, \nu_t^A) \approx \chi(S, \nu^0 + \nu_t^A)$. We first study the best-response behavior of each player. We then analyze the equilibria of the game based on the best-response behavior.

5.2 Best-Response Strategies

We first analyze the best-response strategy for the adversary at each iteration t. For a given choice of S_t, the adversary's best response to S_t is given by

$$\begin{array}{ll} \text{maximize} & \chi(S_t, \nu^0 + \nu_t^A) \\ \text{s.t.} & \nu_t^A \in \mathcal{S}_2 \end{array} \quad (22)$$

The function $\chi(S_t, \nu^0 + \nu_t^A)$ is a convex function of ν_t^A by Theorem 3. Hence the adversary's optimal noise allocation ν_t^A at each iteration can be obtained by solving (22) via convex optimization.

The MAS's problem of choosing the optimal leader set to minimize noise in response to ν_t^A is formulated as

$$\begin{array}{ll} \text{minimize} & \chi(S_t, \nu^0 + \nu_t^A) \\ \text{s.t.} & |S_t| \leq k \end{array} \quad (23)$$

Problem (23) can be solved by supermodular optimization, as shown by the following theorem, proved in [4].

THEOREM 5. *For fixed ν, $\chi(S, \nu)$ is a supermodular function of S.*

While minimizing a supermodular function is NP-hard in general, a greedy algorithm can be used to approximate the optimal leader set S_t [10]. In the algorithm, the leader set $S_t = \emptyset$ initially. At each iteration, the agent v^* satisfying

$$v^* = \arg \max \left\{ v \in V \setminus S_t : \chi(S_t, \nu^0 + \nu_t^A) \right.$$
$$\left. -\chi(S_t \cup \{v\}, \nu^0 + \nu_t^A) \right\} \quad (24)$$

is added to the leader set. The algorithm terminates after k iterations. A pseudocode description as algorithm **BestResponse**-k.

BestResponse-k: Algorithm for selecting up to k leaders in response to an adversary's strategy

Input: Maximum number of leaders, k
Graph topology $G = (V, E)$
Link error variances $\nu_t = \nu_t^0 + \nu_t^A$
Output: Leader set S_t

$S_t \leftarrow \emptyset$, $l \leftarrow 0$	1
while $l < k$	2
$\quad v^* \leftarrow \arg \max \{ v \in V \setminus S_t : \chi(S_t, \nu_t)$	
$\quad -\chi(S_t \cup \{v\}, \nu_t) \}$	3
$\quad S_t \leftarrow S_t \cup \{v^*\}$, $l \leftarrow l + 1$	4
end while	5
return S_t	6

THEOREM 6. *Let S_t^* be the optimal solution to (23). Then the set S returned by **BestResponse**-k satisfies*

$$\chi(S_t, \nu_t^0 + \nu_t^A) \leq \left(1 - \frac{1}{e}\right) \chi(S_t^*, \nu_t^0 + \nu_t^A) + \frac{1}{e} \chi_{max} \quad (25)$$

where $\chi_{max} \triangleq \max_i \sum_{j \in V} \chi(i, j)$.

PROOF. The proof follows from Proposition 4.1 of [10] and the supermodularity of the error χ. $\square$

5.3 Equilibrium Analysis

As discussed in Section 3.3, the MAS owner and the adversary will maximize their utilities by playing a Nash equilibrium strategy at each iteration t. In general, determining

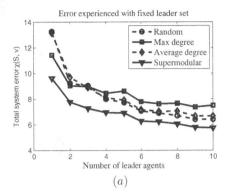

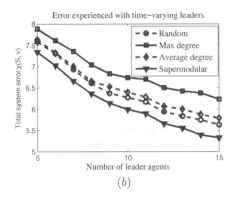

Figure 1: (a) Simulation of selection of a fixed set of leaders in the presence of adversarial noise using random, degree-based, and supermodular algorithms. While all schemes experience a decrease in performance, the supermodular selection approach provides the most robustness to noise. (b) Simulation of the approximate Nash equilibrium that arises from updating the leader set over time. All schemes outperform the case of fixed leader selection, while the supermodular optimization approach outperforms both random and degree-based approaches.

Nash equilibria of two-player games is PPAD-complete [12, Ch. 4.1]. Moreover, in this case, the MAS's best-response strategy is NP-hard to compute. Instead, the following algorithm, first proposed for general two-player games [5], can be used to efficiently compute an approximate mixed-strategy equilibrium. We note that there may be other equilibria, which we will characterize in future work.

The MAS first chooses a set of leaders S. The adversary computes $\hat{\nu}^A$ by solving the best-response problem of (22) based on the leader set S. The MAS approximates the best-response S' to $\hat{\nu}^A$ using **BestResponse**-k.

The MAS's strategy is to choose leader set S with probability $1/2$ and to choose S' with probability $1/2$, corresponding to a mixed strategy $\{(S, 1/2), (S', 1/2)\}$. The adversary's strategy is to choose link error variances $\hat{\nu}^A$ with probability 1. A pseudocode description of the algorithm for approximating a Nash equilibrium is given as algorithm **Approx-NE**.

Approx-NE: Algorithm for computing
an approximate Nash equilibrium

Input: Maximum number of leaders, k
Graph topology $G = (V, E)$ and variances ν^0
Adversary's position y and power constraint P
Output: Noise error variances $\hat{\nu}^A$ for adversary
Mixed strategy $\{(S^{(1)}, p_1), (S^{(2)}, p_2)\}$ for MAS

$S \leftarrow$ **BestResponse**-$k(\nu^0, G, k)$	1
$\hat{\nu}^A \leftarrow$ **NoiseInjection**(ν^0, G, y, P)	2
$S' \leftarrow$ **BestResponse**-$k(\nu^0 + \hat{\nu}^A, G, k)$	3
return $\{(S, 1/2), (S', 1/2)\}, \hat{\nu}^A$	4

The following theorem gives a bound on the approximation error of **Approx-NE**.

THEOREM 7. *Let $\hat{U}_{MAS}$ be the utility of the MAS under the strategy defined above, and let $\hat{U}_A$ be the utility of the adversary. Let U_{MAS}^* be the best-response utility of the MAS to the adversary's strategy, and let U_A^* be the best-response utility of the adversary. Then*

$$\hat{U}_{MAS} \geq \frac{1}{2}\left[\left(1 - \frac{1}{e}\right)U_{MAS}^* - \frac{1}{e}\chi_{max}\right] - \frac{1}{2}\chi_{max} \quad (26)$$

$$\hat{U}_A \geq \frac{1}{2}U_A^* \quad (27)$$

PROOF. Let S^* be the MAS's best response to the adversary's strategy $\hat{\nu}^A$, and let $U_{MAS}(S^*)$ be the resulting utility of the MAS. Let $\mathbf{S}$ be a random variable corresponding to the leader set under the mixed strategy returned by **Approx-NE**. Then under this mixed strategy,

$$\begin{aligned}\mathbf{E}(U_{MAS}(\mathbf{S}, \hat{\nu}^A)) &= U_{MAS}(S, \hat{\nu}^A)Pr(\mathbf{S} = S) \\ &\quad + U_{MAS}(S', \hat{\nu}^A)Pr(\mathbf{S} = S') \\ &\geq -\frac{1}{2}\chi_{max} + \frac{1}{2}\left[\left(1 - \frac{1}{e}\right)U_{MAS}(S^*) \right. \\ &\quad \left. -\frac{1}{e}\chi_{max}\right] \end{aligned} \quad (28)$$

where (28) follows from Theorem 6 and the fact that χ_{max} is an upper bound on the error experienced by the MAS. This proves (26).

Suppose that the adversary's best response to $\{(S, \frac{1}{2}), (S', \frac{1}{2})\}$ is given by ν^{A*}. Then the adversary's payoff from the strategy $\hat{\nu}^A$ is given by

$$\begin{aligned}\mathbf{E}(U_A(\mathbf{S}, \hat{\nu}^A)) &= U_A(S, \hat{\nu}^A)Pr(\mathbf{S} = S) \\ &\quad + U_A(S', \hat{\nu}^A)Pr(\mathbf{S} = S') \\ &= \frac{1}{2}U_A(S, \hat{\nu}^A) + \frac{1}{2}U_A(S', \hat{\nu}^A) \\ &\geq \frac{1}{2}U_A(S, \hat{\nu}^{A*}) \end{aligned} \quad (29)$$

The last inequality follows from the fact that $U_A \geq 0$ and $U_A(S, \hat{\nu}^A) \geq U_A(S, \hat{\nu}^*)$, since $\hat{\nu}^A$ is by definition the best response to leader set S. $\square$

6. SIMULATION STUDY

The performance of leader-follower systems in the presence of adversaries, including the case where the leader set is fixed as well as the case where the leader set varies over time, was analyzed using Matlab^{TM}. Simulations were conducted assuming a set of 100 agents, deployed uniformly at random over a 1000m x1000m square area, with each agent's radio range set to 300m. It was assumed that the environmental noise had variance proportional to the distance between agents. An adversary positioned at random within the deployment area, and with power budget equal to 10^6 was simulated. The path-loss parameter was set to $\alpha = 2$. Each plotted data point represents an average of 30 trials.

For both cases, the proposed leader selection algorithms were compared with three alternative heuristics: random leader selection, selection of the highest-degree nodes as leaders, and selection of the nodes with average degree as leaders.

Case 1 – Fixed leader set: The performance of leader-follower systems under noise injection attack when the leader set is fixed is illustrated in Figure 1(a). The algorithm **Fixed**-k was used to select leaders, with $\beta = 1$ and $\delta = 1$. The supermodular optimization approach **Fixed**-k outperforms the degree-based and random selection heuristics, achieving an error of 5, compared to 7 for random selection and 8 for maximum degree-based selection. Furthermore, we observe that the random selection approach achieves comparable performance to the average degree-based selection, and outperforms selection of high-degree nodes as leaders.

Case 2 – Time-varying leader set: Figure 1(b) shows the total error variance when the leader set is allowed to vary over time, based on the approximate Nash equilibrium computed using **Approx-NE**. By allowing the leader set to vary in response to attack, all of the schemes considered achieve better performance than the case of fixed leaders. The supermodular optimization approach outperforms the other three heuristics, achieving a total error variance of 5.25 when 15 leaders are chosen, compared to an error variance of roughly 6 for the random and average degree heuristics, and an error variance of 6.5 for the maximum degree heuristic. Furthermore, random selection of leaders outperforms selecting high-degree agents to act as leaders.

7. CONCLUSIONS

In this paper, improving the resilience of leader-follower multi-agent systems to noise injection attacks through leader selection was studied. Two leader selection problems were considered: first, the problem of choosing a fixed set of leaders to maximize robustness to a noise injection attack, and second, the problem of choosing a set of leaders that varies over time in response to attacks. Both cases were analyzed within a supermodular game framework. The first case was studied as a Stackelberg game between a MAS owner and an adversary. It was shown that the adversary's optimum strategy can be computed for a given leader set, while the MAS's best choice of leader set can be approximated up to a provable bound. In the second case, a simultaneous game framework was developed and an algorithm for efficiently approximating a mixed-strategy equilibrium was presented. Both cases were analyzed through simulation study, which demonstrated that choosing a varying set of leaders provides better robustness to noise injection than a fixed set, and that for both cases the supermodular optimization approach outperformed other leader selection algorithms.

In future work, we will study leader selection algorithms that improve on the bounds given in Sections 4 and 5. Moreover, we note that an adversary may employ additional techniques in order to disrupt system performance, including removing links from the MAS altogether through denial-of-service attack. We will further study leader selection methods for mitigating these different classes of attack.

8. REFERENCES

[1] T. Alpcan and T. Basar. *Network Security: A Decision and Game-Theoretic Approach.* Cambridge University Press, 2010.

[2] P. Barooah and J. Hespanha. Graph effective resistance and distributed control: Spectral properties and applications. In *45th IEEE Conference on Decision and Control*, pages 3479–3485. IEEE, 2006.

[3] S. Boyd and L. Vandenberghe. *Convex optimization.* Cambridge University Press, 2004.

[4] A. Clark and R. Poovendran. A submodular optimization framework for leader selection in linear multi-agent systems. *Proceedings of the 50th IEEE Conference on Decision and Control and European Control Conference (CDC-ECC)*, 2011.

[5] C. Daskalakis, A. Mehta, and C. Papadimitriou. A note on approximate nash equilibria. *Internet and Network Economics*, pages 297–306, 2006.

[6] P. Doyle and J. Snell. Random walks and electric networks. *Carus mathematical monographs*, 22, 2000.

[7] J. Lawton, R. Beard, and B. Young. A decentralized approach to formation maneuvers. *IEEE Transactions on Robotics and Automation*, 19(6):933–941, 2003.

[8] B. Liu, T. Chu, L. Wang, and G. Xie. Controllability of a leader–follower dynamic network with switching topology. *IEEE Transactions on Automatic Control*, 53(4):1009–1013, 2008.

[9] M. Mesbahi and F. Hadaegh. Graphs, matrix inequalities, and switching for the formation flying control of multiple spacecraft. In *Proceedings of the 1999 American Control Conference*, volume 6, pages 4148–4152, 1999.

[10] G. Nemhauser, L. Wolsey, and M. Fisher. An analysis of approximations for maximizing submodular set functions. *Mathematical Programming*, 14(1):265–294, 1978.

[11] J. Proakis. Spread spectrum signals for digital communications. *Encyclopedia of Telecommunications*, 2001.

[12] Y. Shoham and K. Leyton-Brown. *Multiagent systems: Algorithmic, game-theoretic, and logical foundations.* Cambridge University Press, 2009.

[13] L. Wolsey. An analysis of the greedy algorithm for the submodular set covering problem. *Combinatorica*, 2(4):385–393, 1982.

[14] L. Xiao, S. Boyd, and S. Kim. Distributed average consensus with least-mean-square deviation. *Journal of Parallel and Distributed Computing*, 67(1):33 – 46, 2007.

APPENDIX

In this appendix, proofs of Theorems 2, 3, and 4 are given.

PROOF PROOF OF THEOREM 2. Let $\epsilon > 0$. For each $S \subseteq V$, let

$$K(S) \triangleq \min\{K : |f_k(S) - f(S)| < \epsilon/4 \,\forall k \geq K\}. \quad (30)$$

Further, let $K = \max_S K(S)$. Then for any $S \subseteq T$ and

$v \notin T$, and any $k > K$,

$$f(S) - f(S \cup \{v\}) > f_k(S) - f_k(S \cup \{v\}) - \epsilon/2 \quad (31)$$
$$\geq f_k(T) - f_k(T \cup \{v\}) - \epsilon/2 \quad (32)$$
$$> f(T) - f(T \cup \{v\}) - \epsilon \quad (33)$$

where (31) and (33) follow from the definition of K and (32) follows from the supermodularity of f_k. Eq. (33) implies that $f(S) - f(S \cup \{v\}) \geq f(T) - f(T \cup \{v\})$, and hence f is supermodular as a function of S. $\square$

As a first step towards proving Theorem 3, the following intermediate lemmas are needed.

LEMMA 3. *Let v and J denote vectors in $\mathbf{R}^n$ such that $Lv = J$, $v_i = 0$ for all $i \in S$, $J_u = 0$, and $J_i = 0$ for all $i \in V \setminus (S + u)$.*

PROOF. The equation $Lv = J$ can be written in long form as

$$\begin{pmatrix} L_{ff} & L_{fl} \\ L_{lf} & L_{ll} \end{pmatrix} \begin{pmatrix} v_f \\ v_l \end{pmatrix} = \begin{pmatrix} J_f \\ J_l \end{pmatrix} \quad (34)$$

Substituting $v_l = 0$ yields $L_{ff}v_f = J_f$, which in turn implies that $v_f = L_{ff}^{-1}J_f$. Let e_u denote the vector with a 1 in the u-th position and 0s elsewhere. Then multiplying both sides by e_u^T yields

$$v_u = (L_{ff}^{-1})_{u1}J_1 + \cdots + (L_{ff}^{-1})_{u(n-|S|)}J_{n-|S|} \quad (35)$$

Since $J_i = 0$ for $i \neq u$, (35) reduces to $(L_{ff}^{-1})_{uu}J_u = (L_{ff}^{-1})_{uu} = v_u$, as desired. $\square$

In order to prove the next lemma, the following definition is required.

DEFINITION 4. *A function $\mu : E \to \mathbf{R}$ is a flow if the following conditions hold for any $(i,j) \in E$. First, $\mu_{ij} = -\mu_{ji}$. Second, $\sum_{j \in N(i)} \mu_{ij} = 0$ for $i \in V \setminus (S + u)$. μ is defined to be a unit flow if the additional condition $\sum_{j \in N(u)} \mu_{uj} = 1$ holds.*

The following lemma gives a property of unit flows.

LEMMA 4. *Let $w : V \to \mathbf{R}$ be any function on V and let μ be a flow. Then for any $a, b \in V$,*

$$(w_a - w_b) \sum_{j \in N(a)} \mu_{aj} = \frac{1}{2} \sum_{(i,j) \in E} (w_i - w_j)\mu_{ij} \quad (36)$$

The proof of this lemma can be found in [6, Ch 1]. One final lemma is needed before the proof of Theorem 3.

LEMMA 5. *$(L_{ff}^{-1})_{uu}$ is equivalent to*

$$(L_{ff}^{-1})_{uu} = \min \left\{ \sum_{(i,j) \in E} \nu_{ij}\mu_{ij}^2 : \mu_{ij} \text{ is a unit flow} \right\}$$

PROOF. Let v be as in the statement of Lemma 3, and define $\lambda_{ij} : E \to \mathbf{R}$ by $\lambda_{ij} = \nu_{ij}^{-1}(v_i - v_j)$. First, we show that λ_{ij} is a unit flow. $\lambda_{ij} = -\lambda_{ji}$ follows from the definition. Further, $\sum_{j \in N(i)} \nu_{ij}^{-1}(v_i - v_j) = J_i$, since v is defined by $Lv = J$. Thus $\sum_{j \in N(i)} \lambda_{ij} = 0$ if $i \in V \setminus (S + u)$ and

$\sum_{j \in N(i)} \lambda_{ij} = 1$ if $i = u$, satisfying the second and third requirements for a unit flow.

We next show that

$$\sum_{(i,j) \in E} \nu_{ij}\lambda_{ij}^2 = (L_{ff}^{-1})_{uu} \quad (37)$$

From Lemma 4,

$$(v_u - v_s) \sum_{j \in N(u)} \lambda_{uj} = \frac{1}{2} \sum_{(i,j) \in E} (v_i - v_j)\lambda_{ij} \quad (38)$$

for any $s \in S$. By definition of λ, $(v_i - v_j) = \nu_{ij}\lambda_{ij}$, and so the right hand side of (38) is equivalent to $\frac{1}{2}\sum_{(i,j) \in E} \nu_{ij}\lambda_{ij}^2$. Meanwhile, since λ is a unit flow, the left-hand side of (38) is equal to $v_u - v_s$. By definition, $v_s = 0$, and by Lemma 3, $v_u = (L_{ff}^{-1})_{uu}$.

Now, let μ_{ij} be another unit flow, and note that $\mu_{ij} = \lambda_{ij} + \phi_{ij}$, where ϕ_{ij} is a flow with $\sum_{j \in N(u)} \phi_{uj} = 0$. Then

$$\sum_{(i,j) \in E} \nu_{ij}\mu_{ij}^2 = \sum_{(i,j) \in E} \nu_{ij}(\lambda_{ij} + \phi_{ij})^2$$
$$= \sum_{(i,j)} \nu_{ij}\lambda_{ij}^2 + 2\sum_{(i,j)} \phi_{ij}(v_i - v_j)$$
$$+ \sum_{(i,j) \in E} \nu_{ij}\phi_{ij}^2 \quad (39)$$
$$= \sum_{i,j} \nu_{ij}\lambda_{ij}^2 + 4v_u \sum_{j \in N(u)} \phi_{uj}$$
$$+ \sum_{i,j} \nu_{ij}\phi_{ij}^2 \quad (40)$$
$$= \sum_{i,j} \nu_{ij}\lambda_{ij}^2 + \sum_{i,j} \nu_{ij}\phi_{ij}^2 \quad (41)$$
$$\geq \sum_{i,j} \nu_{ij}\lambda_{ij}^2 \quad (42)$$

where (39) follows by expanding the previous equation and by definition of λ, (40) follows from Lemma 4 and (41) follows from the fact that $\sum_{j \in N(u)} \phi_{uj} = 0$. $\square$

PROOF PROOF OF THEOREM 3. First, note that

$$\sum_{(i,j) \in E} \nu_{ij}\mu_{ij}^2 \quad (43)$$

is linear as a function of ν_{ij}. By Lemma 5, $(L_f^{-1})_{uu}$ is a pointwise minimum of linear functions and is therefore concave. $\square$

The following lemma is needed to prove Theorem 4.

LEMMA 6. *The function $F_\zeta(S)$ defined in (16) is supermodular as a function of S.*

PROOF. By the theory of Riemann integration, $F_\zeta(S)$ can be approximated by a sequence of functions

$$F_\zeta^k(S) = \sum_{l=0}^{L_k} \max \{\chi(S, R(P_l^k)), \zeta\}|C_l^k| \quad (44)$$

where $|\cdot|$ denotes the Lebesgue measure of a set, the sets C_l^k satisfy $|C_l^k| = \delta_k$, with $\delta_k \to 0$ as $k \to \infty$, $P_l \in C_l^k$, and $\mathcal{S}_2 \subseteq \bigcup_{l=0}^{L_k} C_l^k$. Now, since $\chi(S, R)$ is supermodular for fixed R (Theorem 5), $\max \{\chi(S, R), \zeta\}$ is supermodular as a function of S (Lemma 2). $F_\zeta^k(S)$ is therefore a nonnegative weighted sum of supermodular functions, and thus is supermodular by Lemma 1. This implies that $F_\zeta(S)$ is the limit of a sequence of supermodular functions, and so $F_\zeta(S)$ is supermodular by Theorem 2. □

LEMMA 7. *For fixed ζ, for the optimization problem*

$$
\begin{aligned}
minimize \quad & |S| \\
s.t. \quad & F_\zeta(S) \leq \zeta
\end{aligned} \tag{45}
$$

*the greedy algorithm of lines 6-8 in **Fixed**-k returns a set S with*

$$
\frac{|S|}{|S^*|} \leq 1 + \log_e \left\{ \frac{\max_v F_\zeta(\{v\})}{\zeta} \right\}, \tag{46}
$$

where S^* is the optimum solution to (45).

PROOF. The proof follows from Theorem 1 of [13] and the supermodularity of $F_\zeta(S)$. □

PROOF PROOF OF THEOREM 4. From Lemma 7, solving a problem of the form (45) with $\zeta = \zeta^*$ will return a set S with $|S| \geq \beta k$ and β is as in the statement of Theorem 4. Furthermore, the algorithm is guaranteed to reach $\zeta = \zeta^*$, because ζ^j is strictly decreasing as long as $|S^j| \leq \beta k$, which will hold for all $\zeta^j > \zeta^*$. □

A Dynamic Game-Theoretic Approach to Resilient Control System Design for Cascading Failures*

Quanyan Zhu
Coordinated Science Laboratory
University of Illinois at Urbana-Champaign
1308 W. Main St.
Urbana, IL, USA
zhu31@illinois.edu

Tamer Başar
Coordinated Science Laboratory
University of Illinois at Urbana-Champaign
1308 W. Main St.
Urbana, IL, USA
basar1@illinois.edu

ABSTRACT

The migration of many current critical infrastructures, such as power grids and transportations systems, into open public networks has posed many challenges in control systems. Modern control systems face uncertainties not only from the physical world but also from the cyber space. In this paper, we propose a hybrid game-theoretic approach to investigate the coupling between cyber security policy and robust control design. We study in detail the case of cascading failures in industrial control systems and provide a set of coupled optimality criteria in the linear-quadratic case. This approach can be further extended to more general cases of parallel cascading failures.

Categories and Subject Descriptors

C.3 [**Special-Purpose and Application-Based Systems**]: Process Control Systems; D.4.8 [**Performance**]: Stochastic analysis; I.2.8 [**Problem Solving, Control Methods, and Search**]: Control Theory

General Terms

Security, Reliability, Algorithms, Theory

Keywords

Game Theory, Differential Games, Markov Games, Cyber-Physical Systems, Nash Equilibrium

1. INTRODUCTION

Many current critical infrastructures such as power grids and transportation systems are migrating into the open public network. The technological advancement has posed many challenges on the legacy control systems. The classical design of control systems takes into account modeling uncertainties as well as physical disturbances and encompasses a multitude of control design methods such as robust control, adaptive control, and stochastic control. With the growing level of integration with new information technologies, modern control systems face uncertainties not only from the physical world but also from the cyber space. The vulnerabilities of the software deployed in the new control system infrastructure create many potential risks and threats from the attackers. Exploitation of these vulnerabilities can lead to severe damages as have been seen in [1, 2]. It has been reported in [1] that the U.S. power grid was penetrated by cyber spies and the intrusions could have damaged the power grid and other key infrastructure. In [2], it is believed that an inappropriate software update has led to a recent emergency shutdown for 48 hours of a nuclear power plant in Georgia. More recently, it is reported in [3, 4] that a computer worm, Stuxnet, has been spread to target Siemens Supervisory Control And Data Acquisition (SCADA) systems that are configured to control and monitor specific industrial processes.

In this paper, we propose a hybrid game-theoretic approach to address resilient control design issues in modern critical infrastructures. We investigate the coupling between cyber security policy at the cyber level of the system and the robust control design at the physical layer of the system. Resilience of cyber-physical systems addresses two types of disturbances. One source of disturbance comes from the physical environment, which is due to noise or uncertainty. Another source of disturbance comes from the cyber-physical system integration. The uncertainty in cyber events can trigger the system to switch from one operating state to another. Such a disturbance is usually unanticipated by the physical layer control.

2. RELATED WORK

Cascading failures have been widely studied in the literature of complex networks. In [8], authors have presented a model based on the dynamical redistribution of the flow on the network, and they have shown that the breakdown of a single node is sufficient to collapse the efficiency of the entire system if the node is among the ones with largest load. In [7], the authors have used an evolutionary algorithm to improve the resilience of complex networks to cascading failures, and have shown that clustering, modularity

---

*The research was partially supported by the AFOSR MURI Grant FA9550-10-1-0573, and also by an NSA Grant through the Information Trust Institute at the University of Illinois.

and long path lengths all play important roles in the design of robust large-scale infrastructures. The 2003 blackout in North America has motivated the study of cascading failures in power networks. In [6], a hidden failure embedded DC model of power transmission systems has been developed to study the power law distributions observed in North American blackout data. In [5], the authors have investigated criticality in a sizable network with a fairly detailed blackout model and measure blackout size by energy unserved.

The notion of resilience has appeared in the literature of many fields such as psychology, ecology, organizational behavior, networks, and material science [9, 10]. In [11], resilience of a system is defined as the ability of the system to withstand a major disruption within acceptable degradation parameters and to recover within an acceptable time and composite costs and risks. In [12], the author points out that resilience and robustness are not general properties but are relative to specific classes of perturbations. Different from the concept of robustness, resilience of a system to a class of unexpected extreme perturbations is defined as the ability of this system to (i) gracefully degrade its function by altering its structure in an agile way when it is subject to a set of perturbations of this class, and (ii) quickly recover it once the perturbations cease. The notion of resilience in [10], [11], [12] all refer to the ability of a system to withstand an unexpected event and recover after the failure. These definitions provide conceptual background for the development of quantitative methods for resilient control systems.

Metrics for resilient control systems have been studied in [14]. The authors have proposed a 3-layer system model and a resilience curve, and provided metrics for quantitative estimation of system resiliency. In [13, 15], we have introduced a hierarchical security architecture for cyber-physical systems to identify security issues at different layers of the system, and within that framework we have introduced quantitative approaches to enable the study of security issues that lie at the physical, cyber and human levels of the system. In [15, 19, 18], we have used cross-layer methods to understand the coupling between cyber and physical security. In [19], we have studied the impact of delay and packet drop rates on control system performance as a result of defense-in-depth cyber defense. In [18], we have introduced dynamic coupling between cyber defense policy-making and physical layer control design. This recently developed framework serves as the foundational basis for this paper in which we investigate the case of cascading failures in cyber-physical systems.

3. RESILIENT CONTROL SYSTEMS

Industrial control systems (ICSs) are commonly seen in many critical infrastructures such as electricity generation, transmission and distribution, water treatment and manufacturing. The main function of ICSs is to monitor and control physical and chemical processes. In the past few decades, we have seen a growing trend of integrating physical ICSs with cyber space to allow for new degrees of automation and human-machine interactions. The uncertainties and hostilities existing in the cyber environment have brought about emerging concerns for the traditional ICSs. It is of supreme importance to have a system that maintains state awareness and an accepted level of operational normalcy in response to disturbances, including threats of an unexpected and malicious nature [16]. The term *resilient*

control system (RCS) is used to describe systems that have these essential features.

In this section, our aim is to establish a theoretical framework for designing resilient controllers. To address this challenge, we first need to understand the architecture of industrial control systems (ICSs). Here, we adopt a layering perspective toward ICSs. This view-point has been adopted in many large scale system designs such as the Internet, power systems and nuclear power plants. For example, in smart grids, the hierarchical architecture includes economy grid, regulatory grid, electricity market grid, transmission grid and distribution grid. The seven layer OSI model for the Internet provides a set of rules and standards that allow manufacturers and developers to create software and hardware that is compatible with each other.

We hierarchically separate ICSs into 6 layers, namely, physical layer, control layer, communication layer, network layer, supervisory layer and management layer. This hierarchical structure is depicted in Fig. 1.

The physical layer comprises the physical plant to be controlled. The control layer consists of multiple control components, including observers/sensors, intrusion detection systems (IDSs), actuators and other intelligent control components. The physical layer together with the control layer can be viewed as the physical world of the system. On top of these two layers, the communication layer is where we have physical communication channels that can be in the form of wireless channels, the Internet, etc., and the network layer is where the topology and routing of the architecture live. The communication and network layers constitute the cyber world of the system. Supervisory layer coordinates all lower layers by designing and sending appropriate commands. It can be viewed as the brain of the system. Management layer is a higher level decision-making engine, where the decision-makers take an economic perspective towards the resource allocation problems in control systems. Supervisory and management layers are interfaces with humans and hence they contain many human factors and human-made decisions.

The layered architecture can facilitate the understanding of the cross-layer interactions between the physical world and the cyber world. In Fig. 2, we use $x(t)$ and $\theta(t)$ to denote the continuous physical state and the discrete cyber state of the system, which are governed by the laws f and Λ, respectively. The physical state $x(t)$ is subject to disturbances w and can be controlled by u. The cyber state $\theta(t)$ is controlled by the defense mechanism l used by the network administrator as well as the attacker's action a. The hybrid nature of the cross-layer interaction leads to adoption of the hybrid system model described later through (1), (2) and (5).

As mentioned earlier, our goal in this paper is to establish a framework for designing a resilient controller for the hybrid system model described. We view resilient control as a cross-layer control design, which takes into account the given range of deterministic uncertainties at each state as well as the random unexpected events that trigger the transition from one system state to another. Hence, it has the property of disturbance attenuation or rejection to physical uncertainties as well as damage mitigation or resilience to sudden cyber attacks. We first derive resilient control for the closed-loop perfect-state measurement information structure in a general setting with the transition law depending on the

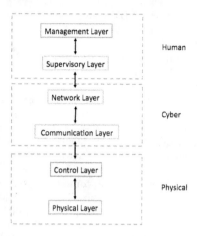

Figure 1: A hierarchical layered architecture of cyber-physical control systems.

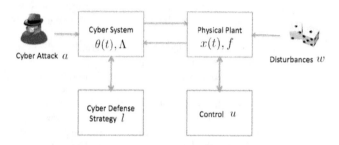

Figure 2: The interactions between the cyber and physical systems are captured by their dynamics governed by the transition law Λ and the dynamical system f. The physical system state $x(t)$ is controlled by u in the presence of disturbances and noises. The cyber state $\theta(t)$ is controlled by the defense mechanism l used by the network administrator as well as the attacker's action a.

control action, and then we simplify the result to the special case of the linear-quadratic problem.

4. SYSTEM MODEL

In this section, we consider an ICS that is subject to possible failures due to either manufacturing faults or malicious attacks. We follow the general framework that has been proposed in [18] to derive a set of coupled optimality criteria to characterize the coupling between cyber and physical systems.

In Fig. 5, we describe the cascading effects in an ICS, where the state $\theta \in \mathcal{S} := \{1, 2, \cdots, N\}$ is the failure state in the system. The dynamics of the system at each state are described by

$$\dot{x}(t) = A^\theta x + B^\theta u + D^\theta w, \quad x(t_0) = x_0. \quad (1)$$

where x_0 is the initial state of the system at time $t = t_0$. $x \in \mathbb{R}^n$, $u \in \mathbb{R}^r$ is the control input, $w \in \mathbb{R}^p$ is the disturbance. $A^\theta, B^\theta, D^\theta, \theta \in \mathcal{S}$, are matrices with real-valued entries and of appropriate dimensions, indexed by θ. By default, state $\theta = 1$ is the normal operating state and state

$\theta = N$ is the terminal failure state. The states $i, 2 \leqslant i \leqslant N - 1$, are intermediate compromised states in which one system component failure leads to another. We assume that the failure states are irreversible, i.e., the system cannot be fixed or brought back to its normal state immediately after faults occur. This is usually due to the fact that the time scale for critical cascading failures is much shorter than the time scale for system maintenance. The transition between the failure states follows a Markov jump process with rate matrix $\lambda = \{\lambda_{ij}\}_{i,j \in \mathcal{S}}$ such that for $i \neq j, \lambda_{ij} \geqslant 0$, $\lambda_{ii} = 1 - \sum_{j \neq i} \lambda_{ij}$, and for $i > j, \lambda_{ij} = 0$. For simplicity, we can use the notation $p_i = \lambda_{i,i+1}, 1 \leqslant i \leqslant N - 1$, as the transition rates between adjacent states, and hence $\lambda_{ii} = 1 - p_i, 1 \leqslant i \leqslant N - 1, p_N = \lambda_{NN}$. The matrices $A^\theta, B^\theta, D^\theta$ and the transition rate matrix λ are generally dependent on a given cyber policy l and attack strategy a.

4.1 Robust Control Design

At the physical control layer, our aim is to design a robust feedback controller μ to reject the worst-case disturbance w by employing an H^∞ control design using a zero-sum game-theoretic approach. We can view the controller as minimizing the following quadratic cost while the disturbance maximizing it.

$$J(\mu, \nu) = \mathbb{E}_\theta \int_{t_0}^{\infty} \left(|x(t)|^2_{Q^\theta} + |u(t)|^2_{R^\theta} - \gamma^2 |w(t)|^2 \right) dt, \quad (2)$$

where μ is a state-feedback control law, ν is a state-feedback disturbance law, and $|\cdot|$ denotes the Euclidean norm with appropriate weighting. $Q^\theta \geqslant 0$, $R^\theta > 0$, $\theta \in \mathcal{S}$, are matrices of appropriate dimensions. Under regularity conditions and for an attenuation level $\gamma > \gamma^*$, the critical attenuation level (see [17, 18] for details), the strategy that guarantees the upper value of the underlying game is in the form of linear state feedback, i.e.,

$$u(t) = \mu(t, x(t), \theta(t) = i) = -(R^i)^{-1} B^{i'} Z_i x(t), \quad (3)$$

where $Z_i, i \in \mathcal{S}$, are positive definite solutions to the following linearly coupled set of Riccati equations

$$A^{i'} Z_i + Z_i A^i - Z_i \left(B^i (R^i)^{-1} B^{i'} - \frac{1}{\gamma^2} D^i D^{i'} \right) Z_i$$
$$+ Q^i + \sum_{j=1}^{N} \lambda_{ij} Z_j = 0, i \in \mathcal{S}. \quad (4)$$

The value of the game when the initial mode state is $\theta = i$ is given by $V^i = x^T Z_i x$.

4.2 Cyber Policies

The cyber policy in an ICS is made by an administrator to protect the system from malicious attacks. Cyber policies are made often on a longer time scale than the physical layer control. Hence we let $k = t/\epsilon$ be the time unit at the cyber level for a sufficiently small $\epsilon > 0$. Different cyber policies can affect different aspects of physical layer control system performance. For example, intrusion detection/prevention systems (IDPSs) at the actuation side of the control can lead to packet drops in the communication channel between the actuator and the plant [22, 20, 21, 19]. Such loss of data packets can be captured by the matrix B^θ. In addition, the cyber policies at the network level can influence the

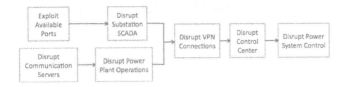

Figure 3: An illustration of sequences of attacks in system systems

```
alert tcp any any -> any 7580 (msg:"ETPRO SCADA
Siemens Tecnomatix FactoryLink CSService GetFile
path Buffer Overflow"; flow:to_server,established;
content:"LEN|00|"; depth:4; byte_test:4,>,
1028,0,little; content:"|99|"; distance:8; within:1;
content:"|99 00 00 00 08 00 00 00 02 06|"; distance:
0; byte_test:4,>,1024,0,big; classtype:attempted-
user;reference:url,digitalbond.com/tools/quickdraw/
vulnerability-rules; sid:1111675; rev:1;)
```

Figure 4: A SCADA IDS rule to detect CSService CSMSG GetFile buffer overflow in Siemens Tecnomatix FactoryLink

transition rate matrix λ because a higher level of security enforcement will lead to lower transition rates between a state i and a worse state $i+1$, $1 \leqslant i \leqslant N-1$. The rate matrix λ is determined by cyber security polices as well as reliability of physical components in the cyber-physical system. In the absence of security considerations, λ has its baseline transition rates only determined by the corresponding reliability models.

At the cyber level, we consider an attacker who uses a sequence of attacks toward achieving his goal of disrupting the services of the system. At each stage, the attacker chooses one possible attack from a set of possible actions based on the state of the system. The action set of an attacker is often characterized by attack graphs [23, 24], which consist of a multi-level hierarchy in a tree structure that captures possible ways of achieving attack goals. In Fig. 3, we illustrate a possible sequence of attacks, where each block can be associated with many different specific actions to accomplish the attack. One possible sequence starts with an exploration and exploitations of vulnerable ports and then disruption of the SCADA system at substations before launching an attack on the control center.

One way to defend a cyber system is to deploy intrusion detection systems (IDSs), which are passive devices that receive and evaluate information sent over a network against a set of signatures. IDS signatures have been developed for most published vulnerabilities and for potentially dangerous activity in common IT protocols. Configuration of IDSs is not a trivial task. The current version of the Snort IDS, for example, has approximately 10,000 signature rules located in fifty categories. Each IDS also comes with a default configuration to use when no additional information or expertise is available. It is not trivial to determine the optimal configuration of an IDS because of the need to understand the quantitative relationship between a wide range of analyzers and tuning parameters. This explains why current IDSs are configured and tuned using a trial-and-error approach. In [22], we have proposed a game-theoretic approach for dy-

namic configuration of IDSs and an online learning technique to search for the optimal configuration policy against an attacker.

For critical infrastructures, a set of SCADA IDS signatures that parallel Snort rules for enterprise IT systems has been designed by Digital Bond's Quickdraw which leverages the existing IDS equipment by developing signatures for control system protocols, devices and vulnerabilities [27]. In Fig. 4, we illustrate a typical SCADA IDS rule, which is used detect a buffer overflow attack. The rule is specifically designed for Siemens Tecnomatix FactoryLink software, which is used for monitoring, supervising, and controlling industrial processes. FactoryLink is commonly used to build applications such as human-machine interface (HMI) systems and SCADA systems. The logging function of FactoryLink is vulnerable to a buffer-overflow caused by the usage of **vsprintf** with a stack buffer of 1024 bytes. The vulnerability can be exploited remotely in various ways like the passing of a big path or filter string in the file related operations [27].

The goal of the network administrator is to configure an optimal set of detection rules to protect the cyber system from attackers. To model the interaction between an attacker and a defender, we use a dynamic game approach. Let $\mathcal{L}^*$ be a finite set of possible system configurations in the network and $\mathcal{A}$ be the finite action set of the attacker. Let $\mathbf{h}(k)$ denote a mixed strategy of the defender over the finite set $\mathcal{L}^*$ at time k and $\mathbf{g}(k)$ denote a mixed strategy of the attacker over the finite set $\mathcal{A}$ at time k. We focus on a class of stationary cyber policies, where mixed strategies of the defender and the attacker are only dependent on the state of the system. We let $\mathbf{H} = [\mathbf{h}_s]_{s=1}^N$ and $\mathbf{G} = [\mathbf{g}_s]_{i=1}^N$ be the stationary strategies for the defender and the attacker, where $\mathbf{h}_s$ and $\mathbf{g}_s$ are respectively mixed strategies of the defender and the attacker that correspond to state $s \in \mathcal{S}$. A defender chooses a stationary strategy to minimize the long-term cost W_β as follows while an attacker chooses one to maximize it.

$$W_\beta(\theta, \mathbf{H}, \mathbf{G}) = \int_{t_0}^\infty e^{-\beta k} \mathbb{E}_{\theta, \mathbf{H}, \mathbf{G}} Y(Z_{s(k)}, k) dk, \quad (5)$$

Here, $\beta > 0$ is a discount factor, $s(k)$ is the state of system at time k, $Y(\cdot)$ is a function of time k and control gain Z_s, which is related to the value of each state through the value functions obtained for (2). Note that Z_θ depends on the cyber policies $(\mathbf{H}, \mathbf{G})$.

A saddle-point equilibrium strategy pair $(\mathbf{H}^*, \mathbf{G}^*)$ is one that achieves the game value w_β^* and needs to satisfy the fixed-point optimality condition

$$\beta w_\beta^*(i) = \mathrm{val}\left\{ Y(\mathbf{H}, \mathbf{G}, i) + \sum_{j \in \mathcal{S}} \lambda_{ij}(\mathbf{H}, \mathbf{G}) w_\beta^*(j) \right\}. \quad (6)$$

Here, we have written $Y(\cdot)$ in terms of the strategy pair $(\mathbf{H}, \mathbf{G})$ and state i through its dependence on Z_i. w_β^* is the value function of the cost functional W_β and val is the saddle-point value operator.

4.3 Optimality Criteria for Cascading Failures

To find the robust control and saddle-point cyber policy for the cyber-physical system (1) under the physical level cost (2) and the cyber level cost (5), we need to solve the set of coupled optimality equations (4) and (6). Let

$Y = x_0^T Z_i x_0$ be the utility of each state i. For the case of cascading failure as depicted in Fig. 5 and linear quadratic robust control design, we can simplify (4) and (6) and arrive at the following set of coupled equations. The optimality criteria for the cyber system are described by

$$\beta w_\beta^*(N) = V^N, \tag{7}$$

$$\beta w_\beta^*(i) = \mathrm{val}\{V^i + p_i w_\beta^*(i+1) - p_i w_\beta^*(i)\}, \tag{8}$$
$$i = 1, \cdots, N-1,$$

$$V^i = x_0^T Z_i x_0.$$

Here, $p_i = \lambda_{i,i+1}, 1 \leqslant i \leqslant N-1$, and V^i is dependent on p_i through Z_i in (4). Note that (8) requires solving for a saddle-point in mixed strategies. Since both players have a finite number of choice for each k, the existence of a saddle-point solution is guaranteed for the zero-sum game in (4), [25, 26].

In addition, the optimality criteria for the optimal control in the linear quadratic case can be reduced to

$$A^{N'} Z_N + Z_N A^N - Z_N \left(B^N (R^N)^{-1} B^{N'} \right.$$
$$\left. -\frac{1}{\gamma^2} D^N D^{N'} \right) Z_N + Q^N = 0, \tag{9}$$

$$A^{i'} Z_i + Z_i A^i - Z_i \left(B^i (R^i)^{-1} B^{i'} - \frac{1}{\gamma^2} D^i D^{i'} \right) Z_i$$
$$+ Q^i + p_i Z_{i+1} = 0, \quad i = 1, \cdots, N-1. \tag{10}$$

Here, γ is a chosen level of attenuation. Under regularity conditions in [17], there exists a finite scalar $\gamma^\infty > 0$ such that for all $\gamma > \gamma^\infty$, solutions to (9) and (10) exist and are unique.

In (8), p_i is dependent on $\mathbf{H}$ and $\mathbf{G}$. At the same time, as a result of solving (10), the value V^i is dependent on p_i and B^i, which are in turn a function of $\mathbf{H}$ and $\mathbf{G}$. The above set of coupled equations can be solved by starting with (9) for obtaining the value of the terminal state V^N. From (7), we can calculate the value v_N^* and then in the next step use (8) and (10) for finding the stationary saddle-point equilibrium strategies $\mathbf{h}_{N-1}^*, \mathbf{g}_{N-1}^*$ at state $\theta = N - 1$, their corresponding transition rate $p_{N-1}^* = \lambda_{N-1,N}(\mathbf{h}_{N-1}^*, \mathbf{g}_{N-1}^*)$ and the Riccati solution Z_{N-1}. We can iterate the process again by using Z_{N-1} in (8) for $i = N - 2$, and the obtained strategy pair $(\mathbf{h}_{N-2}^*, \mathbf{g}_{N-2}^*)$ is used in (10) for solving Z_{N-2}. Hence we can use the backward induction to find Z_1 and $(\mathbf{h}_1^*, \mathbf{g}_1^*)$.

Note that the coupling between equations (9), (10) and (7), (8) demonstrates the interdependence between security at the cyber level and the robustness at the physical level. The holistic viewpoint towards these system properties is essential in addressing the resilience of cyber-physical systems. The coupling between cyber and physical levels of the system is not one-directional but rather reciprocal. The upward resilience from the physical level to the cyber level results from the function Y while the downward resilience from the cyber level to the physical level follows from the dependence of λ on the cyber policies.

5. CONCLUSIONS AND FUTURE WORK

In this paper, we have introduced a dynamic game-theoretic approach to model the interactions between the cyber level policy making and physical level robust control design. We

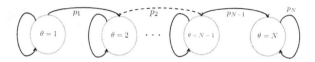

Figure 5: Cascading failures in an ICS

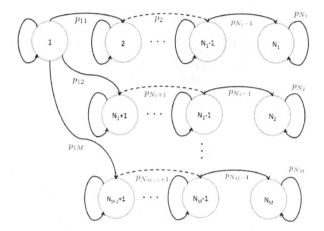

Figure 6: Generalized form of cascading failures in an ICS

have investigated the case of cascading failures where one unanticipated event propagates failures in the system. We have provided a set of coupled optimality conditions in the special case of linear-quadratic systems to characterize the saddle-point equilibrium of cyber defense policy and robust control design. As future work, we will generalize the cascading failure to the case as depicted in Fig. 6. In addition, we will incorporate reinforcement learning schemes such as Q-learning for learning the saddle-point cyber policy online, and study iterative methods to find solutions to the coupled set of optimality equations.

6. REFERENCES

[1] S. Gorman, "Electricity Grid in U.S. Penetrated By Spies," *Wall Street Journal*, April 8, 2009, http://online.wsj.com/article/ SB123914805204099085.html, Retrieved Aug. 16, 2011.

[2] B. Krebs, "Cyber Incident Blamed for Nuclear Power Plant Shutdown", *Washington Post*, June 5, 2008, http://www.washingtonpost.com/wp-dyn/content/ article/2008/06/05/AR2008060501958.html, Retrieved Aug. 16, 2011.

[3] S. Greengard, "The New Face of War", Communications of the ACM, Dec. 2010, vol. 53, no. 12, pp. 20–22.

[4] R. McMillan, "Siemens: Stuxnet worm hit industrial systems," *Computerworld*, Sept. 16, 2010, http:// www.computerworld.com/s/article/print/9185419, Retrieved Aug. 16, 2011.

[5] D.P. Nedic, I. Dobson, D.S. Kirschen, B.A. Carreras, V.E. Lynch, "Criticality in a cascading failure blackout model," *Intl. J. of Electrical Power and Energy Systems*, vol. 28, 2006, pp. 627–633.

[6] J. Chen, J.S. Thorp, I. Dobson, "Cascading dynamics and mitigation assessment in power system disturbances via a hidden failure model," *Intl. J. of Electrical Power and Energy Systems*, vol. 27, no. 4, May 2005, pp. 318–326.

[7] J. Asha and D. Newth, "Optimizing complex networks for resilience against cascading failure," *Physica A*, vol. 380, pp. 673-683, 2007.

[8] P. Crucitti, V. Latora and M. Marchiori, "Model for cascading failures in complex networks," *Phys. Rev. E*, vol. 69, 045104(R), 2004.

[9] R. Hollnagel, D. D. Woods, N. Leveson (eds.), "Resilience engineering: concepts and precepts," Ashgate Publishing Company, 2006.

[10] E. Hollnagel, J. Pariès, D. D. Woods and J. Wreathall, "Resilience Engineering in Practice," Ashgate Publishing Company, 2011.

[11] Y. Y. Haimes, "On the definition of resilience in systems," *Risk Analysis*, vol. 29, no. 4, 2009.

[12] L. Mili, "Taxonomy of the characteristics of power system operating states," 2nd NSF-VT Resilient and Sustainable Critical Infrastructures (RESIN) Workshop, Tuscon, Arizona, January 13-15, 2011.

[13] Q. Zhu, C. Rieger and T. Başar, "A hierarchical security architecture for cyber-physical systems," in Proc. of Intl. Symposium on Resilient Control Systems (ISRCS), Boise, ID, Aug. 9 - 11, 2011.

[14] D. Wei and K. Ji, "Resilient industrial control system (RICS): Concepts, formulation, metrics, and insights," in Proc. of 3rd Intl. Symp. on Resilient Control Systems (ISRCS), 2010.

[15] Q. Zhu and Başar, "A hierarchical security architecture for smart grid," In Z. Han, E. Hossain and V. Poor (Eds.), *Smart Grid Communications and Networking*, Cambridge University Press, 2012.

[16] C.G. Rieger, D.I. Gertman, and M. A. McQueen, "Resilient control systems: next generation design research," In Proc. of the 2nd Conf. on Human System interactions, Catania, Italy, May 21-23, 2009, pp. 629–633.

[17] T. Başar and P. Bernhard, *H-infinity Optimal Control and Related Minimax Design Problems: A Dynamic Game Approach*, Birkhäuser, 1995.

[18] Q. Zhu and T. Başar, "Robust and resilient control design for cyber-physical systems with an application to power systems," in Proc. of 50th IEEE Conference on Decision and Control and European Control Conference, Orlando, Florida, Dec. 12-15, 2011.

[19] Q. Zhu and T. Başar, "Towards a unifying security framework for cyber-physical systems," in Proc. of Workshop on the Foundations of Dependable and Secure Cyber-Physical Systems (FDSCPS-11), CPSWeek 2011, Chicago.

[20] Q. Zhu and T. Başar, "Indices of power in optimal IDS default configuration: theory and examples," in Proc. of 2nd Conference on Decision and Game Theory (GameSec 2011), College Park, MD, USA. Nov. 14 - 15, 2011.

[21] Q. Zhu, H. Tembine and T. Başar, "Network security configuration: a nonzero-sum stochastic game approach," in Proc. of 2010 American Control Conference (ACC), June 30 -July 2, 2010, pp. 1059–1064.

[22] Q. Zhu and T. Başar, "Dynamic policy-based IDS configuration," in Proc. of 48th IEEE Conference on Decision and Control, Shanghai, China, Dec. 2009, Dec. 15-18, 2009, pp. 8600 – 8605.

[23] C.-W. Ten, C.-C. Liu and M. Govindarasu, "Vulnerability assessment of cybersecurity for SCADA systems using attack trees," Power Engineering Society General Meeting, 24-28 June 2007, pp.1–8.

[24] O. Sheyner, J. Haines, S. Jha, R. Lippmann, and J. Wing, "Automated generation and analysis of attack graphs," IEEE Symposium on Security and Privacy, 2002, pp. 273–284.

[25] J. F. Nash, "Equilibrium points in n-person games PNAS," January 1, 1950 vol. 36 no. 1 pp. 48–49.

[26] T. Başar and G. J. Olsder, *Dynamic Noncooperative Game Theory*, SIAM Series in Classics in Applied Mathematics, Philadelphia, January 1999.

[27] Digital Bond, http://www.digitalbond.com/tools/quickdraw/, last accessed on Feb. 20, 2012.

Integrity Attacks on Cyber-Physical Systems*

Yilin Mo
Department of Electrical and Computer
Engineering
Carnegie Mellon University
5000 Forbes Ave, Pittsburgh, PA, 15213
ymo@andrew.cmu.edu

Bruno Sinopoli
Department of Electrical and Computer
Engineering
Carnegie Mellon University
5000 Forbes Ave, Pittsburgh, PA, 15213
bruons@ece.cmu.edu

ABSTRACT

In this paper we consider the integrity attack on Cyber-Physical System(CPS), which is modeled as a discrete linear time-invariant system equipped with a Kalman filter, LQG controller and χ^2 failure detector. An attacker wishes to disturb the system by injecting external control inputs and fake sensor measurements. In order to perform the attack without being detected, the adversary will need to carefully design its actions to fool the failure detector as abnormal sensor measurements will result in an alarm. The adversary's strategy is formulated as a constrained control problem. In this paper, we characterize the reachable set of the system state and estimation error under the attack, which provides a quantitative measure of the resilience of the system. To this end, we will provide an ellipsoidal algorithm to compute the outer approximation of the reachable set. We also prove a necessary condition under which the reachable set is unbounded, indicating that the attacker can successfully destabilize the system.

Categories and Subject Descriptors

B.2.3 [**Reliability, Testing, and Fault-Tolerance**]: Diagnostics

General Terms

Security

Keywords

Cyber-Physical Systems, Reachability analysis, Security

---

*This research is supported in part by CyLab at Carnegie Mellon under grant DAAD19-02-1-0389 from the Army Research Office Foundation and grant NGIT2009100109 from Northrop Grumman Information Technology Inc Cybersecurity Consortium. The views and conclusions contained here are those of the authors and should not be interpreted as necessarily representing the official policies or endorsements, either express or implied, of ARO, CMU, or the U.S. Government or any of its agencies.

1. INTRODUCTION

The concept of Cyber-Physical System (CPS) refers to the embedding of sensing, communication, control and computation into the physical spaces. Today, CPSs can be found in areas as diverse as aerospace, automotive, chemical process control, civil infrastructure, energy, health-care, manufacturing and transportation, where secure operation is usually one of the main concerns. Any successful attack on these safety-critical CPS may significantly hamper the economy (for example, power outrage) or even lead to the loss of human lives (for example, the malfunctioning of automotive). The current CPSs are usually running in isolated networks, which protects the system by limiting the access points of the attacker. However, the next generation of "smarter" CPSs, such as Smart Grids, Vehicular ad-hoc network (VANET) and sensor networks, will make extensive use of widespread networking, which create lots of entry points for the attacker. Stuxnet, the first-ever malware that targets and subverts CPS systems, was first discovered on June 2010, which raises great concerns on CPS security.

The impact of attacks on CPS is discussed in [2]. The authors consider two possible classes of attacks on CPS: Denial of Service (DoS) and deception (or integrity) attacks. The DoS attack prevents the exchange of information, usually either sensor readings or control inputs between subsystems, while a integrity attack affects the data integrity of packets by modifying their payloads. A robust feedback control design against DoS attacks has been discussed in [1]. We feel that integrity attacks can be a subtler attack than DoS as they are in principle more difficult to detect. In this paper we want to analyze the impact of integrity attacks on CPS.

A significant amount of research has been carried out on detect, analyze and handle integrity attacks in CPS. In [5], the authors consider replay attack, which is a special kind of integrity attacks. The authors provide algebraic conditions for the feasibility of replay attack and proposed a detection technique to counter it. In [4], the authors discuss general integrity attacks in wireless sensor networks, where they propose an ellipsoidal approximation method to compute all possible biases the attacker could introduce to the state estimator. However, they are only concerned with state estimation. Therefore, it is not clear what is the impact of integrity attacks on the control performance.

For distributed control systems, Pasqualetti et al. [6] and Sundaram et al. [8] show how to detect and identify malicious behavior in consensus algorithm and wireless control networks respectively, based on the theory of structured linear systems. However, their models are noiseless, which greatly favor the intrusion detection system, since the evolution of the system is deterministic and any deviation from the predetermined trajectory will be detected. In a noisy environment, it is much harder to detect the malicious behavior of the attacker since it may be indistinguishable from the noise.

The effect of integrity attacks on power systems has also been extensively studied. Liu et al. [3] illustrate how an adversary can inject a stealthy input into the measurements to change the state estimation, without being detected by the bad data detector. In [7], the authors consider how to find a sparse stealthy input, which enables the adversary to launch an attack with minimum number of compromised sensors. Xie et al. [9] discuss how an adversary could use such kind of stealthy attacks to gain financial benefit in the electricity market. The main drawbacks of the above approaches is they only consider static systems and estimators. As a result, the applicability of such results to dynamic systems is questionable.

In this paper we model the CPS as a discrete linear time-invariant system equipped with a Kalman filter, LQG controller and χ^2 failure detector. We assume that an attacker wishes to disturb the system by injecting external control inputs and fake sensor measurements. In order to perform the attack without being detected, the adversary also need to carefully design its actions to fool the failure detector. We formulate the adversary's strategy as a constrained control problem and characterize the reachable set of the system state and estimation error under stealthy constraint, which provides a quantitative measure of the resilience of the system. We provide an ellipsoidal algorithm to compute the outer approximation of the reachable set. We also prove a necessary condition under which the reachable set is unbounded, indicating that the attacker can successfully destabilize the system.

The rest of the paper is organized as follows: in Section 2, we introduce the model of CPS by revisiting and adapting Kalman filter, LQG controller and χ^2 failure detector to our scenario. In Section 3, we define the threat model of integrity attacks and formulate it as a constrained control design problem. In Section 4 we discuss how to derive the upper bound for the reachable region. We also prove a necessary condition under which the reachable region is unbounded. An illustrative example is provided in Section 5. Finally Section 6 concludes the paper.

2. SYSTEM DESCRIPTION

In this section we model the CPS as a linear control system, which is equipped with a Kalman filter, a LQG controller and a χ^2 failure detector.

2.1 Physical System

We assume that the physical system has Linear Time Invariant (LTI) dynamics, which take the following form:

$$x_{k+1} = Ax_k + Bu_k + w_k, \qquad (1)$$

where $x_k \in \mathbb{R}^n$ is the vector of physical state variables at time k, $u_k \in \mathbb{R}^p$ is the control input, $w_k \in \mathbb{R}^n$ is the process noise at time k and x_0 is the initial state. w_k, x_0 are independent Gaussian random variables, and $x_0 \sim \mathcal{N}(0, \Sigma)$, $w_k \sim \mathcal{N}(0, Q)$.

2.2 Kalman filter and LQG controller

A sensor network is deployed to monitor the system described in (1). At each step all the sensor readings are collected and sent to a centralized estimator. The observation equation can be written as

$$y_k = Cx_k + v_k, \qquad (2)$$

where $y_k = [y_{k,1}, \ldots, y_{k,m}]^T \in \mathbb{R}^m$ is a vector of measurements from the sensors, and $y_{k,i}$ is the measurement made by sensor i at time k. $v_k \sim \mathcal{N}(0, R)$ is the measurement noise independent of x_0 and w_k.

A Kalman filter is used to compute state estimation $\hat{x}_k$ from observations y_ks:

$$\hat{x}_{0|-1} = 0, \ P_{0|-1} = \Sigma,$$
$$\hat{x}_{k+1|k} = A\hat{x}_k + Bu_k, \ P_{k+1|k} = AP_kA^T + Q,$$
$$K_k = P_{k|k-1}C^T(CP_{k|k-1}C^T + R)^{-1},$$
$$\hat{x}_k = \hat{x}_{k|k-1} + K_k(y_k - C\hat{x}_{k|k-1}),$$
$$P_k = P_{k|k-1} - K_kCP_{k|k-1}.$$

Although the Kalman filter uses a time varying gain K_k, it is well known that this gain will converge if the system is detectable. In practice the Kalman gain usually converges in a few steps. Thus, we can safely assume the Kalman filter to be already in steady state. Let us define

$$P \triangleq \lim_{k\to\infty} P_{k|k-1}, \ K \triangleq PC^T(CPC^T + R)^{-1}. \qquad (3)$$

The update equations of Kalman filter are as follows:

$$\hat{x}_{k+1} = A\hat{x}_k + Bu_k + K[y_{k+1} - C(A\hat{x}_k + Bu_k)], \qquad (4)$$

For future analysis, let us define the residue z_{k+1} at time $k+1$ to be

$$z_{k+1} \triangleq y_{k+1} - C(A\hat{x}_k + Bu_k). \qquad (5)$$

(4) can be simplified as

$$\hat{x}_{k+1} = A\hat{x}_k + Bu_k + Kz_{k+1}. \qquad (6)$$

The estimation error e_k at time k is defined as

$$e_k \triangleq x_k - \hat{x}_k. \qquad (7)$$

An LQG controller is used to stabilize the system by minimizing the following objective function[1]:

$$J = \lim_{T\to\infty} \min_{u_0,\ldots,u_T} E\frac{1}{T}\left[\sum_{k=0}^{T-1}(x_k^TWx_k + u_k^TUu_k)\right], \qquad (8)$$

where W, U are positive semidefinite matrices and u_k is measurable with respect to $y_0, \ldots, y_k$, i.e. u_k is a function of previous observations. It is well known that the optimal controller of the above minimization problem is a fixed gain controller, which takes the following form:

$$u_k = -(B^TSB + U)^{-1}B^TSA\hat{x}_k, \qquad (9)$$

where u_k is the optimal control input and S satisfies the following Riccati equation

$$S = A^TSA + W - A^TSB(B^TSB + U)^{-1}B^TSA. \qquad (10)$$

Let us define $L \triangleq -(B^TSB + U)^{-1}B^TSA$, then $u_k = Lx_{k|k}$.

---

[1] We assume an infinite horizon LQG controller is implemented.

It is easy to see that x_k, e_k are the states of the CPS[2]. Let us define

$$\tilde{x}_k \triangleq \begin{bmatrix} x_k \\ e_k \end{bmatrix} \in \mathbb{R}^{2n} \qquad (11)$$

Hence, we can write the dynamics of CPS as

$$\tilde{x}_{k+1} = \begin{bmatrix} A+BL & -BL \\ 0 & A-KCA \end{bmatrix} \tilde{x}_k$$
$$+ \begin{bmatrix} I & 0 \\ I-KC & -K \end{bmatrix} \begin{bmatrix} w_k \\ v_k \end{bmatrix}$$

It is trivial to prove that the CPS is stable if and only if both matrices $A-KCA$ and $A+BL$ are stable. In the rest of the paper, we will only consider stable CPS. Further, we assume that the CPS is already in steady state, which means that $\{x_k, y_k, \hat{x}_k\}$ are stationary random processes.

REMARK 1. *At the first glance, it seems that our choice of estimator, controller is quite limited. However, the analysis in this paper can be easily generalized to any fixed gain linear estimator and controller.*

2.3 Failure Detector

Failure detectors are often used in CPS to detect abnormal operations. We assume that a χ^2 failure detector is deployed, which computes the following quantity

$$g_k = z_k^T \mathcal{P}^{-1} z_k, \qquad (12)$$

where $\mathcal{P}$ is the covariance matrix of the residue z_k. Since z_k is Gaussian distributed, g_k is χ^2 distributed with m degrees of freedom. As a result, g_k cannot be far away from 0. The χ^2 failure detector will compare g_k with a certain threshold. If g_k is greater than the threshold, then an alarm will be triggered. We assume that the probability of false alarm for the χ^2 detector is P_f.

REMARK 2. *We will show later that the choice of detector is not critical for the analysis to hold. In fact, our result is valid for any detector which computes g_k as*

$$g_k = f(\hat{x}_k, \ldots, \hat{x}_{k-T}, y_k, \ldots, y_{k-T}, z_k, \ldots, z_{k-T}), \qquad (13)$$

where f is an arbitrary continuous function and T is the window size.

3. ATTACK MODEL

In this section we want to describe the integrity attack model on the CPS. To distinguish the compromised system and healthy system, we will use x_k', y_k', u_k' to indicate the states, measurements and control inputs of the compromised system respectively. We assume that an adversary has the following capabilities:

1. The adversary knows the static parameters of the system, namely A, B, C, K, L.

2. The adversary compromised a subset of sensors, and can add arbitrary bias to the reading of compromised sensors. As a result, the modified reading received by the estimator takes the following form:

$$y_k' = Cx_k' + \Gamma y_k^a + v_k, \qquad (14)$$

---

[2]x_k is the states of the physical system and $\hat{x}_k$ is the states of the estimator. Since the transformation from x_k, $\hat{x}_k$ to x_k, e_k is invertible, we could use x_k, e_k as the states of CPS.

where $\Gamma = diag(\gamma_1, \ldots, \gamma_m)$ is the sensor selection matrix such that $\gamma_i = 1$ if the ith sensor is compromised and $\gamma_i = 0$ otherwise. y_k^a is the bias introduced by the attacker.

3. The adversary can inject external control inputs to the system. As a result, the system equation becomes

$$x_{k+1}' = Ax_k' + Bu_k' + B^a u_k^a + w_k, \qquad (15)$$

where $B^a \in \mathbb{R}^{n \times q}$ characterizes the direction of control inputs the attacker could inject to the system.

Let us define $\hat{x}_k'$, z_k', e_k' as the state estimation, residue and estimation error of the compromised system respectively. Moreover, let us define the differences between the healthy and compromised system as

$$\begin{aligned} \Delta x_k &\triangleq & x_k' - x_k, \Delta y_k &\triangleq & y_k' - y_k, \\ \Delta u_k &\triangleq & u_k' - u_k, \Delta \hat{x}_k &\triangleq & \hat{x}_k' - \hat{x}_k, \\ \Delta z_k &\triangleq & z_k' - z_k, \Delta e_k &\triangleq & e_k' - e_k \\ \Delta \tilde{x}_k &\triangleq & \begin{bmatrix} x_k' \\ e_k' \end{bmatrix} - \begin{bmatrix} x_k \\ e_k \end{bmatrix}. \end{aligned} \qquad (16)$$

It can be proved that

$$\Delta \tilde{x}_{k+1} = \begin{bmatrix} A+BL & -BL \\ 0 & A-KCA \end{bmatrix} \Delta \tilde{x}_k$$
$$+ \begin{bmatrix} B^a & 0 \\ B^a - KCB^a & -K\Gamma \end{bmatrix} \begin{bmatrix} u_k^a \\ y_{k+1}^a \end{bmatrix} \qquad (17)$$

and

$$\Delta z_{k+1} = \begin{bmatrix} 0 & CA \end{bmatrix} \Delta \tilde{x}_k + \begin{bmatrix} CB^a & \Gamma \end{bmatrix} \begin{bmatrix} u_k^a \\ y_{k+1}^a \end{bmatrix} \qquad (18)$$

To simplify notations, let us define the following matrices:

$$\begin{aligned} \tilde{A} &\triangleq \begin{bmatrix} A+BL & -BL \\ 0 & A-KCA \end{bmatrix} \in \mathbb{R}^{2n \times 2n}, \\ \tilde{B} &\triangleq \begin{bmatrix} B^a & 0 \\ B^a - KCB^a & -K\Gamma \end{bmatrix} \in \mathbb{R}^{2n \times (q+m)} \\ \tilde{C} &\triangleq \begin{bmatrix} 0 & CA \end{bmatrix} \in \mathbb{R}^{m \times 2n}, \\ \tilde{D} &\triangleq \begin{bmatrix} CB^a & \Gamma \end{bmatrix} \in \mathbb{R}^{m \times (q+m)}. \end{aligned} \qquad (19)$$

and the attacker's action ζ_k^a as

$$\zeta_k^a \triangleq \begin{bmatrix} u_k^a \\ y_{k+1}^a \end{bmatrix}. \qquad (20)$$

Therefore,

$$\Delta \tilde{x}_{k+1} = \tilde{A} \Delta \tilde{x}_k + \tilde{B} \zeta_k^a, \qquad (21)$$

and

$$\Delta z_{k+1} = \tilde{C} \Delta \tilde{x}_k + \tilde{D} \zeta_k^a. \qquad (22)$$

It is clear that $\Delta x_k, \Delta z_k, \Delta e_k$ are functions of the attacker's actions $(\zeta_0^a, \zeta_1^a, \ldots)$. Let us define $\zeta^a = (\zeta_0^a, \zeta_1^a, \ldots)$ as the infinite sequence of the attacker's actions. As a result, we can write $\Delta x_k, \Delta z_k, \Delta e_k$ as $\Delta x_k(\zeta^a)$, $\Delta z_k(\zeta^a)$, $\Delta e_k(\zeta^a)$ respectively. We will omit the parameter ζ^a when there is no confusion.

We assume that the attacker wants its attack to be stealthy. In other words, the attacker wants the failure detector to have a very small probability to detect its presence. Ideally, to achieve this goal, the attacker would choose its action ζ^a, such that the following condition holds for all $k = 0, 1, \ldots$:

$$P(z_k'^T \mathcal{P}^{-1} z_k' > threshold) < \alpha, \qquad (23)$$

where α is a threshold probability chosen by the attacker. However, such probability is hard to compute in general as it involves in integrating a Gaussian distribution over an ellipsoid and hence difficult to enforce. As a result, we assume that attacker would enforce the following condition instead:

$$\|\Delta z_k\| \leq \beta. \forall k = 0, 1, \ldots. \qquad (24)$$

where

$$\|\Delta z_k\| \triangleq \sqrt{(\Delta z_k)^T \mathcal{P}^{-1} \Delta z_k}.$$

REMARK 3. *By triangular inequality, it can be easily seen that*

$$\|z_k'\| \leq \|z_k\| + \beta.$$

Therefore, when $\beta \to 0$, then the probability of detection $P(z_k'^T \mathcal{P}^{-1} z_k' > threshold)$ converges to the false alarm probability P_f, which is in general very small. Moreover, we would like to point out that for general detector of the form (13), the probability of detection always converges to the false alarm probability when $\beta \to 0$. Therefore, by carefully choosing β, (24) is valid for more general detection schemes. Due to linearity, we will assume that $\beta = 1$ for the rest of the paper.

We define the attacker's action ζ^a to be feasible if (24) holds for all k and $\beta = 1$. Moreover, we define the reachable region R_k as

$$R_k \triangleq \{\tilde{x} \in \mathbb{R}^{2n} : \tilde{x} = \Delta \tilde{x}_k(\zeta^a), \text{ for some feasible } \zeta^a\}.$$

and

$$\mathcal{R} \triangleq \bigcup_{k=0}^{\infty} R_k. \qquad (25)$$

REMARK 4. *$\mathcal{R}$ indicates all possible biases an attacker could introduce to the system. Since $x_k' = x_k + \Delta x_k$ and $e_k' = e_k + \Delta e_k$, and x_k, e_k are stationary Gaussian process, we can immediately derive the statistics of x_k', e_k' from $\mathcal{R}$. As a result, we will focus ourselves on characterizing the reachable set $\mathcal{R}$.*

4. MAIN RESULTS

In this section we want to characterize the shape of the reachable region $\mathcal{R}$. We will provide an outer approximation of $\mathcal{R}$ based on ellipsoidal approximation. Moreover, we provide a necessary condition for $\mathcal{R}$ to be unbounded, which indicates that the attacker could destabilize the system by introducing an arbitrary large bias.

4.1 Outer Approximation of $\mathcal{R}$

First, let us define the following sets:

$$T_0 \triangleq \mathbb{R}^{2n},$$
$$T_{i+1} \triangleq \{\tilde{x} \in \mathbb{R}^{2n} : \exists \zeta, \text{ such that } \tilde{A}\tilde{x} + \tilde{B}\zeta \in T_i, \qquad (26)$$
$$\text{and } \|\tilde{C}\tilde{x} + \tilde{D}\zeta\| \leq 1\}.$$

The following theorem shows that T_i is a superset of the reach region $\mathcal{R}$.

THEOREM 1. *The following properties hold for $\mathcal{R}$ and T_is:*

1. *For any $\tilde{x} \in \mathcal{R}$, there exists a ζ, such that*

$$\tilde{A}\tilde{x} + \tilde{B}\zeta \in \mathcal{R},$$

and

$$\|\tilde{C}\tilde{x} + \tilde{D}\zeta\| \leq 1.$$

2. *$T_{i+1} \subseteq T_i, \forall i$.*

3. *$\mathcal{R} \subseteq T_i, \forall i$.*

PROOF. 1. Since $\tilde{x} \in \mathcal{R}$, we know that

$$\tilde{x} = \Delta \tilde{x}_k(\zeta^a),$$

for some k and feasible ζ^a. Now choose $\zeta = \zeta_k^a$. Hence,

$$\tilde{A}\tilde{x} + \tilde{B}\zeta = \Delta \tilde{x}_{k+1}(\zeta^a) \in \mathcal{R},$$

and

$$\|\tilde{C}\tilde{x} + \tilde{D}\zeta\| = \|\Delta z_{k+1}(\zeta^a)\| \leq 1,$$

which concludes the proof.

2. Since $T_1 \subseteq T_0 = \mathbb{R}^{2n}$, it is trivial to prove that $T_{i+1} \subseteq T_i$ for all i by induction.

3. Since $\mathcal{R} \subseteq T_0 = \mathbb{R}^{2n}$, it is trivial to prove that $\mathcal{R} \subseteq T_i$ for all i by induction.

$\square$

Due to Theorem 1, we know that T_i is an outer approximation of $\mathcal{R}$. Moreover, T_i is monotonically decrease. Therefore, we can use $\lim_{i \to \infty} T_i$ as the outer approximation of $\mathcal{R}$. However, the exact shape of T_i is still numerically difficult to compute as i goes to infinity. Therefore, we will try to compute an ellipsoidal superset of T_i. To this end, let us suppose that T_i is outer approximated by the following ellipsoid:

$$T_i \subseteq \mathcal{E}_{2n}(\tilde{Q}_i),$$

where $\tilde{Q}_i \in \mathbb{R}^{2n \times 2n}$ is positive semidefinite, and $\mathcal{E}_l(S)$ is defined as the following ellipsoid

$$\mathcal{E}_l(S) \triangleq \{x \in \mathbb{R}^l : x^T S x \leq 1\}.$$

It is trivial to see that since $T_0 = \mathbb{R}^{2n}$, $\tilde{Q}_0 = 0$. Our goal is to find a recursive algorithm to evaluate $\tilde{Q}_i$.

Let us choose an arbitrary $\tilde{x} \in T_{i+1}$ and ζ, such that

$$\tilde{A}\tilde{x} + \tilde{B}\zeta \in T_i, \|\tilde{C}\tilde{x} + \tilde{D}\zeta\| \leq 1.$$

Since T_i is outer approximated by $\mathcal{E}_{2n}(\tilde{Q}_i)$, we know that

$$\begin{bmatrix} \tilde{x}^T & \zeta^T \end{bmatrix} \begin{bmatrix} \tilde{A}^T \tilde{Q}_i \tilde{A} & \tilde{A}^T \tilde{Q}_i \tilde{B} \\ \tilde{A}^T \tilde{Q}_i \tilde{B} & \tilde{B}^T \tilde{Q}_i \tilde{B} \end{bmatrix} \begin{bmatrix} \tilde{x} \\ \zeta \end{bmatrix} \leq 1.$$

Moreover,

$$\begin{bmatrix} \tilde{x}^T & \zeta^T \end{bmatrix} \begin{bmatrix} \tilde{C}^T \mathcal{P}^{-1} \tilde{C} & \tilde{C}^T \mathcal{P}^{-1} \tilde{D} \\ \tilde{C}^T \mathcal{P}^{-1} \tilde{D} & \tilde{D}^T \mathcal{P}^{-1} \tilde{D} \end{bmatrix} \begin{bmatrix} \tilde{x} \\ \zeta \end{bmatrix} \leq 1.$$

Therefore, $[\tilde{x}^T, \zeta^T]^T$ must jointly lies in the intersection of the following two $2n + p + q$ dimension ellipsoids:

$$\begin{bmatrix} \tilde{x} \\ \zeta \end{bmatrix} \in \mathcal{E}_{2n+q+m} \left(\begin{bmatrix} \tilde{A}^T \tilde{Q}_i \tilde{A} & \tilde{A}^T \tilde{Q}_i \tilde{B} \\ \tilde{B}^T \tilde{Q}_i \tilde{A} & \tilde{B}^T \tilde{Q}_i \tilde{B} \end{bmatrix} \right)$$
$$\bigcap \mathcal{E}_{2n+q+m} \left(\begin{bmatrix} \tilde{C}^T \mathcal{P}^{-1} \tilde{C} & \tilde{C}^T \mathcal{P}^{-1} \tilde{D} \\ \tilde{D}^T \mathcal{P}^{-1} \tilde{C} & \tilde{D}^T \mathcal{P}^{-1} \tilde{D} \end{bmatrix} \right).$$

One can prove that an outer approximation of the intersection is given by

$$\left[\begin{array}{c} \tilde{x} \\ \zeta \end{array}\right] \in \mathcal{E}_{2n+q+m}\left(\left[\begin{array}{cc} \tilde{A}^T\tilde{Q}_i\tilde{A} & \tilde{A}^T\tilde{Q}_i\tilde{B} \\ \tilde{B}^T\tilde{Q}_i\tilde{A} & \tilde{B}^T\tilde{Q}_i\tilde{B} \end{array}\right]\right)$$

$$\bigcap \mathcal{E}_{2n+q+m}\left(\left[\begin{array}{cc} \tilde{C}^T\mathcal{P}^{-1}\tilde{C} & \tilde{C}^T\mathcal{P}^{-1}\tilde{D} \\ \tilde{D}^T\mathcal{P}^{-1}\tilde{C} & \tilde{D}^T\mathcal{P}^{-1}\tilde{D} \end{array}\right]\right)$$

$$\subseteq \mathcal{E}_{2n+q+m}\left(\frac{1}{2}\left[\begin{array}{cc} \tilde{A}^T\tilde{Q}_i\tilde{A} & \tilde{A}^T\tilde{Q}_i\tilde{B} \\ \tilde{B}^T\tilde{Q}_i\tilde{A} & \tilde{B}^T\tilde{Q}_i\tilde{B} \end{array}\right]\right.$$

$$\left.+\frac{1}{2}\left[\begin{array}{cc} \tilde{C}^T\mathcal{P}^{-1}\tilde{C} & \tilde{C}^T\mathcal{P}^{-1}\tilde{D} \\ \tilde{D}^T\mathcal{P}^{-1}\tilde{C} & \tilde{D}^T\mathcal{P}^{-1}\tilde{D} \end{array}\right]\right).$$

Finally, using the Schur complement, we can project a high dimensional ellipsoid in $\mathbb{R}^{2n+q+m}$ to $\mathbb{R}^{2n}$ to obtain $\tilde{Q}_{i+1}$ as follows:

$$\begin{aligned} \tilde{Q}_{i+1} = \frac{1}{2}\Big[& \tilde{A}^T\tilde{Q}_i\tilde{A} + \tilde{C}^T\mathcal{P}^{-1}\tilde{C} \\ & -(\tilde{A}^T\tilde{Q}_i\tilde{B} + \tilde{C}^T\mathcal{P}^{-1}\tilde{D}) \\ & \times(\tilde{B}^T\tilde{Q}_i\tilde{B} + \tilde{D}^T\mathcal{P}^{-1}\tilde{D})^+ \\ & \times(\tilde{B}^T\tilde{Q}_i\tilde{A} + \tilde{D}^T\mathcal{P}^{-1}\tilde{C})\Big], \end{aligned} \quad (27)$$

where $^+$ is the Moore-Penrose pseudoinverse.

4.2 Stability analysis

In this subsection, we want to characterize the boundedness of $\mathcal{R}$. An unbounded $\mathcal{R}$ indicates that the attacker could destabilize the system by introducing an arbitrary large bias. The following theorem provides a necessary condition for $\mathcal{R}$ to be unbounded.

THEOREM 2. *The reachable region $\mathcal{R}$ is unbounded only if there exist a vector $v \in \mathbb{R}^n$ and a matrix $L^a \in \mathbb{R}^{q\times n}$, such that*

  1. *v is an eigenvector of $A + B^aL^a$, the corresponding eigenvalue of which is λ.*

  2. *Cv belongs to the column space of Γ or $\lambda = 0$.*

REMARK 5. *It is worth noticing that the shape of $\mathcal{R}$ depends on the choice of estimation and controller gain K, L in general. However, the necessary condition is independent of K, L. In other words, if the necessary condition holds, then the system has an inherent vulnerability which cannot be fixed by simply redesigning the estimator and controller.*

The rest of the subsection is devoted to proving Theorem 2. First we want to show that Δx_k is bounded if and only if Δe_k is bounded. From definition,

$$\Delta x_k = \Delta e_k + \Delta\hat{x}_k,$$

and

$$\Delta\hat{x}_{k+1} = (A + BL)\Delta\hat{x}_k + K\Delta z_{k+1}.$$

Since we assume that the system is closed-loop stable, which implies that $A + BL$ is stable, and $\|\Delta z_k\| \leq 1$, $\Delta\hat{x}_k$ must be bounded. Thus, the boundedness of Δx_k is equivalent to the boundedness of Δe_k. Therefore, we only need to focus on Δe_k and thus we could simplify (21),(22) as

$$\Delta e_{k+1} = (A-KCA)\Delta e_k+(B^a-KCB^a)u_k^a-K\Gamma y_{k+1}^a, \quad (28)$$

$$\Delta z_{k+1} = CA\Delta e_k + CB^au_k^a + \Gamma y_{k+1}^a. \quad (29)$$

To further simplify notations, we define the following matrices:

$$\begin{aligned} \mathcal{A} &\triangleq A - KCA \in \mathbb{R}^{n\times n}, \\ \mathcal{B} &\triangleq \left[\begin{array}{cc} B^a - KCB^a & -K\Gamma \end{array}\right] \in \mathbb{R}^{n\times(q+m)} \\ \mathcal{C} &\triangleq CA \in \mathbb{R}^{m\times n}, \\ \mathcal{D} &\triangleq \tilde{D} \in \mathbb{R}^{m\times(q+m)}. \end{aligned} \quad (30)$$

Thus, we can write (28) and (29) as

$$\begin{aligned} \Delta e_{k+1} &= \mathcal{A}\Delta e_k + \mathcal{B}\zeta_k, \\ \Delta z_{k+1} &= \mathcal{C}\Delta e_k + \mathcal{D}\zeta_k, \end{aligned}$$

LEMMA 1. *There exists feasible attacker's action ζ^a such that $\Delta e_k(\zeta^a)$ is unbounded only if there exist a vector $v \in \mathbb{R}^n$ and a matrix $\mathcal{L} \in \mathbb{R}^{(q+m)\times n}$, such that*

  1. *v is an eigenvector of $\mathcal{A} + \mathcal{B}\mathcal{L}$*

  2. *$(\mathcal{C} + \mathcal{D}\mathcal{L})v = 0$*

PROOF. The proof is quite long and is hence reported in the appendix for the sake of legibility. □

Now we are ready to prove the Theorem 2.

PROOF. By Lemma 1, we know that $\mathcal{R}$ is unbounded only when there exist a vector $v \in \mathbb{R}.$ and a matrix $\mathcal{L} \in \mathbb{R}^{(q+m)\times n}$, such that

  1. *v is an eigenvector of $\mathcal{A} + \mathcal{B}\mathcal{L}$,*

  2. *$(\mathcal{C} + \mathcal{D}\mathcal{L})v = 0$*

Now let us write $\mathcal{L}$ as

$$\mathcal{L} = \left[\begin{array}{c} L^a \\ M \end{array}\right]$$

where $L^a \in \mathbb{R}^{q\times n}$ and $M \in \mathbb{R}^{m\times n}$. Since v satisfies $(\mathcal{C} + \mathcal{D}\mathcal{L})v = 0$, we have

$$(CA + CB^aL^a + \Gamma M)v = 0. \quad (31)$$

Now by the fact that v is an eigenvector of $\mathcal{A} + \mathcal{B}\mathcal{L}$, we have

$$(A - KCA + B^aL^a - KCB^aL^a - K\Gamma M)v = \lambda v, \quad (32)$$

where λ is the corresponding eigenvalue. Combining (31) and (32), we have

$$\begin{aligned} (A + B^aL^a)v - K(CA + CB^aL^a + \Gamma M)v &= (A + B^aL^a)v \\ &= \lambda v. \end{aligned} \quad (33)$$

Therefore, v is also an eigenvector of $A + B^aL^a$. Now by (31) and (33), we have

$$\lambda Cv = -\Gamma Mv.$$

The right-hand side of equation belongs to the column space of Γ. Therefore, either $\lambda = 0$ or Cv belongs to the column space of Γ, which concludes the proof. □

5. ILLUSTRATIVE EXAMPLE

In this section, we will provide a numerical example to illustrate the effects of integrity attack on CPS.

Consider a vehicle which is moving along the x-axis. The state space includes position x and velocity v of the vehicle. As a result, the discrete-time system dynamics are as follows:

$$v_{k+1} = v_k + w_{k,1} + u_k,$$
$$x_{k+1} = x_k + v_k + w_{k,2}, \tag{34}$$

which can be written in the matrix form as

$$X_{k+1} = \begin{bmatrix} 1 & 0 \\ 1 & 1 \end{bmatrix} X_k + w_k + \begin{bmatrix} 1 \\ 0 \end{bmatrix} u_k, \tag{35}$$

where

$$X_k = \begin{bmatrix} v \\ x \end{bmatrix}, \; w_k = \begin{bmatrix} w_{k,1} \\ w_{k,2} \end{bmatrix}. \tag{36}$$

Suppose two sensors are measuring velocity and position respectively. Hence

$$y_k = X_k + v_k. \tag{37}$$

We assume that the covariance of the noise is $Q = R = I$. The steady state Kalman gain in this case is

$$K = \begin{bmatrix} 0.5939 & 0.0793 \\ 0.0793 & 0.6944 \end{bmatrix}. \tag{38}$$

Moreover, we assume that the LQG cost $W = I$ and $U = 1$. Therefore, the control gain is given by

$$L = \begin{bmatrix} -1.2439 & -0.4221 \end{bmatrix} \tag{39}$$

We consider two cases, where either the velocity sensor or the position sensor is compromised, i.e. $\Gamma = [1,0]'$ or $\Gamma = [0,1]'$. We assume that the attacker does not inject external control input, i.e. $B^a = [0,0]'$ for both cases.

Figure 1 shows the outer approximation of $\mathcal{R}$ when the velocity sensor is compromised. From the simulation we can conclude that the reachable region $\mathcal{R}$ is bounded. Therefore the attacker cannot destabilize the system by simply compromising velocity sensor.

Figure 2 shows the outer approximation of $\mathcal{R}$ when the position sensor is compromised. It can be seen that the outer approximation is unbounded (The ellipse degenerates into two straight lines), which implies that the attacker can arbitrarily manipulate the position of the vehicle. In fact, one can check that $v = [0,1]'$ and $L^a = 0$ satisfies the necessary conditions listed in Theorem 2.

6. CONCLUSION

In this paper we consider the integrity attack on Cyber-Physical System(CPS). We formalize the adversary's strategy as a constrained control problem and characterize the shape and boundedness of the reachable set of the system state and estimation error under the attack, which provides a quantitative measure of the resilience of the system.

7. REFERENCES

[1] S. Amin, A. Cardenas, and S. S. Sastry. Safe and secure networked control systems under denial-of-service attacks. In *Hybrid Systems: Computation and Control*, pages 31–45. Lecture Notes in Computer Science. Springer Berlin / Heidelberg, April 2009.

[2] A. A. Cárdenas, S. Amin, and S. Sastry. Secure control: Towards survivable cyber-physical systems. In *Distributed Computing Systems Workshops, 2008. ICDCS '08. 28th International Conference on*, pages 495–500, June 2008.

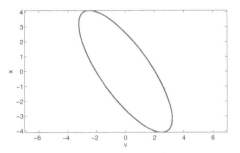

Figure 1: Outer Approximation When Velocity Sensor is Compromised

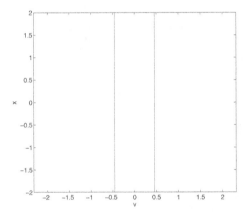

Figure 2: Outer Approximation When Position Sensor is Compromised

[3] Y. Liu, M. Reiter, and P. Ning. False data injection attacks against state estimation in electric power grids. In *Proceedings of the 16th ACM conference on Computer and communications security*, 2009.

[4] Y. Mo, E. Garone, A. Casavola, and B. Sinopoli. False data injection attacks against state estimation in wireless sensor networks. In *Proc. 49th IEEE Conf. Decision and Control (CDC)*, pages 5967–5972, 2010.

[5] Y. Mo and B. Sinopoli. Secure control against replay attacks. In *Proc. 47th Annual Allerton Conf. Communication, Control, and Computing Allerton 2009*, pages 911–918, 2009.

[6] F. Pasqualetti, A. Bicchi, and F. Bullo. Consensus computation in unreliable networks: A system theoretic approach. *IEEE Transactions on Automatic Control*, Feb. 2010. To appear.

[7] H. Sandberg, A. Teixeira, and K. H. Johansson. On security indices for state estimators in power networks. In *First Workshop on Secure Control Systems*, 2010.

[8] S. Sundaram, M. Pajic, C. Hadjicostis, R. Mangharam,

and G. J. Pappas. The wireless control network: monitoring for malicious behavior. In *IEEE Conference on Decision and Contro*, Atlanta, GA, Dec 2010.

[9] L. Xie, Y. Mo, and B. Sinopoli. False data injection attacks in electricity markets. In *IEEE Int'l Conf. on Smart Grid Communications (SmartGridComm)*, pages 226–231, Oct. 2010.

8. APPENDIX

Before proving Lemma 1, we want to define the following sets: $S_0 \triangleq \mathbb{R}^n$ and

$$S_{i+1} \triangleq \{e \in \mathbb{R}^n : \exists \zeta, \mathcal{A}e + \mathcal{B}\zeta \in S_i,$$
$$\|\mathcal{C}e + \mathcal{D}\zeta)\|_\infty \leq 1\}.$$

REMARK 6. *Due to the equivalence of norms in $\mathbb{R}^n$ and linearity of the system, we could use infinity norm instead of $\|\cdot\|_{\mathcal{P}-1}$ without affecting the stability result.*

Let us also define

$$\mathcal{S} \triangleq \bigcap_{i=0}^{\infty} S_i.$$

The following lemma characterizes some important properties of S_i and $\mathcal{S}$:

LEMMA 2. *The following statements of $\mathcal{S}$ and S_i hold:*

1. $S_{i+1} \subseteq S_i$.

2. *S_i takes the following form:*

$$S_i = \{e \in \mathbb{R}^n : \mathcal{A}_i e \leq b_i\}, \quad (40)$$

where $\mathcal{A}_i$ is a matrix and b_i is a vector of proper dimensions and the comparison is entry-wise.

3. *$\mathcal{S}$ is convex and closed.*

4. *If $e \in \mathcal{S}$, then $\alpha e \in \mathcal{S}$, where $\alpha \in [-1, 1]$.*

5. *Suppose that subspaces $\mathcal{V}, \mathcal{V}' \subseteq \mathcal{S}$, then the direct sum $\mathcal{V} \oplus \mathcal{V}' \subseteq \mathcal{S}$.*

6. *If $\mathcal{S}$ is unbounded, then $\mathcal{S}$ contains a subspace $\mathcal{V} \neq \{0\}$.*

7. *For any $e \in \mathcal{S}$, there exists an ζ, such that*

$$\mathcal{A}e + \mathcal{B}\zeta \in \mathcal{S}, \|\mathcal{C}e + \mathcal{D}\zeta\|_\infty \leq 1. \quad (41)$$

PROOF. 1. Since $S_0 = \mathbb{R}^n$, $S_1 \subseteq S_0$. The statement can be easily proved by induction.

2. Since we use infinite norm in the definition of S_i, this can also be shown by induction.

3. It is trivial to see that S_i is convex and closed for each i. Hence, their intersection $\mathcal{S}$ is also convex and closed.

4. Since S_i is symmetric, $\mathcal{S}$ is also symmetric. Using the convexity of $\mathcal{S}$, we can finish the proof.

5. This is a direct consequence of the convexity of $\mathcal{S}$.

6. Suppose that $e_1, e_2, \ldots$ is an unbounded sequence in $\mathcal{S}$. Without loss of generality, we assume that

$$\lim_{i \to \infty} e_i / \|e_i\|_\infty = e^0, \lim_{i \to \infty} \|e_i\|_\infty = \infty.$$

Now pick an arbitrary $\alpha \in \mathbb{R}$. There exists N, such that for all $i \geq N$, $\alpha/\|e_i\|_\infty \in [-1, 1]$, which implies that

$$\frac{\alpha}{\|e_i\|_\infty} e_i \in \mathcal{S}.$$

Take the limit on the left side and use the fact that $\mathcal{S}$ is closed, we have $\alpha e^0 \in \mathcal{S}$ for all α. Hence, $\mathcal{S}$ contains $span(e^0)$.

7. From the definition of S_i, if $e \in \mathcal{S}$, there exists ζ_i for each i such that

$$\mathcal{A}e + \mathcal{B}\zeta_i \in S_i, \|\mathcal{C}e + \mathcal{D}\zeta_i\|_\infty \leq 1. \quad (42)$$

Without loss of generality, let us pick such ζ_is with minimal infinite norm. Suppose that ζ_i converges to ζ^*. For each i, we know that if $j \geq i$, then

$$\mathcal{A}e + \mathcal{B}\zeta_j \in S_j \subseteq S_i.$$

Take the limit on the left-hand side and use the fact that S_i is closed, we have

$$\mathcal{A}e + \mathcal{B}\zeta^* = \lim_{j \to \infty} \mathcal{A}e + \mathcal{B}\zeta_j \in S_i, \forall i.$$

Therefore

$$\mathcal{A}e + \mathcal{B}\zeta^* \in \bigcap_{i=0}^{\infty} S_i = \mathcal{S}.$$

Moreover,

$$\|\mathcal{C}e + \mathcal{D}\zeta^*\|_\infty = \lim_{i \to \infty} \|\mathcal{C}e + \mathcal{D}\zeta_i\|_\infty \leq 1$$

Hence, ζ^* is the required vector for (41). As a result, we only need to prove that $\{\zeta_i\}$ converges or at least contains a converging subsequence. We will prove that by contradiction. Suppose $\{\zeta_i\}$ does not contains any converging subsequence. Due to Bolzano Weierstrass Theorem, $\{\zeta_i\}$ must be unbounded. Again, by Bolzano Weierstrass theorem, there exists $\zeta_{i_1}, \zeta_{i_2}, \ldots$, such that

$$\lim_{j \to \infty} \|\zeta_{i_j}\|_\infty = \infty, \zeta^0 = \lim_{j \to \infty} \zeta_{i_j} / \|\zeta_{i_j}\|_\infty.$$

We now have

$$\lim_{j \to \infty} \frac{\|\mathcal{C}e + \mathcal{D}\zeta_{i_j}\|_\infty}{\|\zeta_{i_j}\|_\infty} = \|\mathcal{D}\zeta^0\|_\infty \leq \lim_{j \to \infty} 1/\|\zeta_{i_j}\|_\infty = 0.$$

Hence $\mathcal{D}\zeta^0 = 0$. Pick an arbitrary $\alpha \in \mathbb{R}$ and $l \in \mathbb{N}$. There exists an N such that if $j \geq N$, then

$$\frac{\alpha}{\|\zeta_{i_j}\|_\infty} \in [-1, 1], \text{ and } i_j \geq l + 1.$$

As a result,

$$\frac{\alpha}{\|\zeta_{i_j}\|_\infty}(\mathcal{A}e + \mathcal{B}\zeta_{i_j}) \in S_{i_j} \subseteq S_l.$$

Take the limit on the left side and use the fact that S_l is closed, we have

$$\alpha \mathcal{B}\zeta^0 \in S_l, \forall \alpha.$$

As a result, $span(\mathcal{B}\zeta^0) \in S_i$. Therefore, $\mathcal{A}_i \mathcal{B}\zeta^0 = 0$ for all i, which implies that for any $\alpha \in \mathbb{R}$,

$$\mathcal{A}e + \mathcal{B}(\zeta_{i_j} - \alpha\zeta^0) \in S_{i_j},$$
$$\|\mathcal{C}e + \mathcal{D}(\zeta_{i_j} - \alpha\zeta^0)]\|_\infty \leq 1.$$

Therefore, the fact that ζ_{i_j} goes to infinity contradicts the minimality of ζ_{i_j}, which completes the proof.

$\square$

Now we are ready to prove Lemma 1.

PROOF. Similar to the proof of Theorem 1, we can prove that the reachable region of Δe_k is contained in $\alpha\mathcal{S}$, where $\alpha > 0$ is a constant. As a result, $\mathcal{S}$ is unbounded. By

Lemma 2, we know that there exists a subspace $\mathcal{V} \subseteq \mathcal{S}$. Moreover we can assume $\mathcal{V}$ is maximal subspace contained in $\mathcal{S}$ due to Lemma 2(5).

Now pick an arbitrary vector e in $\mathcal{V}$. We know there exists $\zeta_k \in \mathbb{R}^p$, $k \in \mathbb{N}$ such that

$$\mathcal{A}(ke) + \mathcal{B}\zeta_k \in \mathcal{S}, \|\mathcal{C}(ke) + \mathcal{D}\zeta_k\|_\infty \leq 1.$$

We will pick such ζ_k with minimal norm. By similar argument as in Lemma 2, we can prove that $\sup_k \|\zeta_k\|/k$ must be finite. By Bolzano Weierstrass theorem, there exists $\zeta_{i_1}, \zeta_{i_2}, \ldots$, such that

$$\lim_{j \to \infty} \zeta_{i_j}/i_j = \zeta^*.$$

Similar to Lemma 2, we can also prove that

$$\|\mathcal{C}e + \mathcal{D}\zeta^*\| = 0.$$

and

$$span(\mathcal{A}e + \mathcal{B}\zeta^*) \subseteq \mathcal{S}.$$

Thus, $span(\mathcal{A}e + \mathcal{B}\zeta^*) \subseteq \mathcal{V}$ due to the maximality of $\mathcal{V}$.

Now suppose $e_0, \ldots, e_j$ form a basis for $\mathcal{V}$. For every e_i, there exists ζ_i^*, such that $\mathcal{A}e_i + \mathcal{B}\zeta_i^* \in \mathcal{V}$ and $\mathcal{C}e_i + \mathcal{D}\zeta_i^* = 0$. Hence, we could find a matrix $\mathcal{L}$, such that $\zeta_i^* = \mathcal{L}e_i$, for all e_i, which implies that $(\mathcal{A} + \mathcal{B}\mathcal{L})\mathcal{V} \subseteq \mathcal{V}$ and $(\mathcal{C} + \mathcal{D}\mathcal{L})\mathcal{V} = 0$. Therefore, there exists $v \in \mathcal{V}$, such that v is the eigenvector of $\mathcal{A} + \mathcal{B}\mathcal{L}$, and $(\mathcal{C} + \mathcal{D}\mathcal{L})v = 0$. $\square$

Attack Models and Scenarios for Networked Control Systems

André Teixeira,　Daniel Pérez,　Henrik Sandberg,　Karl H. Johansson

ACCESS Linnaeus Center
Automatic Control Laboratory
KTH - Royal Institute of Technology
Osquldas väg 10
SE-10044 Stockholm, Sweden
andretei, danielph, hsan, kallej@kth.se

ABSTRACT

Cyber-secure networked control is modeled, analyzed, and experimentally illustrated in this paper. An attack space defined by the adversary's system knowledge, disclosure, and disruption resources is introduced. Adversaries constrained by these resources are modeled for a networked control system architecture. It is shown that attack scenarios corresponding to replay, zero dynamics, and bias injection attacks can be analyzed using this framework. An experimental setup based on a quadruple-tank process controlled over a wireless network is used to illustrate the attack scenarios, their consequences, and potential counter-measures.

Categories and Subject Descriptors

K.6.5 [**Management of Computing and Information Systems**]: Security and Protection—*unauthorized access*; C.3 [**Special-Purpose and Application-Based Systems**]: Process control systems

Keywords

Cyber-physical systems, security, attack space, secure control systems

1. INTRODUCTION

Safe and reliable operation of infrastructures is of major societal importance. These systems need to be engineered in such a way so that they can be continuously monitored, coordinated, and controlled despite a variety of potential system disturbances. Given the strict operating requirements and system complexity, such systems are operated through IT infrastructures enabling the timely data flow between digital controllers, sensors, and actuators. However, the use of non-proprietary communication networks and heterogeneous IT components has made these cyber-physical systems vulnerable to cyber threats. One such example are the

power transmission networks operated through Supervisory Control and Data Acquisition (SCADA) systems. The measurement and control data in these systems are commonly transmitted through unprotected channels, leaving the system vulnerable to several threats [7]. In fact cyber attacks on power networks operated by SCADA systems have been reported in the media [8].

There exists a vast literature on computer security focusing on three main properties of data and IT services, namely confidentiality, integrity, and availability [3]. Confidentiality relates to the non-disclosure of data by unauthorized parties. Integrity on the other hand concerns the trustworthiness of data, meaning there is no unauthorized change of the data contents or properties, while availability means that timely access to the data or system functionalities is ensured. Unlike other IT systems where cyber-security mainly involves the protection of data, cyber attacks on networked control systems may influence the physical processes through the communication infrastructure due to feedback loops. Therefore networked control system security needs to consider the existing threats at both the cyber and physical layers. These threats can be captured in the attack space illustrated in Figure 1, which also depicts several attack scenarios described in this work. For instance, two typical examples of cyber attacks considered in IT security can be found in Figure 1, the eavesdropping attack and the Denial-of-Service (DoS) attack.

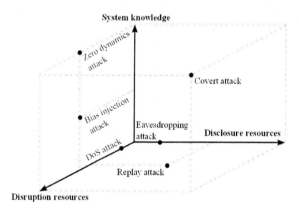

Figure 1: The cyber-physical attack space.

We propose three dimensions for the attack space: the adversary's *a priori* system model knowledge and his disclosure and disruption resources. The *a priori* system knowledge can be used by the attacker to construct more complex attacks, possibly harder to detect and with more severe consequences. Similarly, the disclosure resources enable the attacker to obtain sensitive information about the system during the attack by violating the data confidentiality. Note that disclosure resources cannot be used to disrupt the system operation, which is the case of the eavesdropping attack illustrated in Figure 1. On the other hand, disruption resources can be used to affect the system operation, which happens for instance when data integrity or availability properties are violated. One such example is the DoS attack illustrated in Figure 1, where the data required for correctly operating the system is made unavailable.

Control theory has contributed with frameworks to handle model uncertainties and disturbances [20] as well as fault diagnosis and mitigation [5, 10], which can then be used to detect and attenuate the consequences of cyber attacks on networked control systems. Some of these tools are therefore considered as part of the networked control system and will be used to analyze the consequences of cyber attacks.

1.1 Related Work

Cyber attacks on control systems compromising measurement and actuator data integrity and availability have been considered in [4], where the authors modeled their effects on the physical dynamics. Availability attacks have been further analyzed in [1, 9] for resource constrained attackers with full-state information. Particularly, this work considered DoS attacks in which the attacker could jam the communication channels and prevent measurement and actuator data from reaching its destination, rendering the data unavailable. A particular instance of the DoS attack in which the attacker does not have any *a priori* system knowledge [1] is represented in the attack space in Figure 1.

Deception attacks compromising integrity have recently received more attention. A particular kind of deception attacks, i.e. replay attacks on the sensor measurements, has been analyzed in [14]. The authors considered the case where all the existing sensors were attacked and proposed suitable counter-measures to detect the attack. In this attack scenario the attacker does not have any system knowledge but is able to access and corrupt the sensor data, thus having disclosure and disruptive resources, as depicted in Figure 1.

Another class of deception attacks, false-data injection attacks, has also been studied in recent work. For instance, in the case of power networks, an attacker with perfect model knowledge has been initially considered in [13]. The work in [12] considered stealthy attacks with limited resources and proposed improved detection methods, while [16] analyzed the minimum number of sensors required for stealthy attacks, based on which measurement security metrics were proposed. The consequences of these attacks have also been analyzed in [18, 19]. The models used are static, hence these attack scenarios are closest to the bias injection attack shown in Figure 1.

Data injection attacks on dynamic control systems were also considered. In [17] the author characterizes the set of attack policies for covert (undetectable) false-data injection attacks with detailed model knowledge and full access to all sensor and actuator channels, while [15] described the set of undetectable false-data injection attacks for omniscient attackers with full-state information, but possibly compromising only a subset of the existing sensors and actuators. In these attack scenarios confidentiality was also violated, as the attacker had access to either measurement and actuator data or full-state information. These attacks are therefore placed close to the boundaries of the attack space, as illustrated in Figure 1 for the covert attack, while the framework in [15] addresses attacks on the top plane where full model knowledge is considered.

1.2 Contributions and Outline

Most of the recent work on cyber-security of control systems has considered scenarios where the attacker has access to a large set of resources and knowledge, thus being placed close to the boundaries of the attack space in Figure 1. Therefore a large part of the attack space has not been addressed. In particular, the class of detectable attacks that do not trigger conventional alarms has yet to be covered in depth.

In this paper we consider a typical control architecture for the networked control system under both cyber and physical attacks. Given this architecture, a generic adversary model applicable to several attack scenarios is discussed and the attack resources are mapped to the corresponding dimensions of the attack space. Three stealthy attack scenarios are discussed in more detail to better illustrate the proposed adversary model and the concept of attack space.

One of the attack scenarios analyzed corresponds to a particular type of detectable attack, the bias injection attack. Although this attack may be detected, it requires limited model knowledge and no information about the system state. Stealthiness conditions are provided, as well as a methodology to assess the attack impact on the physical state of the system.

The attack scenarios analyzed in the paper have been staged at our testbed for security of control systems. The testbed architecture and results from the staged attacks are presented and discussed.

The outline of the paper is as follows. The system architecture and model are described in Section 2, while Section 3 contains the adversary model and a detailed description of the attack resources on each dimension of the attack space. The framework introduced in the previous sections is then illustrated for three particular attack scenarios in Section 4. The results of the experiments for each attack scenario in a secure control systems testbed are presented and discussed in Section 5, followed by conclusions in Section 6.

2. NETWORKED CONTROL SYSTEM

In this section we describe the networked control system structure, where we consider three main components: the physical plant and communication network, the feedback controller, and the anomaly detector.

2.1 Physical Plant and Communication Network

The physical plant is modeled in a discrete-time state-space form,

$$\mathcal{P} : \begin{cases} x_{k+1} = Ax_k + B\tilde{u}_k + Gw_k + Ff_k \\ y_k = Cx_k + v_k \end{cases}, \quad (1)$$

where $x_k \in \mathbb{R}^n$ is the state variable, $\tilde{u}_k \in \mathbb{R}^q$ the control actions applied to the process, $y_k \in \mathbb{R}^p$ the measurements from the sensors at the sampling instant $k \in \mathbb{Z}$, and $f_k \in \mathbb{R}^d$ is the unknown signal representing the effects of anomalies, usually denoted as fault signal in the fault diagnosis literature [6]. The process and measurement noise, $w_k \in \mathbb{R}^n$ and $v_k \in \mathbb{R}^p$, represent the discrepancies between the model and the real process, due to unmodeled dynamics or disturbances, for instance, and we assume their means are respectively bounded by δ_w and δ_v, i.e. $\bar{w} = \|\mathbb{E}\{w_k\}\| \leq \delta_w$ and $\bar{v} = \|\mathbb{E}\{v_k\}\| \leq \delta_v$.

The physical plant operation is supported by a communication network through which the sensor measurements and actuator data are transmitted, which at the plant side correspond to y_k and $\tilde{u}_k$, respectively. At the controller side we denote the sensor and actuator data by $\tilde{y}_k \in \mathbb{R}^p$ and $u_k \in \mathbb{R}^q$ respectively. Since the communication network may be unreliable, the data exchanged between the plant and the controller may be altered, resulting in discrepancies in the data at the plant and controller ends. In this paper we do not consider the usual communication network effects such as packet losses and delays. Instead we focus on data corruption due to malicious cyber attacks, as described in Section 3. Therefore the communication network is supposed to be reliable, not affecting the data flowing through it.

Given the physical plant model (1) and assuming an ideal communication network, the networked control system is said to have a *nominal behavior* if $f_k = 0$, $\tilde{u}_k = u_k$, and $\tilde{y}_k = y_k$. The absence of either one of these condition results in an abnormal behavior of the system.

2.2 Feedback Controller

In order to comply with performance requirements in the presence of the unknown process and measurement noises, we consider that the physical plant is controlled by an appropriate linear time-invariant feedback controller [20]. The output feedback controller can be written in a state-space form as

$$\mathcal{F}: \begin{cases} z_{k+1} = A_c z_k + B_c \tilde{y}_k \\ u_k = C_c z_k + D_c \tilde{y}_k \end{cases} \quad (2)$$

where the states of the controller, $z_k \in \mathbb{R}^m$, may include the process state and tracking error estimates. Given the plant and communication network models, the controller is supposed to be designed so that acceptable performance is achieved under nominal behavior.

2.3 Anomaly Detector

In this section we consider the anomaly detector that monitors the system to detect possible anomalies, i.e. deviations from the nominal behavior. We consider that the anomaly detector is collocated with the controller, therefore it only has access to $\tilde{y}_k$ and u_k to evaluate the behavior of the plant.

Several approaches to detecting malfunctions in control systems are available in the fault diagnosis literature [6,10]. Here we consider the following observer-based Fault Detection Filter

$$\mathcal{D}: \begin{cases} \hat{x}_{k|k} = A\hat{x}_{k-1|k-1} + Bu_{k-1} + K(\tilde{y}_k - \hat{y}_{k|k-1}) \\ r_k = V(\tilde{y}_k - \hat{y}_{k|k}) \end{cases}, \quad (3)$$

where $\hat{x}_{k|k} \in \mathbb{R}^n$ is the state estimate given measurements up until time k and $r_k \in \mathbb{R}^{p_d}$ the residue, which is evaluated in order to detect and locate existing anomalies.

The anomaly detector is designed so that

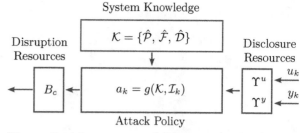

Figure 2: Adversary model for a point in the attack space in Figure 1.

1. under nominal behavior of the system (i.e., $f_k = 0$, $u_k = \tilde{u}_k$, $y_k = \tilde{y}_k$), the expected value of the residue converges asymptotically to a neighborhood of zero, i.e., $\lim_{k \to \infty} \|\mathbb{E}\{r_k\}\| \leq \delta_r$, with $\delta_r \in \mathbb{R}^+$;

2. the residue is sensitive to the anomalies ($f_k \not\equiv 0$).

An alarm is triggered if the residue meets

$$\|r_k\| \geq \delta_r + \delta_\alpha, \quad (4)$$

where $\delta_\alpha \in \mathbb{R}^+$ is chosen so that the false alarm rate does not exceed a given $\alpha \in [0, 1]$.

3. ADVERSARY MODELS

The adversary model considered in this paper is illustrated in Figure 2 and is composed of an attack policy and the adversary resources i.e., the system model knowledge, the disclosure resources, and the disruption resources. The attack policy is described by

$$a_k = g(\mathcal{K}, \mathcal{I}_k). \quad (5)$$

Each of the attack policy components can be mapped to a specific axis of the attack space in Figure 1: $\mathcal{K} = \{\hat{\mathcal{P}}, \hat{\mathcal{F}}, \hat{\mathcal{D}}\}$ is the *a priori* system knowledge possessed by the attacker, $\mathcal{I}_k$ corresponds to the set of sensor and actuator data available to the attacker at time k, thus being mapped to the disclosure resources, while a_k is the attack vector at time k that may affect the system behavior using the disruption resources captured by B_c.

In this section we describe the networked control system under attack with respect to the attack vector a_k. Then we detail the adversary's system knowledge, the disclosure resources, and the disruption resources. Models of the attack vector a_k for particular disruption resources are also given.

3.1 Networked Control System under Attack

The system components under attack are now characterized for the attack vector a_k. Considering the plant and controller states to be stacked as $\eta_k = [x_k^\top \ z_k^\top]^\top$, the dynamics of the closed-loop system composed by $\mathcal{P}$ and $\mathcal{F}$ under the effect of a_k can be written as

$$\eta_{k+1} = \mathbf{A}_c \eta_k + \mathbf{B}_c a_k + \mathbf{G}_c \begin{bmatrix} w_k \\ v_k \end{bmatrix}$$

$$\tilde{y}_k = \mathbf{C}_c \eta_k + \mathbf{D}_c a_k + \mathbf{H}_c \begin{bmatrix} w_k \\ v_k \end{bmatrix}, \quad (6)$$

where the system matrices are

$$\mathbf{A}_c = \begin{bmatrix} A + BD_cC & BC_c \\ B_cC & A_c \end{bmatrix}, \quad \mathbf{G}_c = \begin{bmatrix} G & BD_c \\ 0 & B_c \end{bmatrix},$$

$$\mathbf{C}_c = \begin{bmatrix} C & 0 \end{bmatrix}, \quad\quad\quad \mathbf{H}_c = \begin{bmatrix} 0 & I \end{bmatrix},$$

and $\mathbf{B}_c$ and $\mathbf{D}_c$ capture the way in which the attack vector a_k affects the plant and controller. These matrices are characterized for some attack scenarios in Section 3.4.

Similarly, using $\mathcal{P}$ and $\mathcal{D}$ as in (1) and (3), respectively, the anomaly detector error dynamics under attack are described by

$$
\begin{aligned}
\xi_{k|k} &= \mathbf{A}_e\xi_{k-1|k-1} + \mathbf{B}_e a_{k-1} + \mathbf{G}_e \begin{bmatrix} w_{k-1} \\ v_k \end{bmatrix} \\
r_k &= \mathbf{C}_e\xi_{k-1|k-1} + \mathbf{D}_e a_{k-1} + \mathbf{H}_e \begin{bmatrix} w_{k-1} \\ v_k \end{bmatrix},
\end{aligned}
\tag{7}
$$

where $\xi_{k|k} \in \mathbb{R}^n$ is the estimation error and

$$
\begin{aligned}
\mathbf{A}_e &= (I - KC)A, & \mathbf{G}_e &= \begin{bmatrix} (I-KC)G & -K \end{bmatrix}, \\
\mathbf{C}_e &= VC(I - KC)A, & \mathbf{H}_e &= \begin{bmatrix} VC(I-KC)G & V(I-CK) \end{bmatrix}.
\end{aligned}
$$

The matrices $\mathbf{B}_e$ and $\mathbf{D}_e$ are specific to the available disruptive resources and are characterized in Section 3.4.

3.2 System Knowledge

The amount of *a priori* knowledge regarding the control system is a core component of the adversary model, as it may be used, for instance, to render the attack undetectable. In general, we may consider that the adversary approximately knows the model of the plant ($\hat{\mathcal{P}}$) and the algorithms used in the feedback controller ($\hat{\mathcal{F}}$) and the anomaly detector ($\hat{\mathcal{D}}$), thus denoting the adversary knowledge by $\mathcal{K} = \{\hat{\mathcal{P}}, \hat{\mathcal{F}}, \hat{\mathcal{D}}\}$. Figure 1 illustrates several types of attack scenarios with different amounts of required system knowledge. In particular, note that the replay attacks do not need much knowledge of the system components.

3.3 Disclosure Resources

The disclosure resources enable the attacker to gather sequences of data from the calculated control actions u_k and the real measurements y_k through disclosure attacks. Denote $\mathcal{R}_C^u \subseteq \{1, \ldots, q\}$ and $\mathcal{R}_C^y \subseteq \{1, \ldots, p\}$ as the disclosure resources, i.e. set of actuator and sensor channels that can be accessed during disclosure attacks, and let $\mathcal{I}_k$ be the control and measurement data sequence gathered by the attacker from time k_0 to k. The disclosure attacks can then be modeled as

$$\mathcal{I}_k := \mathcal{I}_{k-1} \cup \begin{bmatrix} \Upsilon^u & 0 \\ 0 & \Upsilon^y \end{bmatrix} \begin{bmatrix} u_k \\ y_k \end{bmatrix}, \tag{8}$$

where $\Upsilon^u \in \mathbb{B}^{|\mathcal{R}_C^u| \times q}$ and $\Upsilon^y \in \mathbb{B}^{|\mathcal{R}_C^y| \times p}$ are the binary incidence matrices mapping the data channels to the corresponding data gathered by the attacker and $\mathcal{I}_{k_0} = \emptyset$.

As seen in the above description of disclosure attacks, the physical dynamics of the system are not affected by these type of attacks. Instead, these attacks gather intelligence that may enable more complex attacks, such as the replay attacks depicted in Figure 1.

3.4 Disruption Resources

As seen in (6) and (7), disruption resources are related to the attack vector a_k and may be used to affect the several components of the system. The way a particular attack disturbs the system operation depends not only on the respective resources, but also on the nature of the attack. For instance, a physical attack directly perturbs the system dynamics, whereas a cyber attack disturbs the system through the cyber-physical couplings. To better illustrate this discussion we now consider physical, data deception, and data DoS attacks.

3.4.1 Physical Attack

Physical attacks may occur in control systems, often in conjunction with cyber attacks. For instance, in [2] water was pumped out of an irrigation system while the water level measurements were corrupted so that the attack remained stealthy. Since physical attacks are similar to the fault signals f_k in (1), in the following sections we consider f_k to be the physical attack modifying the plant dynamics as

$$
\begin{aligned}
x_{k+1} &= Ax_k + B\tilde{u}_k + Gw_k + Ff_k \\
y_k &= Cx_k.
\end{aligned}
$$

Considering $a_k = f_k$, the resulting system dynamics are described by (6) and (7) with

$$\mathbf{B}_c = \begin{bmatrix} F \\ 0 \end{bmatrix}, \quad\quad \mathbf{D}_c = 0,$$

$$\mathbf{B}_e = (I - KC)F, \quad \mathbf{D}_e = VC(I - KC)F.$$

Note that the disruption resources in this attack are captured in the matrix F.

3.4.2 Data Deception Attack

The deception attacks modify the control actions u_k and sensor measurements y_k from their calculated or real values to the corrupted signals $\tilde{u}_k$ and $\tilde{y}_k$, respectively. Denoting $\mathcal{R}_I^u \subseteq \{1, \ldots, q\}$ and $\mathcal{R}_I^y \subseteq \{1, \ldots, p\}$ as the deception resources, i.e. set of actuator and sensor channels that can be affected, the deception attacks are modeled as

$$
\begin{aligned}
\tilde{u}_k &:= u_k + \Gamma^u b_k^u \\
\tilde{y}_k &:= y_k + \Gamma^y b_k^y
\end{aligned}
\tag{9}
$$

where the signals $b_k^u \in \mathbb{R}^{|\mathcal{R}_I^u|}$ and $b_k^y \in \mathbb{R}^{|\mathcal{R}_I^y|}$ represent the data corruption and $\Gamma^u \in \mathbb{B}^{q \times |\mathcal{R}_I^u|}$ and $\Gamma^y \in \mathbb{B}^{p \times |\mathcal{R}_I^y|}$ ($\mathbb{B} := \{0, 1\}$) are the binary incidence matrices mapping the data corruption to the respective data channels. The matrices Γ^u and Γ^y indicate which data channels can be accessed by the attacker and are therefore directly related to the attacker resources in deception attacks.

Defining $a_k = [b_k^{u\top} \ b_{k+1}^{y\top} \ b_k^{y\top}]^\top$, the system dynamics are given by (6) and (7) with

$$\mathbf{B}_c = \begin{bmatrix} B\Gamma^u & 0 & BD_c\Gamma^y \\ 0 & 0 & B_c\Gamma^y \end{bmatrix}, \quad \mathbf{D}_c = \begin{bmatrix} 0 & 0 & \Gamma^y \end{bmatrix},$$

$$
\begin{aligned}
\mathbf{B}_e &= \begin{bmatrix} (I-KC)B\Gamma^u & -K\Gamma^y & 0 \end{bmatrix}, \\
\mathbf{D}_e &= \begin{bmatrix} VC(I-KC)B\Gamma^u & V(I-CK)\Gamma^y & 0 \end{bmatrix}.
\end{aligned}
$$

Note that deception attacks do not possess any disclosure capabilities, as depicted in Figure 1 for examples of deception attacks such as the bias injection attack.

3.4.3 Data Denial-of-Service Attack

The DoS attacks prevent the actuator and sensor data from reaching their respective destinations and should therefore be modeled as the absence of data, for instance $u_k = \emptyset$ if all the actuator data was jammed. However such a model would not fit the framework in (6) and (7) where a_k is assumed to be a real valued vector. Hence we consider instead one of the typical mechanisms used by digital controllers to deal with the absence of data, in which the absent data is considered to be zero. Denoting $\mathcal{R}_A^u \subseteq \{1, \ldots, q\}$ and $\mathcal{R}_A^y \subseteq \{1, \ldots, p\}$ as the set of actuator and sensor channels that can be jammed, we can model DoS attacks as deception attacks in (9) with

$$
\begin{aligned}
b_k^u &:= -S_k^u \Gamma^{u\top} u_k \\
b_k^y &:= -S_k^y \Gamma^{y\top} y_k
\end{aligned}
\tag{10}
$$

where $S_k^u \in \mathbb{B}^{|\mathcal{R}_A^u| \times |\mathcal{R}_A^u|}$ and $S_k^y \in \mathbb{B}^{|\mathcal{R}_A^y| \times |\mathcal{R}_A^y|}$ are boolean diagonal matrices where the $i-$th diagonal entry indicates whether a DoS attack is performed ($[S_k^{(\cdot)}]_{ii} = 1$) or not ($[S_k^{(\cdot)}]_{ii} = 0$) on the corresponding channel. Therefore DoS attacks on the data are a type of disruptive attacks, as depicted in Figure 1.

4. ATTACK SCENARIOS

In this section we discuss the general goal of an attacker and likely choices of the attack policy $g(\cdot, \cdot)$. In particular we consider three attack scenarios with stealthiness constraints under the framework introduced in the previous sections. For each scenario we comment on the attacker's capabilities along each dimension of the attack space in Figure 1 and formulate the corresponding stealthy attack policy. These scenarios are illustrated by experiments on a process control testbed in Section 5.

4.1 Attack Goals and Constraints

The attack scenarios need to also include the intent of the attacker, namely the attack goals and constraints shaping the attack policy. The attack goals can stated in terms of the attack impact on the system operation, while the constraints may be related to the attack detectability. In this paper we focus on the latter and consider stealthy attacks. Furthermore, we consider the disruptive attack component consists of only physical and data deception attacks, and thus we consider the attack vector $a_k = [f_k^\top \quad b_k^{u\top} \quad b_{k+1}^{y\top} \quad b_k^{y\top}]^\top$.

Given the anomaly detector described in Section 2 and denoting $\mathcal{A}_{k_0}^{k_f} = \{a_{k_0}, \ldots, a_{k_f}\}$ as the attack signal, the set of stealthy attacks are defined as follows.

DEFINITION 1. *The attack signal $\mathcal{A}_{k_0}^{k_f}$ is stealthy if $\|r_k\| < \delta_r + \delta_\alpha \forall k \geq k_0$.*

Note that the above definition is dependent on the initial state of the system at k_0, as well as the noise terms w_k and v_k.

Since the closed-loop system (6) and the anomaly detector (7) under physical and data deception attacks are linear systems, each of these systems can be separated in two components, the nominal component with $a_k = 0 \forall k$ and the following systems

$$
\begin{aligned}
\eta_{k+1} &= \mathbf{A}_c \eta_k + \mathbf{B}_c a_k \\
\tilde{y}_k^a &= \mathbf{C}_c \eta_k + \mathbf{D}_c a_k
\end{aligned}
\tag{11}
$$

and

$$
\begin{aligned}
\xi_{k|k} &= \mathbf{A}_e \xi_{k-1|k-1} + \mathbf{B}_e a_{k-1} \\
r_k^a &= \mathbf{C}_e \xi_{k-1|k-1} + \mathbf{D}_e a_{k-1},
\end{aligned}
\tag{12}
$$

with $\eta_0 = \xi_{0|0} = 0$.

Assuming the system to be in nominal behavior before the attack, using the triangle inequality and linearity property we have $\|r_k^a\| \leq \delta_\alpha \Rightarrow \|r_k\| \leq \delta_r + \delta_\alpha$, leading to the following definition:

DEFINITION 2. *The attack signal $\mathcal{A}_{k_0}^{k_f}$ is $\alpha-$stealthy with respect to $\mathcal{D}$ if $\|r_k^a\| < \delta_\alpha \forall k \geq k_0$.*

Albeit more conservative than Definition 1, this definition only depends on the attack signals $\mathcal{A}_{k_0}^{k_f}$. Similarly, the impact of attacks on the closed-loop system can also be analyzed by looking at the linear system (11).

4.2 Replay Attack

In replay attacks the adversary first performs a disclosure attack from $k = k_0$ until k_r, gathering sequences of data $\mathcal{I}_{k_r}$, and then begins replaying the recorded data at time $k = k_r + 1$ until the end of the attack at $k = k_f$, as illustrated in Figure 3. In the scenario considered here, the attacker is also able to perform a physical attack while replaying the recorded data.

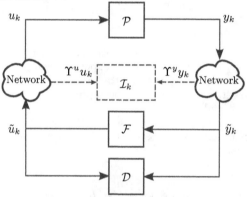

(a) Phase I of the replay attack (13).

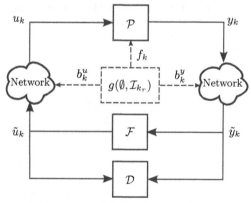

(b) Phase II of the replay attack (14).

Figure 3: Schematic of the replay attack.

Attack policy

Similar to the work in [14], assuming $\mathcal{R}_C^{(\cdot)} = \mathcal{R}_I^{(\cdot)}$, meaning that the attacker can corrupt the digital channels from which the data sequences are gathered, the replay attack policy can be described as

$$\text{Phase I:} \quad \begin{aligned} a_k &= 0 \\ \mathcal{I}_k &= \mathcal{I}_{k-1} \cup \begin{bmatrix} \Upsilon^u & 0 \\ 0 & \Upsilon^y \end{bmatrix} \begin{bmatrix} u_k \\ y_k \end{bmatrix}, \end{aligned} \quad (13)$$

with $k_0 \leq k \leq k_r$ and $\mathcal{I}_{k_0} = \emptyset$ and

$$\text{Phase II:} \quad \begin{aligned} a_k &= \begin{bmatrix} g_f(\mathcal{K}, \mathcal{I}_{k_r}) \\ \Upsilon^u(u_{k-T} - u_k) \\ \Upsilon^y(y_{k+1-T} - y_{k+1}) \\ \Upsilon^y(y_{k-T} - y_k) \end{bmatrix} \\ \mathcal{I}_k &= \mathcal{I}_{k-1}, \end{aligned} \quad (14)$$

where $T = k_r - 1 + k_0$ and $k_r + 1 \leq k \leq k_f$. An interesting instance of this attack scenario consists of applying a pre-defined physical attack to the plant, while using replay attacks to render the attack stealthy. In this case the physical attack signal f_k corresponds to an open-loop signal, $f_k = g_f(k)$.

Disclosure resources

The disclosure capabilities required to stage this attack correspond to the data channels that can be eavesdropped by the attacks, namely $\mathcal{R}_C^u$ and $\mathcal{R}_C^y$.

Disruption resources

In this case the deception capabilities correspond to the data channels that the attacker can tamper, $\mathcal{R}_I^u$ and $\mathcal{R}_I^y$. In particular, for replay attacks the attacker can only tamper data channels from which data has been previously recorded, i.e. $\mathcal{R}_I^u \subseteq \mathcal{R}_C^u$ and $\mathcal{R}_I^y \subseteq \mathcal{R}_C^y$.

Direct disruption of the physical system through the signal f_k depends on direct access to the physical system, modeled by the matrix F in (1).

System knowledge

Note that no *a priori* knowledge on the system model is needed for the cyber component of the attack, namely the data disclosure and deception attack, as seen in the attack policy (13) and (14). As for the physical attack, f_k, the required knowledge is scenario dependent. In the scenario considered in the experiments described in Section 5, this component was modeled as an open-loop signal, $f_k = g_f(k)$.

Stealthiness constraints

The work in [14] provided conditions under which replay attacks with access to all measurement data channels are stealthy. However, these attacks are not guaranteed to be stealthy when only a subset of the data channels is attacked. In this case, the stealthiness constraint may require additional knowledge of the system model. For instance, the experiment presented in Section 5 required knowledge of the physical system structure, so that f_k only excited the attacked measurements.

4.3 Zero Dynamics Attack

Recalling that for attacks with only physical and data deception components the plant and anomaly detector are linear systems, (11) and (12) respectively, Definition 2 states that these type of attacks are 0−stealthy if $r_k^a = 0$, $k = k_0, \ldots, k_f$. The idea of 0−stealthy attacks then consists of

designing an attack policy and attack signal $\mathcal{A}_{k_0}^{k_f}$ so that the residue r_k does not change due to the attack.

A particular subset of 0−stealthy attacks are characterized in the following lemma:

LEMMA 1. *The attack signal $\mathcal{A}_{k_0}^{k_f}$ is 0−stealthy with respect to any $\mathcal{D}$ if $\tilde{y}_k^a = 0$, $\forall k \geq k_0$.*

PROOF. Consider the attacked components of the controller and the anomaly detector in (11) and (12) with $\hat{x}_0^a = \xi_{0|0}^a = 0$. From the controller dynamics it directly follows that $\tilde{y}_k^a = 0$, $\forall k \geq k_0$ results in $u_k^a = 0$, $\forall k \geq k_0$, as the input to the controller ($\tilde{y}_k^a$) is zero. Since $\hat{x}_0^a = 0$ and $\tilde{y}_k^a = u_k^a = 0$, $\forall k \geq k_0$, meaning that the detector's inputs are zero, we then conclude $r_k^a = 0$, $\forall k \geq k_0$. □

Both the definition of 0−stealthy attacks and Lemma 1 indicate that these attacks are decoupled from the outputs of linear systems, r_k and y_k respectively. Hence finding 0−stealthy attack signals relates to the output zeroing problem or zero dynamics studied in the control theory literature [20]. Note that such attack requires the perfect knowledge of the plant dynamics P and the attack signal is then based on the open-loop prediction of the output changes due to the attack, as illustrated in Figure 4 where $\mathcal{K}_z$ denote the zero dynamics and there is no disclosure of sensor or actuator data.

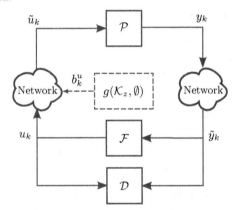

Figure 4: Schematic of the zero dynamics attack.

In Section 5 a particular instance of this attack was considered, where only the actuator data is corrupted. The zero attack policy thus corresponds to the transmission zero dynamics of the plant, which is now described. The plant dynamics due to an attack on the actuator data are described by

$$\begin{aligned} x_{k+1}^a &= A x_k^a + B a_k \\ \tilde{y}_k^a &= C x_k^a \end{aligned} \quad (15)$$

with $a_k = b_k^u$. Given the discrete-time system (15) with B having full column rank, the transmission zeros can be calculated as the values $\nu \in \mathbb{C}$ that cause the matrix $P(\nu)$ to lose rank, where

$$P(\nu) = \begin{bmatrix} \nu I - A & -B \\ C & 0 \end{bmatrix}. \quad (16)$$

Those values are called minimum phase or non-minimum phase zeros depending on whether they are stable or unstable zeros, respectively. In discrete-time systems a zero is stable if $|\nu| < 1$ and unstable otherwise.

Attack policy

The attack policy then corresponds to the input sequence (a_k) that makes the outputs of the process $(\tilde{y}_k^a)$ identically zero for all k and is illustrated in Figure 4. It can be shown [20] that the solution to this problem is given by the sequence

$$a_k = g\nu^k, \qquad (17)$$

where g is the input zero direction for the chosen zero ν. The input zero direction can be obtained by solving the following equation

$$\begin{bmatrix} \nu I - A & -B \\ C & 0 \end{bmatrix} \begin{bmatrix} x_0 \\ g \end{bmatrix} = \begin{bmatrix} 0 \\ 0 \end{bmatrix}. \qquad (18)$$

where x_0 is the initial state for which the input sequence (17) results in an identically zero output, $\tilde{y}_k^a = 0 \,\forall k$. If the zero is stable, that is $|\nu| < 1$, the attack will asymptotically decay to zero, thus having little effect on the plant. However, in the case of unstable zeros the attack grows geometrically, which could cause a great damage to the process.

Disclosure resources

This attack scenario considers an open-loop attack policy and so no disclosure capabilities are required, resulting in $\mathcal{R}_C^u = \mathcal{R}_C^y = \emptyset$ and $\mathcal{I}_k^u = \mathcal{I}_k^u = \emptyset \,\forall k$.

Disruption resources

The disruption capabilities in this attack scenario correspond to the ability of performing deception attacks on the actuator data channels. Therefore the required resources are $\mathcal{R}_I^u = \{1, \ldots, q\}$, $\mathcal{R}_I^y = \emptyset$, and $F = 0$

System knowledge

The ability to compute the open-loop attack policy (17) requires the perfect knowledge zero dynamics (18), which we denote as $\mathcal{K}_z$. Note that computing the zero dynamics requires perfect knowledge of the plant dynamics, namely A, B, and C. No knowledge of the feedback controller or anomaly detector is assumed in this scenario.

Stealthiness constraint

Note that the transmission zero attack is 0−stealthy only if $x_0^a = x_0$. However the initial condition of the system under attack x_0^a is defined to be zero at the beginning of the attack. Therefore stealthiness of the attack may be violated for large differences between $x_0^a = 0$ and x_0.

4.4 Bias Injection Attack

Here a particular scenario of false-data injection is considered, where the attacker's goal is to inject a constant bias in the system without being detected. For this scenario, the class of α−stealthy attacks is characterized at steady-state and a method to evaluate the corresponding impact is proposed. Furthermore, we derive the policy yielding the largest impact on the system.

Denote a_∞ as the bias to be injected and recall the anomaly detector dynamics under attack given by (7). The steady-state detectability of the attack is then dependent on the steady-state value of the residual

$$r_\infty^a = \left(\mathbf{C}_e(I - \mathbf{A}_e)^{-1}\mathbf{B}_e + \mathbf{D}_e\right) a_\infty =: G_{ra} a_\infty. \qquad (19)$$

The largest α−stealthy attacks are then characterized by

$$\|G_{ra} a_\infty\|_2 = \delta_\alpha. \qquad (20)$$

Although attacks satisfying (20) could be detected during the transient, incipient attack signals slowly converging to a_∞ may go undetected, as it is shown in the experiments in Section 5.

The impact of such attacks can be evaluated using the closed-loop dynamics under attack given by (6). Recalling that $\eta_k = [x_k^\top \;\; z_k^\top]^\top$, the steady-state impact on the state is given by

$$x_\infty^a = [I \;\; 0] (I - \mathbf{A}_c)^{-1} \mathbf{B}_c a_\infty =: G_{xa} a_\infty. \qquad (21)$$

Largest 2−norm state bias. The α−stealthy attack yielding the largest bias in the 2−norm sense can be computed by solving

$$\max_{a_\infty} \|G_{xa} a_\infty\|_2^2 \qquad (22)$$

$$\text{s.t.} \quad \|G_{ra} a_\infty\|_2^2 \leq \delta_\alpha^2.$$

Note that this problem is unbounded unless

$$\ker(G_{ra}) \subseteq \ker(G_{xa}),$$

where $\ker(A)$ denotes the null space of A, and the solution is trivial. Therefore in this section we consider the non-trivial case in which the previous condition holds.

The above optimization problem can be transformed into a generalized eigenvalue problem and the corresponding optimal solution characterized in terms of generalized eigenvalues and eigenvectors. Denote λ^* and v^* as the largest generalized eigenvalue and corresponding unit-norm eigenvector of the matrix pencil $G_{xa}^\top G_{xa} - \lambda G_{ra}^\top G_{ra}$, satisfying

$$(G_{xa}^\top G_{xa} - \lambda^* G_{ra}^\top G_{ra})v^* = 0.$$

It can be shown that the optimal solution to the optimization problem (22) is given by

$$a_\infty^* = \frac{\delta_\alpha}{\|G_{ra} v^*\|_2} v^*, \qquad (23)$$

and the corresponding optimal value is $\|G_{xa} a_\infty\|_2^2 = \lambda^* \delta_\alpha^2$.

Largest infinity-norm state bias. Similarly, the α−stealthy attack yielding the largest bias in the infinity-norm sense is the solution to the following optimization problem

$$\max_{a_\infty} \|G_{xa} a_\infty\|_\infty \qquad (24)$$

$$\text{s.t.} \quad \|G_{ra} a_\infty\|_2 \leq \delta_\alpha.$$

A possible method to solve this problem is to observe that

$$\|G_{xa} a_\infty\|_\infty = \max_i \|e_i^\top G_{xa} a_\infty\|_2,$$

where the vector e_i is i−th column of the identity matrix. Thus one can transform the optimization problem (24) into a set of problems with the same structure as (22), obtaining

$$\max_i \max_{a_\infty^i} \left\|e_i^\top G_{xa} a_\infty^i\right\|_\infty \qquad (25)$$

$$\text{s.t.} \quad \left\|G_{ra} a_\infty^i\right\|_2 \leq \delta_\alpha.$$

Denote λ_i^* as the largest generalized eigenvalue of the matrix pencil $G_{xa}^\top e_i e_i^\top G_{xa} - \lambda G_{ra}^\top G_{ra}$. Letting $\lambda^* = \max_i \lambda_i^*$ and v^* be the corresponding generalized eigenvector, the optimal attack is given by (23) and the corresponding optimal value is $\|G_{xa} a_\infty\|_\infty = \sqrt{\lambda^*}\delta_\alpha$.

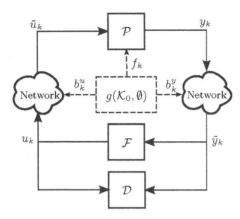

Figure 5: Schematic of the bias injection attack.

Attack policy

The bias injection attack is illustrated in Figure 5. The steady-state attack policy yielding the maximum impact on the physical system is given by (23). For the transient, we consider that the attacker uses a linear low-pass filter so that the data corruptions are slowly converging to the steady-state values. As an example, for a set of identical first-order filters the open-loop attack sequence is described by

$$a_{k+1} = \beta a_k + (1 - \beta)a_\infty^\star, \qquad (26)$$

where $0 < \beta < 1$ and $a_0 = 0$.

Disclosure resources

Similarly to the zero attack, no disclosure capabilities are required for this attack, since the attack policy is open-loop. Therefore we have $\mathcal{R}_C^u = \mathcal{R}_C^y = \emptyset$ and $\mathcal{I}_k^u = \mathcal{I}_k^u = \emptyset \, \forall k$.

Disruption resources

The biases may be added to both the actuator and sensor data, hence the required resources are $\mathcal{R}_I^u \subseteq \{1, \dots, q\}$, $\mathcal{R}_I^y \subseteq \{1, \dots, p\}$. Since no physical attack is performed, we have $F = 0$.

System knowledge

As seen in (22), the open-loop attack policy (26) requires the knowledge of the closed-loop system and anomaly detector steady-state gains G_{ra} and G_{xa}, which we denoted as $\mathcal{K}_0$ as shown in Figure 5.

Stealthiness constraint

Note that the steady-state value of the data corruption $a_\infty^\star$ is only necessary for the attack to be α-stealthy, since the transients are disregarded. In practice, however, it has been observed in the Fault Diagnosis literature that incipient faults with slow dynamics are hard to detect [5]. Therefore the low-pass filter dynamics in (26) could be designed sufficiently slow as to difficult detection.

5. EXPERIMENTS

In this section we present our testbed and report experiments on staged cyber attacks following the different scenarios described in the previous section.

5.1 Quadruple-Tank Process

Our testbed consists of a Quadruple-Tank Process (QTP) [11] controlled through a wireless communication network, as shown in Figure 6.

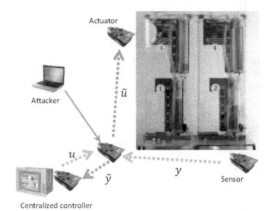

Figure 6: Schematic diagram of the testbed with the Quadruple-Tank Process and a multi-hop communication network.

The plant model can be found in [11]

$$\dot{h}_1 = -\frac{a_1}{A_1}\sqrt{2gh_1} + \frac{a_3}{A_1}\sqrt{2gh_3} + \frac{\gamma_1 k_1}{A_1}u_1,$$
$$\dot{h}_2 = -\frac{a_2}{A_2}\sqrt{2gh_2} + \frac{a_4}{A_2}\sqrt{2gh_4} + \frac{\gamma_2 k_2}{A_2}u_2,$$
$$\dot{h}_3 = -\frac{a_3}{A_3}\sqrt{2gh_3} + \frac{(1-\gamma_2)k_2}{A_3}u_2,$$
$$\dot{h}_4 = -\frac{a_4}{A_4}\sqrt{2gh_4} + \frac{(1-\gamma_1)k_1}{A_4}u_1,$$

$$(27)$$

where h_i are the heights of water in each tank, A_i the cross-section area of the tanks, a_i the cross-section area of the outlet hole, k_i the pump constants, γ_i the flow ratios and g the gravity acceleration. The nonlinear plant model is linearized for a given operating point.

The QTP is controlled using a centralized controller running in a remote computer and a wireless network is used for the communications. A Kalman-filter-based anomaly detector is also running in the remote computer and alarms are triggered according to (4), for which we computed $\delta_r = 0.15$ and chose $\delta_\alpha = 0.25$ for illustration purposes. The communication network is multi-hop, having one additional wireless device relaying the data, as illustrated in Figure 6.

5.2 Replay Attack

In this scenario, the QTP is operating at a constant setpoint and a hacker wants to steal water from the tank 4, the upper tank on the right side. The attacker has been able to hack one of the relay nodes that is between the sensor 2 (y_2) and the controller in a way that data from the real sensor can be recorded. Furthermore the attacker is able to replace the measurements sent to the controller with the recorded data. An example of this attack is presented in the Figure 7, where the attacker replays past data from y_2 while stealing water from tank 4. As we can see, the residue stays almost constant and therefore the attack is not detected, while there is a significant drop in water level in tanks 2 and 4.

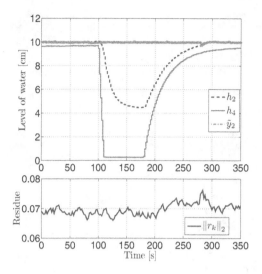

Figure 7: Results for the replay attack performed against sensor 2 from $t \approx 100s$ to $t \approx 280s$. Additionally, the attacker opens the tap of tank 4 at $t \approx 100s$ and closes it at $t \approx 180s$.

5.3 Zero Dynamics Attack

The QTP has a non-minimum phase configuration in which the plant contains an unstable zero. In this case, as discussed in Section 4.3, an attacker able to corrupt all the actuator channels may launch a false-data injection attack where the false-data follows the transmission zero dynamics, rendering the attack undetectable. This scenario is illustrated in Figure 8.

The attack remains undetected for quite some time as expected from the theory, even though the QTP is a nonlinear process. However, the fast increment of the attack signal causes saturation of the water levels after some sampling periods, as seen in Figure 8. From that moment the system dynamics change and therefore the attack signal no longer corresponds to the zero dynamics and will be detected, although it may have already damaged the system. Thus these attacks are particularly dangerous in processes that have unstable zero dynamics and in which the actuators are over-dimensioned, allowing the adversary to perform longer attacks before saturating.

5.4 Bias Injection Attack

Figure 9 shows the maximum attack impacts for all the combinations of compromised sensors and actuators in the QTP. The blue area represents the possible impacts in the process for a given number of attackable channels. As we can see, when the adversary can attack more than two channels the impact is unbounded (assuming linear dynamics), although in practice this is prevented due to saturation, as previously shown for the zero dynamics attack.

The results for the case where u_1 and y_1 are respectively corrupted with b_∞^u and b_∞^y are presented in the Figure 10, where the attacker aimed at maximizing the state bias in the infinity-norm sense while remaining stealthy. The false bias was slowly injected using a first-order low-pass filter and the following steady-state value $a_\infty = [b_\infty^u \; b_\infty^y]^\top = [2.15 \; -9.42]^\top$.

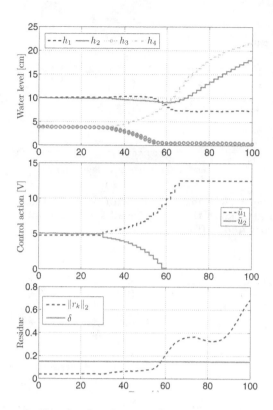

Figure 8: Results for the zero dynamics attack starting at $t \approx 30s$. Tank 3 is emptied at $t \approx 55s$, resulting in a steep increase in the residual since the linearized model is no longer valid.

6. CONCLUSIONS

In this paper we have analyzed the security of networked control systems. A novel attack space based on the attacker's system knowledge, disclosure, and disruption resources was proposed and the corresponding adversary model described. Attack scenarios corresponding to replay, zero dynamics, and bias injection attacks were analyzed using this framework. In particular the maximum impact of stealthy bias injection attacks was derived and it was shown that the corresponding policy does not require perfect model knowledge. These attack scenarios were illustrated using an experimental setup based on a quadruple-tank process controlled over a wireless network.

7. ACKNOWLEDGMENTS

This work was supported in part by the European Commission through the VIKING project, the Swedish Research Council under Grants 2007-6350 and 2009-4565, and the Knut and Alice Wallenberg Foundation.

8. REFERENCES

[1] S. Amin, A. Cárdenas, and S. Sastry. Safe and secure networked control systems under denial-of-service attacks. In *Hybrid Systems: Computation and Control*, pages 31–45. Lecture Notes in Computer Science. Springer Berlin / Heidelberg, April 2009.

[2] S. Amin, X. Litrico, S. S. Sastry, and A. M. Bayen. Stealthy deception attacks on water scada systems. In

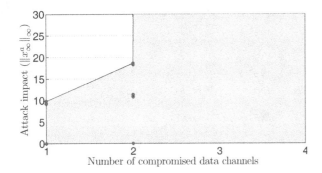

Figure 9: Maximum impact of stealthy bias injection attacks in the QTP for all sets of compromised sensors and actuators.

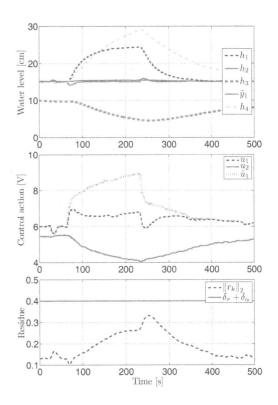

Figure 10: Results for the bias attack against the actuator 1 and sensor 1 in the minimum phase QTP. The attack is launched using a low-pass filter in the instant $t \approx 70s$ and stopped at $t \approx 230s$.

Proc. of the 13th ACM Int. Conf. on Hybrid systems: computation and control, HSCC '10, New York, NY, USA, 2010. ACM.

[3] M. Bishop. *Computer Security: Art and Science*. Addison-Wesley Professional, 2002.

[4] A. Cárdenas, S. Amin, and S. Sastry. Research challenges for the security of control systems. In *Proc. 3rd USENIX Workshop on Hot topics in security*, July 2008.

[5] J. Chen and R. J. Patton. *Robust Model-Based Fault Diagnosis for Dynamic Systems*. Kluwer Academic Publishers, 1999.

[6] S. X. Ding. *Model-based Fault Diagnosis Techniques: Design Schemes*. Springer Verlag, 2008.

[7] A. Giani, S. Sastry, K. H. Johansson, and H. Sandberg. The VIKING project: an initiative on resilient control of power networks. In *Proc. 2nd Int. Symp. on Resilient Control Systems*, Idaho Falls, ID, USA, Aug. 2009.

[8] S. Gorman. Electricity grid in U.S. penetrated by spies. *The Wall Street Journal*, page A1, April 8th 2009.

[9] A. Gupta, C. Langbort, and T. Başar. Optimal control in the presence of an intelligent jammer with limited actions. In *Proc. of the 49th IEEE Conf. on Decision and Control (CDC)*, Dec. 2010.

[10] I. Hwang, S. Kim, Y. Kim, and C. E. Seah. A survey of fault detection, isolation, and reconfiguration methods. *IEEE Transactions on Control Systems Technology*, 18(3):636–653, May 2010.

[11] K. Johansson. The quadruple-tank process: a multivariable laboratory process with an adjustable zero. *IEEE Transactions on Control Systems Technology*, 8(3):456–465, May 2000.

[12] O. Kosut, L. Jia, R. Thomas, and L. Tong. Malicious data attacks on smart grid state estimation: Attack strategies and countermeasures. In *Proc. of IEEE SmartGridComm*, Oct. 2010.

[13] Y. Liu, M. K. Reiter, and P. Ning. False data injection attacks against state estimation in electric power grids. In *Proc. 16th ACM Conf. on Computer and Communications Security*, pages 21–32, New York, NY, USA, 2009.

[14] Y. Mo and B. Sinopoli. Secure control against replay attack. In *47th Annual Allerton Conference on Communication, Control, and Computing*, Oct. 2009.

[15] F. Pasqualetti, F. Dorfler, and F. Bullo. Cyber-physical attacks in power networks: Models, fundamental limitations and monitor design. In *Proc. of the 50th IEEE Conf. on Decision and Control and European Control Conference*, Orlando, FL, USA, Dec. 2011.

[16] H. Sandberg, A. Teixeira, and K. H. Johansson. On security indices for state estimators in power networks. In *Preprints of the First Workshop on Secure Control Systems, CPSWEEK 2010*, Stockholm, Sweden, April 2010.

[17] R. Smith. A decoupled feedback structure for covertly appropriating networked control systems. In *Proc. of the 18th IFAC World Congress*, Milano, Italy, August-September 2011.

[18] A. Teixeira, H. Sandberg, G. Dán, and K. H. Johansson. Optimal power flow: Closing the loop over corrupted data. In *Proc. American Control Conference*, 2012. Accepted.

[19] L. Xie, Y. Mo, and B. Sinopoli. False data injection attacks in electricity markets. In *First IEEE International Conference on Smart Grid Communications*, Oct. 2010.

[20] K. Zhou, J. C. Doyle, and K. Glover. *Robust and Optimal Control*. Prentice-Hall, Inc., Upper Saddle River, NJ, USA, 1996.

Distributed Detection and Isolation of Topology Attacks in Power Networks

James Weimer
ACCESS Linnaeus Centre
School of Electrical
Engineering
KTH Royal Institute of
Technology
Stockholm, Sweden 10044
weimerj@kth.se

Soummya Kar
Department of Electrical and
Computer Engineering
Carnegie Mellon University
Pittsburgh, PA. USA 15213
soummyak@cmu.edu

Karl Henrik Johansson
ACCESS Linnaeus Centre
School of Electrical
Engineering
KTH Royal Institute of
Technology
Stockholm, Sweden 10044
kallej@kth.se

ABSTRACT

This paper addresses the issue of detecting and isolating topology attacks in power networks. A topology attack, unlike a data attack and power injection attack, alters the physical dynamics of the power network by removing bus interconnections. These attacks can manifest as both cyber and physical attacks. A physical topology attack occurs when a bus interconnection is physically broken, while a cyber topology attack occurs when incorrect information about the network topology is transmitted to the system estimator and incorporated as the truth. To detect topology attacks, a stochastic hypothesis testing problem is considered assuming noisy measurements are obtained by periodically sampling a dynamic process described by the networked swing equation dynamics, modified to assume stochastic power injections. A centralized approach to network topology detection and isolation is introduced as a two-part scheme consisting of topology detection followed by topology isolation, assuming a topology attack exists. To address the complexity issues arising with performing centralized detection in large-scale power networks, a decentralized approach is presented that uses only local measurements to detect the presence of a topology attack. Simulation results illustrate that both the centralized and decentralized approaches accurately detect and isolate topology attacks.

Categories and Subject Descriptors

G.3 [**Mathematics of Computing**]: Probability and Statistics

General Terms

Theory, Security

Keywords

Distributed hypothesis testing, Distributed fault detection, Power networks

1. INTRODUCTION

As systems become more integrated into their physical environment and grow in size and complexity, the automatic detection of system faults has become increasingly important. While most of the model-based fault detection and isolation (FDI) literature focuses on centralized systems where the FDI scheme has access to all the available information [1–3], in large-scale systems centralized approaches may be prohibitively costly due to the required communication infrastructure, energy requirements, and computational complexity. For large-scale interconnected dynamical systems, such as power networks, distributed control and monitoring is more suitable [4].

Power networks are large-scale spatially distributed systems. As a critical infrastructure, they possess strict safety and reliability constraints [5]. State monitoring of the system is essential to guarantee safety, and is typically implemented in a centralized control center through a single state estimator. The core methodology for state estimation of power systems dates back to 1970, [6, 7]. Due to the low sampling frequency of the sensors in these systems a steady state approach is taken, which only allows for an over-constrained operation of the system to ensure reliability. Furthermore, faults are handled mainly by hardware devices deployed in the field, so local events leading to cascade failures may pass undetected, since the global state of the system is not taken into account. In recent years, measurement units with higher sampling rate have been developed, e.g. Phaser Measurement Units (PMU), opening the way to dynamic state estimators and observer-based fault detection schemes taking in account the dynamics of the system. Such centralized FDI schemes have been proposed in the recent literature, see [8, 9]. And more recently, extensions to distributed FDI methods has been proposed [10–13].

While there has been much research on model-based FDI within power systems for data attacks and power injection attacks, all these dynamic approaches assume an underlying model based on bus interconnections. In this work, we consider the problem of detecting topological attacks on the network occurring when bus interconnections are broke. These attacks include physical attacks, such as physically destroying an inter-bus connection, and cyber attacks on the transmission of information regarding the topological condition of the network, such as transmitting the wrong network topology configuration. The problem of detecting topological attacks is formulated for a linearized stochastic representation of the swing-equation. Both centralized and decentralized detectors are developed and evaluated using a simulated electrical power grid.

The remainder of this paper is organized as follows. In the following section we present an overview of binary hypothesis testing. Section 3 introduces the topology detection problem considered in this work. Centralized and decentralized solutions to the topology detection problem are described in Section 4 and Section 5, respectively. Section 6 provides simulation results using both 9-bus and 118-bus power networks. The final section provides a discussion and outlines future work.

2. PRELIMINARIES

This section provides a brief summary of the classical test for accepting the null hypothesis in a binary hypothesis testing problem developed by [14]. A binary hypothesis testing problem between a simple null hypothesis, H_0, and a simple alternative hypothesis, H_1, is written as

$$H_0 : \tilde{z} \sim f_0(z) \quad \text{vs.} \quad H_1 : \tilde{z} \sim f_1(z), \tag{1}$$

where $f_0(z)$ and $f_1(z)$ are the distributions of the observation random variables, $\tilde{z}$, under the null and alternative hypotheses, respectively. Given an observation, z, a test for deciding between the null and alternative hypotheses, $\phi(z) \in \{H_0, H_1\}$, is required to satisfy a performance constraint on the probability of false alarm, namely

$$P[\phi(z) = H_1|H_0] \leq \alpha. \tag{2}$$

where $P[x|y]$ denotes the probability of x occurring conditioned on y being true. A test for rejecting the null hypothesis (accepting the alternative hypothesis), such that the performance constraint is satisfied, results from a worst case analysis of Wald's approximation (as discussed in [14]) where

$$l(z) \geq -\ln \alpha \Longrightarrow P[\phi(z) = H_1|H_0] \leq \alpha. \tag{3}$$

and

$$l(z) = \ln f_1(z) - \ln f_0(z). \tag{4}$$

is the log-likelihood ratio. Applying Wald's approximation results in a conservative test that over-constrains the performance and is commonly employed when testing hypotheses containing complex distributions since the threshold for the resulting test is independent of the underlying distributions. The above test for rejecting H_0 will be used in this paper to develop a sequential test for detecting network topology faults.

3. PROBLEM FORMULATION

We consider an electrical power network of N interconnected buses. We assume there exists an underlying interconnection graph, $\mathcal{G}(\mathcal{V}, \mathcal{E})$, between the N buses, where $\mathcal{V} \triangleq \{i\}_1^N$ is the vertex set, with $i \in \mathcal{V}$ corresponding to bus i, and $\mathcal{E} \subseteq \mathcal{V} \times \mathcal{V}$ is the fault-free edge set of the graph.

The undirected edge $\{i, j\}$ is incident on vertices i and j if buses i and j are assumed to share an interconnection. We introduce a parameter $\theta \subseteq \mathcal{E}$, such that

$$\mathcal{N}_{i,\theta} = \{j \in \mathcal{V} : \{i, j\} \in \theta\} \tag{5}$$

defines the neighborhood of bus i assuming the interconnection specified by the edge set θ. The phase angle associated with each bus $i \in \mathcal{V}$, δ_i, has continuous-time double integrator dynamics given by the so-called swing equation [15]

$$m_i \ddot{\delta}_i(t) + d_i \dot{\delta}_i(t) = u_i(t) + w_i(t) - \sum_{j \in \mathcal{N}_{i,\Theta}} P_{ij}(t) \tag{6}$$

where $\delta_i(0) = \dot{\delta}_i(0) = 0$ is the initial condition, m_i and d_i are the inertia and damping coefficients, respectively, P_{ij} is the active power flow from bus i to j, $w_i(t)$ is the scalar zero-mean Gaussian process noise with covariance W_i, and $u_i(t)$ is the piecewise constant mechanical input power such that for a sampling period of T_s

$$u_i(t) = u_{k,i} \quad \forall \quad T_s k \leq t \leq T_s(k+1) \tag{7}$$

Each bus is sampled periodically at the same rate of the mechanical input power using noisy sensors according to

$$\begin{aligned} y_{k,i,1} &= \delta_i(T_s k) + v_{k,i,1} \\ y_{k,i,2} &= \dot{\delta}_i(T_s k) + v_{k,i,2} \end{aligned} \tag{8}$$

where $v_{k,i,j}$ is a scalar zero-mean Gaussian measurement noise with variance $V_{i,j}$.

We assume there are no power losses nor ground admittances and let $V_i = |V_i| e^{j\delta_i}$ be the complex voltage of bus i such that the active power flow between bus i and bus l, P_{il}, is

$$P_{il}(t) = k_{il} \sin(\delta_i(t) - \delta_l(t)) \tag{9}$$

where $k_{il} = |V_i| |V_l| b_{il}$ and b_{il} is the susceptance of the power line connecting buses i and l. In the remainder of this work, we revert to the standard $\{i, j\}$ indexing convention where j represents an index and not the complex operator. Assuming the phase angle differences between interconnected buses are small, then

$$\sin(\delta_i(t) - \delta_j(t)) \approx \delta_i(t) - \delta_j(t) \tag{10}$$

and (6) can be written in its linear form as

$$m_i \ddot{\delta}_i(t) + d_i \dot{\delta}_i(t) = u_i(t) + w_i(t) - \sum_{j \in N_{i,\theta}} k_{ij}(\delta_i(t) - \delta_j(t)) \tag{11}$$

The linear process in (11) can be written using a continuous-time state-space formulation as

$$\dot{x}(t) = A_c(\theta)x(t) + B_c(u(t) + w(t)), \tag{12}$$

where,

$$\begin{aligned} x(t) &= \begin{bmatrix} \delta_1(t) & \cdots & \delta_N(t) & \dot{\delta}_1(t) & \cdots & \dot{\delta}_N(t) \end{bmatrix}^\top \\ u(t) &= \begin{bmatrix} u_{k,1} & \cdots & u_{k,N} \end{bmatrix}^\top \\ w(t) &= \begin{bmatrix} w_1(t) & \cdots & w_N(t) \end{bmatrix}^\top \sim N[0, W_c] \end{aligned} \tag{13}$$

and, by defining $\mathcal{L}_\theta$ to be the graph Laplacian assuming the edges specified by θ,

$$A_c(\theta) = \begin{bmatrix} 0_N & I_N \\ -\bar{M}\mathcal{L}_\theta & -\bar{M}\bar{D} \end{bmatrix}$$

$$B_c = \begin{bmatrix} 0 \\ \bar{M} \end{bmatrix}$$

$$\bar{M} = \mathrm{diag}\left(\frac{1}{m_1}, \cdots, \frac{1}{m_N}\right) \quad (14)$$

$$\bar{D} = \mathrm{diag}\,(d_1, \cdots, d_N)$$

$$W_c = \mathrm{diag}\,(W_1, \cdots, W_N)$$

By discretizing the continuous-time state-space model in (12), a discrete-time state-space model, including the measurement model in (8), can be written as

$$\begin{aligned} x_{k+1} &= A_\theta x_k + B_\theta u_k + w_{k,\theta} \\ y_k &= x_k + v_k \end{aligned}, \quad (15)$$

where,

$$x_k = x(T_s k)$$

$$u_k = u(T_s k)$$

$$y_k = \begin{bmatrix} y_{k,1,1} & \cdots & y_{k,N,1} & y_{k,1,2} & \cdots & y_{k,N,2} \end{bmatrix}^T$$

$$v_k = \begin{bmatrix} v_{k,1,1} & \cdots & v_{k,N,1} & v_{k,1,2} & \cdots & v_{k,N,2} \end{bmatrix}^T, \quad (16)$$

$$v_k \sim N\,[0, V]$$

$$w_{k,\theta} \sim N\,[0, W_\theta]$$

and

$$A_\theta = e^{A_c(\theta)T_s}$$

$$B_\theta = \left(\int_0^{T_s} e^{A_c(\theta)\tau} d\tau\right) B$$

$$W_\theta = \int_0^{T_s} e^{A_c(\theta)\tau} B W_c B^T e^{A_c(\theta)\tau} d\tau \quad (17)$$

$$V = \mathrm{diag}\,(V_{1,1}, \cdots, V_{N,1}, V_{1,2}, \cdots, V_{N,2})$$

For the above formulation, many researchers have considered the detection and isolation of data attacks on the input, u_k, and output, y_k [10]. However, these approaches all assume the underlying dynamical model is accurate. In this work, we consider the problem of detecting topological attacks on the network. These attacks include physical attacks on an inter-bus connection (such as physically destroying an inter-bus connection) and cyber attacks on the transmission of information regarding the topological condition of the network (such as transmitting the wrong network topology configuration). To simplify the following discussion, we assume that at most one edge has been removed from the fault-free network topology and write distribution of the sensor measurements, conditioned on the previous measurements and parameterized by $\Theta \subseteq \mathcal{E}$, as

$$f_\theta(y_k) = N\,[\mu_{k,\theta}, \Sigma_{k,\theta}]. \quad (18)$$

where

$$\begin{aligned} \mu_{k,\theta} &= m_{k|k-1,\theta} \\ \Sigma_{k,\theta} &= S_{k|k-1,\theta} + V \end{aligned} \quad (19)$$

and $m_{k|k-1,\theta}$ and $S_{k|k-1,\theta}$ are the *a priori* mean and *a priori* covariance, respectively, of the minimum mean-squared error state estimate, calculated recursively using a Kalman filter

as

$$\begin{aligned} m_{k+1|k,\theta} &= A_\theta m_{k|k,\theta} + B_\theta u_k \\ S_{k+1|k,\theta} &= A_\theta S_{k|k,\theta} A_\theta^T + W_\theta \\ K_{k,\theta} &= S_{k|k-1,\theta} \left[S_{k|k-1,\theta} + V\right]^{-1} \quad (20) \\ m_{k|k,\theta} &= (I - K_{k,\theta}) m_{k|k-1,\theta} + K_{k,\theta} r_k \\ S_{k|k,\theta} &= (I - K_{k,\theta}) S_{k|k-1,\theta} \end{aligned}$$

To formulate a test for network topology attacks, we define $\Theta_{ij} \triangleq \mathcal{E}\backslash\{i,j\}$ to be a potential edge set and write the set of all possible edge sets as $\Theta = \{\Theta_{ij}|\{i,j\} \in \mathcal{E}\}$. Applying this notation, we consider the following M-ary hypothesis testing problem

$$\begin{aligned} H_0 &: \theta = \mathcal{E} \\ H_{1,2} &: \theta = \Theta_{1,2} \\ &\vdots \quad (21) \\ H_{N,N-1} &: \theta = \Theta_{N,N-1} \end{aligned}$$

where the hypothesis testing problem simultaneously tests the null hypothesis, H_0, which assumes no edges have been removed, against all possible alternative hypotheses, H_{ij}, representing the removal of a single edge. We note that if an edge is not contained in the fault-free network topology, $\{i,j\} \notin \mathcal{E}$, then $\mathcal{E} \equiv \Theta_{N,N-1}$ and hypothesis H_{ij} is excluded from the set of alternative hypotheses since it is statistically equivalent to the null hypothesis, H_0. To decide between the hypotheses, we introduce a test on the measurements,

$$\phi(\vec{y}_k) \in \{H_0\} \cup \{H_{ij}|\{i,j\} \in \mathcal{E}\} \quad (22)$$

where

$$\vec{y}_k \triangleq \begin{bmatrix} y_0^T, \ldots, y_k^T \end{bmatrix}^T \quad (23)$$

is the time-concatenated vector of the measurements. The test $\phi(\vec{y}_k)$ can either accept the null hypothesis ($\phi(\vec{y}_k) = H_0$), or reject the null hypothesis and accept one of the alternative hypotheses ($\phi(\vec{y}_k) \in \{H_{ij}|\{i,j\} \in \mathcal{E}\}$). The decision to accept or reject the null hypothesis is made according to a design constraint on the probability of *false alarm* such that

$$P\,[\phi(\vec{y}_k) = H_{ij}|H_0] \leq \alpha \quad \forall\{i,j\} \in \mathcal{E} \quad (24)$$

where α is the maximum probability of false alarm. In words, we require that the probability of accepting an alternative hypothesis when the null hypothesis is correct must be less than the maximum probability of false alarm. The following sections consider the topology detection problem formulated in (21)-(24) for centralized and distributed approaches, respectively.

4. CENTRALIZED TOPOLOGICAL DETECTION

In this section we present a centralized approach to performing the hypothesis testing problem in (21) assuming the performance constraints in (24). Under this assumption, we present a two-part method for detecting and isolating network topology attacks consisting of *topology attack detection* and *topology attack isolation*. Topology attack detection is concerned with identifying whether any attack or no attack is present in the network, while topology attack isolation identifies the most likely topology attack. For topology attack detection, we write the M-ary hypothesis testing problem in (21) as a binary hypothesis testing problem between a simple null hypothesis, H_0, and a composite alternative, $\neg H_0$, as

$$H_0 : \theta = \mathcal{E} \quad \text{vs.} \quad \neg H_0 : \theta \in \Theta \qquad (25)$$

Performing the test for (25) involves solving $|\mathcal{E}|$ independent binary hypothesis testing problems simultaneously, where a topology fault is detected if any of the hypothesis testing problems accept the alternative hypothesis (rejects the null hypothesis). The distribution of the measurements under each hypothesis in (25) is parameterized by the assumed network topology of the hypothesis. From (18), we observe that the hypothesis testing problem in (25) is a test on the measurements whose distributions for each parameter under each hypothesis are Gaussian with different means and different covariances. Determining a test threshold for a binary test between Gaussian distributions with different means and covariances is known to be complicated [16], thus we apply the results from Section 2 and introduce the following test for testing H_0 vs. $\neg H_0$

$$\hat{\phi}(\vec{y}_k) = \begin{cases} H_0 & \text{if } \max_{\theta \in \Theta} \hat{l}_\theta(\vec{y}_k) \leq -\ln \alpha \\ \neg H_0 & \text{else} \end{cases} \qquad (26)$$

where, $\hat{l}_\theta(\vec{y}_k)$ is a recursively-bounded log-likelihood ratio written as

$$\begin{aligned}
\hat{l}_\theta(\vec{y}_k) =& \max\left\{ 0, \bar{l}_\theta(\vec{y}_k) \right\} \\
\bar{l}_\theta(\vec{y}_k) =& \hat{l}_\theta(\vec{y}_{k-1}) + \ln|\Sigma_{k,\mathcal{E}}| - \ln|\Sigma_{k,\theta}| \\
&+ (y_k - \mu_{k,\mathcal{E}})^T \Sigma_{k,\mathcal{E}}^{-1} (y_k - \mu_{k,\mathcal{E}}) \\
&- (y_k - \mu_{k,\theta})^T \Sigma_{k,\theta}^{-1} (y_k - \mu_{k,\theta})
\end{aligned} \qquad (27)$$

The recursively-bounded log-likelihood ratio, $\hat{l}_\theta(\vec{y}_k)$, employs a sequential change-detection approach to test whether to accept the null hypothesis or accept the alternative hypothesis based on whether the recent measurements indicate the alternative hypothesis is more likely. If any of the binary test, $\hat{\phi}(\vec{y}_k)$, rejects the null hypothesis (accepts the alternative hypothesis), then topology isolation is performed to isolate the most likely attack. This is performed by maximizing the recursively-bounded log-likelihood ratio over the alternative hypotheses, namely

$$\max_{\theta \in \Theta} \hat{l}_\theta(\vec{y}_k) > -\ln \alpha \implies \phi(\vec{y}_k) = H_{ij} \qquad (28)$$

In words, upon rejecting the null hypothesis, the topology attack is isolated by selecting the attack that best explains the measurements. In this section, we introduced a sequential test for detecting network topology attacks using all the available measurements. In the following section we develop a distributed approach which uses only local measurements to detect topology attacks.

5. DISTRIBUTED TOPOLOGICAL DETECTION

For large-scale systems, such as power transmission networks, communication and computational constraints can prohibit the real-time implementation of a centralized detection and isolation scheme. In this section, we present a distributed approach for detecting and isolating topology at-

tacks based strictly on local information. To formulate the distributed topology detection scheme, we introduce

$$y_{k,\Theta_{ij}} = Q_{\Theta_{ij}} y_k \qquad (29)$$

where $Q_{\Theta_{ij}}$ is the binary selection matrix with full row rank and columns which contain a unit entry if and only if the corresponding element of y_k is contained in the combined neighborhood of the vertices of the edge $\{i, j\}$. For each $\theta \subset \mathcal{E}$, the distribution of the local measurements, independent of the previously local measurements, is written as

$$f_\theta(y_{k,\theta}) = N\left[\hat{\mu}_{k,\theta}, \hat{\Sigma}_{k,\theta} \right]. \qquad (30)$$

where

$$\begin{aligned}
\hat{\mu}_{k,\theta} &= Q_\theta \hat{m}_{k|k-1,\theta} \\
\Sigma_{k,\theta} &= Q_\theta \left(\hat{S}_{k|k-1,\theta} + V \right) Q_\theta^T
\end{aligned} \qquad (31)$$

and $\hat{m}_{k|k-1,\theta}$ and $\hat{S}_{k|k-1,\theta}$ are the *a priori* state mean and covariance, respectively, and are calculated recursively using a Kalman filter based on only local measurements as

$$\begin{aligned}
\hat{m}_{k+1|k,\theta} =& A_\theta \hat{m}_{k|k,\theta} + B_\theta u_k \\
\hat{S}_{k+1|k,\theta} =& A_\theta \hat{S}_{k|k,\theta} A_\theta^T + W_\theta \\
\hat{K}_{k,\theta} =& \hat{S}_{k|k-1,\theta} Q_\theta^T \left[Q_\theta \left(\hat{S}_{k|k-1,\theta} + V \right) Q_\theta^T \right]^{-1} \\
\hat{m}_{k|k,\theta} =& \left(I - \hat{K}_{k,\theta} Q_\theta \right) \hat{m}_{k|k-1,\theta} + \hat{K}_{k,\theta} y_{k,\theta} \\
\hat{S}_{k|k,\theta} =& \left(I - \hat{K}_{k,\theta} Q_\theta \right) \hat{S}_{k|k-1,\theta}
\end{aligned} \qquad (32)$$

Additionally, we define the time concatenation of the local measurements as

$$\vec{y}_{k,\theta} \triangleq \left[y_{0,\theta}^T, \dots, y_{k,\theta}^T \right]^T. \qquad (33)$$

To distribute topology attack detection as presented in the previous section, we implement the composite binary hypothesis testing problem in (25) using a collection of distributed simple binary hypothesis testing problems between the null hypothesis, H_0, and a unique alternative hypothesis, H_{ij}, each of which is implemented using only local measurements, $\vec{y}_{k,\theta}$, and written as

$$H_0 : \theta = \mathcal{E} \quad \text{vs.} \quad H_{ij} : \theta = \Theta_{ij} \qquad (34)$$

In the distributed scheme, there are $|\mathcal{E}|$ independent binary hypothesis testing problems performed simultaneously and a topology fault is detected if any of the hypothesis testing problems accept the alternative hypothesis (rejects the null hypothesis). Following the same reasoning as in the centralized scheme, we introduce a test for the hypothesis testing problem in (34) as

$$\hat{\phi}_{\Theta_{ij}}(\vec{y}_{k,\Theta ij}) = \begin{cases} H_0 & \text{if } \hat{l}_{\Theta_{ij}}(\vec{y}_{k,\Theta ij}) \leq -\ln \alpha \\ H_{ij} & \text{else} \end{cases} \qquad (35)$$

Upon detecting a topology attack using local measurements, the corresponding recursive log-likelihood ratio value is transmitted to the central estimator and compared with the other (if any) recursive log-likelihood ratios associated with any other binary tests that reject the null hypothesis. As a heuristic, the topology isolation is performed according to

$$\max_{\Theta_{ij} \in \Theta} \hat{l}_{\Theta_{ij}}(\vec{y}_{k,\Theta_{ij}}) > -\ln \alpha \implies \phi(\vec{y}_k) = H_{ij} \qquad (36)$$

In words, the topology attack is isolated selecting the attack that best explains the local measurements. The complexity involved in computing the distributed statistics is significantly less since the matrix inverse involved in performing the Kalman filter is proportional to the number of sensor measurement. Thus, using only local sensor measurements in the distributed case results in significant computational savings. In this section, we introduced a distributed sequential test for detecting network topology attacks using only local measurements.

6. SIMULATION RESULTS

In this section we evaluate the centralized and decentralized approaches to topology detection using both 9-bus and 118-bus power networks. For comparison between the centralized and decentralized performance, this section first considers a 9-bus power network as defined by the MAT-POWER toolbox [17]. The connectivity graph of the 9-bus system is illustrated in Fig. 1. The power injections and

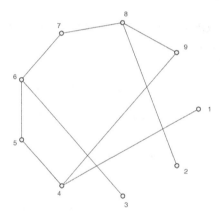

Figure 1: Connectivity graph of 9-bus power network

loading are assumed to have an expected value equivalent to the DC steady-state solution as defined by the MAT-POWER toolbox, namely

$$u(t) = \begin{bmatrix} 67 & 163 & 85 & 0 & -90 & 0 & -100 & 0 & -125 \end{bmatrix}^\top \qquad (37)$$

with process noise covariance, W, and measurement noise covariance, V, defined as

$$W = 10I \quad \text{and} \quad V = 0.1I \qquad (38)$$

We assume a sampling period of 0.02 seconds, which is comparable with current PMU measurement technologies and assume the inertia and damping coefficients, $m = \{m_1, \ldots, m_9\}$ and $d = \{d_1, \ldots, d_9\}$, respectively, are

$$m = \left\{ \begin{matrix} 8.9304, 8.8462, 8.5269, 0.0008, 0.0008, \\ 0.0008, 0.0008, 0.0009, 0.0009 \end{matrix} \right\}$$
$$d = \left\{ \begin{matrix} 3.0920, 3.6539, 3.4160, 0.0004, 0.0004, \\ 0.0003, 0.0004, 0.0004, 0.0003 \end{matrix} \right\} \qquad (39)$$

where the first three buses contain generators which have significantly greater inertia than the non-generation buses as captured by their respective inertia and damping coefficient magnitudes [15]. The voltage phase angle trajectory assuming edge $\{4, 5\}$ is removed at time $t = 0.5s$ is shown in Fig. 2 From the state trajectory we observe that the phase

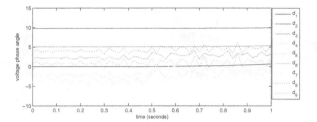

Figure 2: 9-bus voltage phase trajectories (in degrees) versus time (in seconds).

change caused by removing the edge between bus 4 and bus 5 does not result in a safety critical situation since the DC voltage phase angle between buses remains small (between 45 degrees). We specifically consider this situation when evaluating detection and isolation capabilities since drastic changes in phase are much easier to detect and isolate.

For testing purposes, we assume a maximum probability of false alarm as $\alpha = 10^{-4}$ and plot the time evolution of the test statistics as calculated using the centralized approach (assuming all measurements) and the decentralized approach (assuming only local measurements) against the decision threshold in Fig. 3. In Fig. 3, the centralized test statistic trajectories are displayed in the upper subplot while the decentralized test statistic trajectories are shown in the lower subplot. For both plots, the statistic corresponding the actual error (removal of the edge between bus 4 and bus 5) is denoted by the solid black line, while the dotted and dashed lines correspond to all other test statistic trajectories.

We observe from the results in Fig. 3 that detection in both the centralized and decentralized approaches occurs within one sample of the error, indicating detection of a topology attack is quick and accurate. In terms of isolation, we observe that in the centralized case, isolation is performed correctly and remains correct throughout the entire statistic trajectory. In the distributed case, isolation is initially correct, but occasionally leads to incorrect isolation as the statistics evolve. We assert that accurate initial detection and isolation is most important since action would be taken immediately to remedy the situation. Moreover, once the voltage phase angle reaches a steady state value, DC analysis on the phase change can be applied to identify the topology change. Thus, we are primarily concerned with the transient detection and isolation of topology attacks, and observe that both the centralized and decentralized approaches yield promising results.

In terms of the comparative performance between the decentralized and centralized approaches, we observe that the centralized approach is more accurate than the decentralized, which is expected since the centralized approach uses much more information to both detect and isolate. It is clear in Fig. 3 that the decentralized approach is prone to a higher probability of false alarm than the centralized approach as

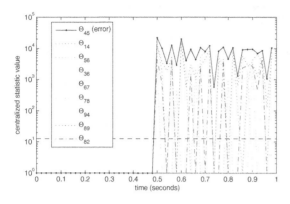

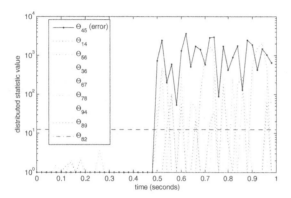

Figure 3: 9-bus power network : centralized test statistics (top) and decentralized test statistics (bottom) vs. time step.

indicated by the peaks in the statistic trajectories in the decentralized approach during the period when no errors are present (time zero to time 0.5 seconds). Although both approaches use the same threshold (which ensures the maximum probability of false alarm is bounded by α), the difference in their actual probability of false alarm is attributed to the conservative nature of Wald's approximation.

To evaluate performance of the distributed approach in a large-scale power network, we consider consider a 118-bus network as defined by the MATPOWER toolbox [17]. In this simulation, and similar to the 9-bus network, we assume a DC-operating point as defined by the MATPOWER toolbox while measuring and perturbing the system using the same noise profiles (but of larger dimension). In this simulation, we assume a topology attack on the edge between bus 5 and bus 6. Figure 4 indicates the trajectory of the statistic corresponding to the actual topology attack (solid black line) versus the maximum of all other statistic trajectories corresponding to all other topology attacks (dotted red line). In Fig. 4, we observe that the distributed approach to detection and isolation accurately detects and isolates the attack quickly. Moreover, the computational complexity of performing decentralized testing is greatly reduced since only

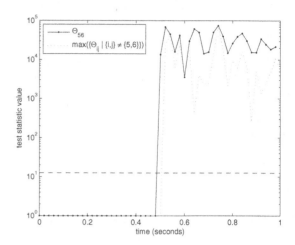

Figure 4: 118-bus power network: decentralized test statistics vs. time step.

local sensor measurements are selected for inclusion in the local tests.

7. DISCUSSION AND FUTURE WORK

This work considers the detection of topology attacks in second-order network systems, with specific application to power networks. A DC-power analysis is employed to generate the well known swing-equation dynamics that when linearized is dependent upon the power network connectivity graph. A decentralized approach to detection and isolation is proposed that is evaluated using the state-of-the-art MATPOWER simulation toolbox. Results indicate the the decentralized approach is well suited for large-scale detection and isolation in networked systems.

Future work on this topic include applying principles of invariance to develop test statistics that evolve independent of non-hypothesized topology attacks. These approaches have shown promise in power networks when isolating power injection attacks; however, topology attacks present much more difficult scenarios when discrete sensing is assumed since plant discretization results in systems that are heavily dependent on the assumed network laplacian. Additionally, we envision future distributed detection schemes to incorporate collaboration between different agents (tests) where agents iteratively exchange information with each other over a communication graph (possibly different from the physical graph). These approaches have been shown to yield promising results in distributed gossip based approaches for collaborative hypothesis testing [18].

8. ACKNOWLEDGMENTS

This work is supported by the Swedish Energy Agency, the Swedish Governmental Agency for Innovation Systems (VINNOVA), the Swedish Foundation for Strategic Research (SSF), and the Knut and Alice Wallenberg Foundation.

9. REFERENCES

[1] R. Isermann, "Model-based fault detection and diagnosis: status and applications," in *Proceedings of the 16th IFAC Symposium on Automatic Control in*

Aerospace, St. Petersburg, Russia, June 2004, pp. 71–85.

[2] S. X. Ding, *Model-based Fault Diagnosis Techniques: Design Schemes.* Springer Verlag, 2008.

[3] J. Chen and R. J. Patton, *Robust Model-Based Fault Diagnosis for Dynamic Systems.* Kluwer Academic Publishers, 1999.

[4] D. D. Siljak, *Decentralized control of complex systems.* Academic Press, 1991.

[5] M. Shahidehpour, W. F. Tinney, and Y. Fu, "Impact of security on power systems operation," *Proceedings of the IEEE*, vol. 93, no. 11, pp. 2013–2025, Nov. 2005.

[6] F. C. Schweppe and J. Wildes, "Power system static-state estimation, part I: Exact model," *IEEE Transactions on Power Apparatus and Systems*, vol. 89, no. 1, pp. 120–125, January 1970.

[7] A. Abur and A. Exposito, *Power System State Estimation: Theory and Implementation.* Marcel-Dekker, 2004.

[8] E. Scholtz and B. Lesieutre, "Graphical observer design suitable for large-scale DAE power systems," in *Proceedings of the IEEE Conf. on Decision and Control*, Cancun, Dec. 2008, pp. 2955–2960.

[9] M. Aldeen and F. Crusca, "Observer-based fault detection and identification scheme for power systems," in *IEE Proceedings - Generation, Transmission and Distribution*, vol. 153, no. 1, Jan. 2006, pp. 71–79.

[10] I. Shames, A. M. H. Teixeira, H. Sandberg, and K. H. Johansson, "Distributed fault detection for interconnected second-order systems with applications to power networks," in *IN FIRST WORKSHOP ON SECURE CONTROL SYSTEMS*, 2010.

[11] S. X. Ding, P. Zhang, C. Chihaia, W. Li, Y. Wang, and E. L. Ding, "Advanced design scheme for fault tolerant distributed networked control systems," in *Proceedings of the 17th IFAC World Congress*, Seoul, Korea, July 2008, pp. 13 569 – 13 574.

[12] W. H. Chung, J. L. Speyer, and R. H. Chen, "A decentralized fault detection filter," *Journal of Dynamic Systems, Measurement, and Control*, vol. 123, no. 2, pp. 237–247, 2001. [Online]. Available: http://link.aip.org/link/?JDS/123/237/1

[13] F. Pasqualetti, A. Bicchi, and F. Bullo, "Consensus computation in unreliable networks: A system theoretic approach," *IEEE Transactions on Automatic Control*, 2010, submitted, available online at http://www.fabiopas.it/papers/FP-AB-FB-10a.pdf.

[14] A. Wald, *Sequential Analysis.* John Wiley & Sons, Inc., New York, 1947.

[15] P. Kundur, *Power System Stability and Control.* McGraw-Hill Professional, 1994.

[16] L. L. Scharf, *Statistical Signal Processing, Detection, Estimation, and Time Series Analysis.* Addison-Welsley Publishing Company Inc., Reading, Massachusetts, 1991.

[17] R. D. Zimmerman, Carlos, and D. . Gan, "MATPOWER: A MATLAB Power System Simulation Package, Version 3.1b2, User's Manual," Power Systems Engineering Research Center, Tech. Rep., 2006. [Online]. Available: http://www.pserc.cornell.edu/matpower/

[18] S. Kar, S. Aldosari, and J. M. F. Moura, "Topology for distributed inference on graphs," *Jun. 2006 [Online]. Available: http://www.arxiv. org/abs/cs/0606052.*

NCS Security Experimentation using DETER

Alefiya Hussain
USC/Information Sciences Institute
hussain@isi.edu

Saurabh Amin
MIT-CEE
amins@mit.edu

ABSTRACT

Numerous efforts are underway to develop testing and experimentation tools to evaluate the performance of networked control systems (NCS) and supervisory control and data acquisition (SCADA) systems. These tools offer varying levels of fidelity and scale. Yet, researchers lack an experimentation framework for systematic testing and evaluation of NCS reliability and security under a wide range of failure scenarios. In this paper, we propose a modular experimentation framework that integrates the NCS semantics with the DETERLab cyber security experimentation facilities. We develop several attack scenarios with realistic network topology and network traffic configurations to evaluate the impact of denial of service (DoS) attacks on scalar linear systems. We characterize the impact of the attack dynamics on six plants located at various levels in a hierarchical topology. Our results suggest that emulation-based evaluations can provide novel insights about the network-induced security and reliability failures in large scale NCS.

Categories and Subject Descriptors

C.4 [**Performance of Systems**]: Reliability,availability, and serviceability

General Terms

Experimentation, Reliability, Security

Keywords

Robust Control, Network Security, Experimentation

1. INTRODUCTION

Networked control systems (NCS), which are increasingly being used for operational management of large-scale physical infrastructures, inherit the vulnerabilities of commercial IT solutions. In recent years, numerous studies have focused on the interconnected physical and cyber-based processes of NCS and next-generation supervisory control and data acquisition (SCADA) systems. The

interdependence between random failures caused due to sensor-actuator faults and adversarial failures caused due to malicious software are especially important [20]. Several theoretical analyses build on well known classes of attacker-defender models, and apply tools from robust control and game theory, to derive safety and performance bounds for a wide range of NCS models [16]. However, in order to develop practically implementable diagnostic tools and real-time response mechanisms, these attacker-defender models should be benchmarked and evaluated against real-world threat scenarios. Indeed, experimental research in network security highlights the accuracy and level of modeling detail, and focuses on techniques for security evaluation by combining real and simulated components. Such experimental research is necessary to complement theoretical performance bounds. It will enable researchers to address new developments in smart infrastructures that face emerging threats, and yet account for the challenges of realism, fidelity, and scale as these networked systems expand in size and functionality.

Several efforts are currently underway for testing and evaluation of new IT security solutions and secure control algorithms for NCS and SCADA systems. There is a diverse body of literature which studies the co-simulation of NCS and SCADA processes using Matlab, Modelica, Ptolemy, and other hybrid system simulation tools with simulated network models using ns2, OMNet++, SSFnet [1, 4, 5, 10, 12, 17, 13, 18]. These approaches are sufficient to study NCS performance under unreliable communication networks with delay, jitter, and packet loss. However, for the purpose of cyber security testing and evaluation for NCS and SCADA systems, emulation-based experiments offer a richer class of scenarios. At present, multiple government-industry initiatives are exploring testbed research and development for NCS and SCADA system applications. The DHS Control Systems Security Program (CSSP) and the DOE-OE Control System Security National SCADA Testbed (NSTB) [17] have offered the red-team and blue-team training exercises for asset owners and vendors across different utility sectors over the past three years. The current and past red and blue configurations involved prototyped tools on a limited basis to see if the applications would install and operate on real control systems. Testing done at the DoE national laboratories has also generated considerable interest in extending the existing SCADA training architectures to include testing of a wider range of security scenarios, and making this extension accessible as an academic research testbed.

Our goal is to use the network security testing tools available at the DETERLab facilities to study network attacks for NCS systems. The integration of the NCS models into DETERLab has a potential to offer a unique opportunity to use the large scale network testing capabilities to generate realistic network attacks and

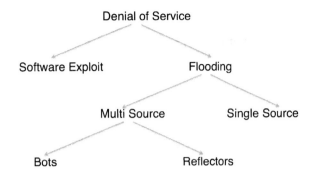

Figure 1: A taxonomy of DoS attacks based on the volume of attack packets and the number of attackers. [14].

validate resilient control algorithms for maintaining the safety and security of NCS. In particular, we integrate the dynamics of multiple NCS with a hierarchically structured network topology, where the individual NCS face different levels of flood-based denial of service (DoS) attacks. We represent the communication network with different models of background traffic and network topology. The system dynamics is mathematically represented by scalar linear system and our goal is to study the evolution and closed-loop stability under a range of attack scenarios. In our experiments, the forward network path from the plant to the controller, the backward network path from the controller to the plant, or both are flooded with a large volume of attack packets that compete for bandwidth and storage (queuing) resources at the routers. In this paper we are primarily focused on flood-based DoS attacks which impact the timely delivery of the plant and controller feedback. There are other classes of attacks, such as *deception* attacks, where the integrity of the control data is compromised. They are not discussed in this paper.

In Section 2, we briefly discusses the taxonomy of DoS attacks in networked systems and summarizes the existing capabilities of DETERLab. In Section 3, we introduce an experimentation model of NCS and discuss our approach for testbed-based emulation. We are specifically focused on using real–world attack tools and mechanisms along with representative models of topology and cross traffic to systematically evaluate the security of linear dynamical systems. In Section 4, we evaluate the impact of the attack on the security and stability of a plant. Specifically, how the attack characteristics, such as, attacker–plant location, start time, and packet size, impact the closed feedback loop between the plant and the controller. Our results suggest that emulation-based evaluations provide novel insights into network-induced security and reliability failures in large scale NCS.

2. DOS ATTACKS

In this section we summarize the taxonomy of DoS attacks on the Internet and discuss how the taxonomy is applicable to NCS and SCADA systems that directly or indirectly use network connectivity for their operation. This taxonomy does not include DoS attacks to NCS communicating over the wireless networks. We then discuss how the DETERLab facilities and tools can be used for evaluating NCS safety and security against DoS attacks.

2.1 Taxonomy

In a DoS attack on the Internet, a malicious user exploits the network connectivity to cripple the services offered by a victim server, often by simply exhausting the resources at the victim. Typically, these resources include network bandwidth, computational

power, or operating system data structures. A DoS attack can be either a single-source attack originating at a single host, or a multi-source attack where multiple hosts coordinate to flood the victim with a large volume of attack packets. A multi-source attack is also called a distributed denial of service (DDoS) attack. Sophisticated attack tools that automate the procedure of compromising hosts and launching such attacks are readily available on the Internet.

To launch a DDoS attack, a malicious user compromises Internet hosts and installs attack tools on the host also known as a zombies or bots. The bots is now available to attack any victim on command. With full control of the bots, the attacker can construct any packet including illegal packets, such as packets with incorrect header field values, or an invalid combination of flags. Figure 1 presents a broad classification of DoS attacks, namely, software exploits and flooding attacks.

Software exploit attacks target specific software bugs in the system or an application, and can potentially disable the victim machine with a single or a few packets. A well known example is the SCADA Modbus attack, where a remote attacker can force a programmable logic controller (PLC) device or Modbus TCP servers to repeatedly power cycle by sending a TCP request containing the 08 Diagnostics function code with sub function 01 [19]. Additionally, East et. al [8], have documented several software exploits on the DNP3 protocol for SCADA system. For example, the DFC Flag attack demonstrates that an attacker can generate spoofed, illegal packets with the flag set to incorrectly signal the master that the remote device is busy.

Flooding attacks result from one or more attackers sending incessant streams of packets aimed at overwhelming link bandwidth or computing resources at the victim. These attacks can be further classified into (a) bot directed floods, and (b) reflector attacks.

In *bot directed flooding attacks*, a malicious user installs attack tools on the host machine to generate a flood of illegal packets. Examples include, attacks that send a flood of TCP requests to a sensor node resulting in power exhaustion at the node [10] and attacks that create a flood of DNP3 messages between the master and the remote devices [8]. Several canned attack tools are available on the Internet, such as Trinoo, Tribal Flood Network, and SCADA server/client attack tools, that can generate flooding attacks using a combination of protocols.

Reflector attacks are used to hide the identity of the attacker and/or to amplify an attack. A reflector is any host that responds to network request. For example, a web servers or ftp servers that respond to TCP SYN requests with a TCP SYN-ACK packets, and a host that respond to echo requests with echo replies. Servers may be used as reflectors by spoofing the victim's IP address in the source field of the request, tricking the reflector into directing its response to the victim. Unlike directed attacks, reflector attacks require well-formed packets to solicit a reply. If many reflector machines are employed, such an attack can easily overwhelm the victim without adversely affecting the reflectors or triggering the local IDS. Reflectors can also be used as amplifiers by sending packets to the broadcast address on the reflector network, soliciting a response from every host on the LAN. Unlike directed floods that represent improperly secured hosts, reflectors are often hosts intentionally providing Internet services, and hence reflector attacks may be more difficult to block.

2.2 Attack Generation

The DETERLab facility provides a rich set of resources, tools, and methodologies to conduct high-fidelity, large scale network and cyber security experiments [3, 6]. This facility has been operational since 2003 and is operated by the USC Information Sciences In-

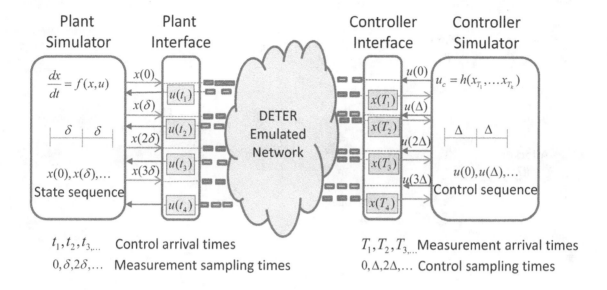

Plant Simulator

$$\frac{dx}{dt} = f(x,u)$$

$x(0)$
$x(\delta)$
$\delta \quad \delta$
$x(0), x(\delta),...$
State sequence

Plant Interface

$x(0)$
$u(t_1)$
$x(\delta)$
$u(t_2)$
$x(2\delta)$
$u(t_3)$
$x(3\delta)$
$u(t_4)$

DETER Emulated Network

Controller Interface

$u(0)$
$x(T_1)$
$u(\Delta)$
$x(T_2)$
$u(2\Delta)$
$x(T_3)$
$u(3\Delta)$
$x(T_4)$

Controller Simulator

$u_c = h(x_{T_1},...x_{T_k})$

$\Delta \quad \Delta$
$u(0), u(\Delta),...$
Control sequence

$t_1, t_2, t_{3,...}$ Control arrival times
$0, \delta, 2\delta,...$ Measurement sampling times

$T_1, T_2, T_{3,...}$ Measurement arrival times
$0, \Delta, 2\Delta,...$ Control sampling times

Figure 2: NCS emulation on the DETER Testbed

stitute, UC Berkeley, and Sparta Inc. As of December 2011, the DETER testbed has supported more than 2000 experimenters and students experimenting with a diverse set of cyber security technologies. The main thrusts of research on the testbed include DoS attacks, worm propagation and analysis, botnets, and anomaly detection in networks.

Using DETERLab for evaluation of NCS systems allows the experimenter to replicate the interactions between the NCS components, and the attackers with high-fidelity and accuracy. The NCS components, such as the plants and the controllers, can be implemented as simulation, emulation, or real components with the interface discussed in Section 3. The attack traffic can be generated using either real–world attack tools mentioned in the previous section or modeled attack tools provided by the DETERLab facility. Several real–world attack tools are available in binary or executable format and can be activated on the suggested operating systems and end host configuration. The DETERLab facilities also provides a range of DoS attack tools that model the various attack methodologies, command and control structures, attack volumes, and attack types, with easy to use graphical user interfaces. These tools together provide a unique balance between experiment control and realism.

We note that there are several experimentation environments available or currently under development for NCS and SCADA systems. Each offers a different levels of fidelity and scale [4, 17, 5]. We believe that the DETERLab tools and facilities complement these efforts. In particular, it allows the experimenter to closely replicate the real–world end host and cyber attack models. This enables systematic and consistent evaluation of physical control systems in such environments.

3. EXPERIMENTATION FRAMEWORK

In this section, we discuss the framework for integrating NCS semantics with the DETER testbed to systematically explore the impact of network attacks on evolution and stability of such systems. Our approach is to combine NCS system tools and simulation with DETERLab tools and methodologies for networking and cyber security testing and evaluation. The experimentation framework is

shown in Figure 2 and has three main components: the physical system dynamics, the physical-to-cyber network interface, and the cyber network dynamics.

In our framework, the NCS plant is remotely connected to a controller over a shared network. The plant–controller communication is hence subjected to network and shared medium effects, such as, delays, jitter, and packet losses. In addition, in presence of cyber security incidents, the communication can also be subjected to malicious losses or corruption.

The physical system dynamics of a NCS can be represented as a simulation, an emulation, or by real control system such as the interconnected four-tank water system. In this paper we implement a simulation based scalar linear system. The physical-to-cyber network interface translates between the physical and the event-based network dynamics. The cyber network dynamics can be represented as a simulation, an emulation, or an operational network such as the Internet. In this paper, we emulate the network and cyber security dynamics on the DETERLab facilities. In this paper we specifically focus on the study of DoS attacks on control systems. We now discuss each of these components in more detail.

Physical System Dynamics: In our framework, the plant is represented by an ordinary differential equation (ODE) simulation engine and the controller by a simple output feedback policy that has been designed for target-tracking in the absence of the attacks. We build on NCS co-simulation technique developed by Branicky et. al [1]. In our experiments, the NCS dynamics are defined as follows:

$$\dot{x}(t) = Ax(t) + u(t)$$
$$y(t) = x(t)$$
$$u = K[R(t) - y(t)]$$

where $x(t)$ denotes the plant state, $y(t)$ the output, $u(t)$ the control input, and $R(t)$ the reference trajectory signal. A represents the system matrix and K represents the controller gain matrix, In this paper, we restrict our attention to scalar dynamics.

Network Interface: The network interfaces are located both at the plant and the controller. This enables the integration of NCS dynamics with the event-based communication semantics of the DE-

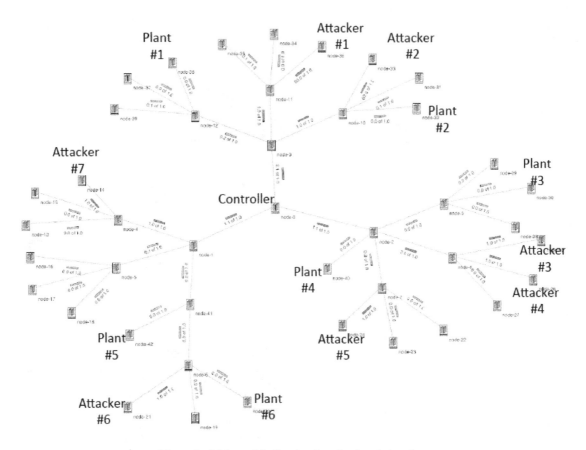

Figure 3: A hierarchically structured network topology

TER testbed. The interface is responsible for sending and receiving data signals across the emulated testbed network. At pre-specified times, represented as δ, the plant simulator provides samples of the system state. This is presented as a time stamped output signal to the interface. The plant interface sends the data over the emulated network to the controller, but retains it until the end of the time-interval δ.

Upon receipt of the plant system state, the controller interface passes the data to the controller system. The controller calculates a control input and sends it back to the controller interface at periodic intervals Δ. The controller interface then forwards the control input on to the network. Upon receipt of the control input, the plant interface immediately forwards the control input to the plant system. The plant incorporates the control input and updates the current plant state. The plant then computes the next projected plant state.

In order to account for asynchronous and out-of-order system state arrivals, at both the plant and controller interfaces, the system has the capability to roll-back and roll-forward their respective updates.

Cyber Network Dynamics The middle section, shown as a cloud, represents the DETER testbed experimentation network that emulates topology and traffic dynamics between the plant and the controller. Such a communication network is typically modeled with two primary layers; (a) the physical topology and routing structure of the network components, and (b) the network traffic layer between the network components [15].

Selecting representative topologies for the communication network has been a subject of significant research over the last several years. It is challenging since the Internet structure constantly evolves and deployed NCS or SCADA systems rarely make their underlying network topologies publicly available due to security reasons [9, 4]. Further, the network routing structure is also impacted by the link-level communication technologies, such as wireless, satellite, or wired networks. For example, wireless mobile networks have a dynamic topological and routing structure that evolves with the movement of the nodes while wired networks have a relatively static topological structure that does not change frequently. The DETER testbed is primarily a wired testbed and offers several topology generation tools and sample topology catalogs for experimentation [7].

The second layer, the traffic in the experimentation framework is determined by the various servers, clients, and attackers in the network. To accurately model the wide-area networks and the Internet, cyber security experiments typically model three different types of network traffic; (i) *background traffic*, for example, web server and web client traffic which is congestion reactive, the (ii) *foreground traffic* that is under study, for example, control traffic in a NCS system, and (iii) *malicious or selfish traffic* such as, attack traffic in a DoS attack, or constant-rate traffic generated by selfish nodes. This type of traffic is not congestion reactive. The three types of traffic interleave to create a complex set of dynamics that can be captured with high fidelity in an emulation-based environment such as a testbed. They are discussed in detail in Section 4. DETER provides a diverse set of traffic generators, including Harpoon,TCP replay, Apache wget clients for background and foreground traffic, and real and emulated DoS attack traffic and worm traffic generators [7].

Modularizing the experimentation framework enables us to rapidly evolve the models to systematically explore the structural and functional aspects of the system. This allows addressing existing security threats, identifying new threats, and meeting the challenges of fidelity, scale, and complexity. In the next section, we discuss the specific experimentation scenarios along with metrics and measurements for exploring the impact of DoS attacks on a NCS system in an emulated testbed environment.

4. EVALUATION

Using the experimentation framework presented in the previous section, we now systematically evaluate the impact of a DoS attack on the networked control system. We first discuss how we parametrize our experimentation framework, specifically, the network topology and the network traffic, and then present our results.

4.1 Emulation Parameters

Our goal is to employ the experimentation framework to create a rich and complex evaluation scenario that will allow the assessment of a multi-source flooding DoS attack on the networked control system. We model complexity in both topology and traffic. We employ network topologies appropriate for the analyses of DoS attacks. We interleave background web traffic, foreground control traffic, and malicious DoS attack traffic, as expected on a real network. We use real–world attack tools to capture the complexity of the attack dynamics.

While there are several ways to model the underlying topology, as discussed in Section 3, we employ a hierarchically structured network topology, with the controller at the root of the hierarchy, and a homogeneous ensemble of six plants located at various levels in the hierarchical tree network. The parameters A and K are chosen from [1], and are identical for all plants. The bandwidth at each link is configured at 1Mbps.

The location of various plants is depicted in Figure 3. The topology has three subnets, and each subnet has two plants. Starting from the top, and going clockwise, the first subnet has both plants located at the leaf nodes, the second subnet has a plant at a leaf node and a plant located at tree–depth level one from the controller, and the third subnet has a plant at a leaf node and a plant located at tree–depth level two from the controller.

We deploy attackers at seven leaf nodes in the network as shown in the Figure 3. Each attacker generates a DoS attack, with a real–world tool called punk [14], that sends a maximum rate stream of TCP segments, where the source address and the source and destination ports are randomized. The size of the attack packet can be configured when the attack is launched and then the attacker generates attack packets at the maximum rate of the network interface. The attack victim is the controller located at the root of the tree. In addition, all the leaf nodes also generate webtraffic that traverses the network [7].

Consequently, plants are located at various levels in the topology. It allows systematic study of the impact of the attack on the control signals at different levels of aggregation of the attack and control traffic.

4.2 Effect of Location

We first study the impact of the DoS attacks on plants that are located at different levels in the topology. In the Figure 4, the y-axis plots the output state from the plants #3, #4, and #5, at any point in time. Each plant is located at a different tree-depth level, specifically; (a) Plant #4 located one tree-depth level from the controller, (b) Plant #5 located two tree-depth levels from the controller, (c) Plant #3 located at a leaf node.

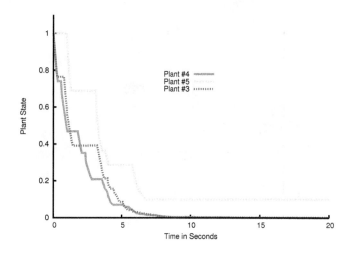

Figure 4: Impact of attack at various locations in the topology

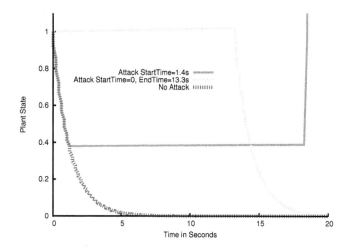

Figure 5: Effect of Start time of the attack on the plant

The attackers are configured to generate 40 byte attack packets using real–world attack tools. The aggregation of the attack traffic in the topology impacts the convergence of the plant state. As observed from the graph, each plant is subjected to a different plant convergence dynamic during the attack. When we varied the size of the attack packet, from the minimum size of 40 bytes to a large packet of 1040 bytes, we observed plant #5 and plant #3 converged very slowly and sometimes failed to converge. We observed plant #4, that is located two hops from the controller, was significantly more stable than plants located at deeper levels in the topology.

These results indicate that parsimonious analytical models may not capture the complex interaction between the various topology and traffic components.

4.3 Effect of Start time

We study the impact of the attack start time on the plant stability. In Figure 5, y-axis plots the output state from plant #3 at any point in time. Under the no attack condition, all the plants stabilize and converge. Since NCS rely on real-time feedback, both packet delays and packet losses affect the NCS stability. The route between plant #3 and the controller, is impacted by three attackers send-

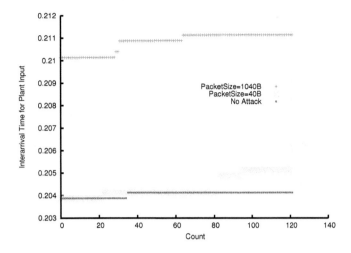

Figure 6: Effect of an attack on the Inter-arrival time of the plant state

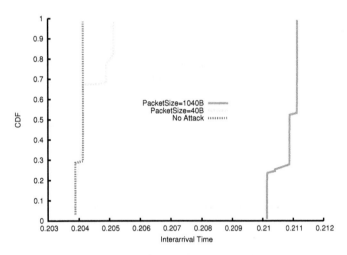

Figure 7: CDF of the Inter-arrival time

ing packets at the maximum rate with a packet size of 40 bytes. In this section we discuss the stability of plant #3 as it is farthest away from the controller and is exposed to the maximum number of attackers.

We investigate two scenarios; (a) when the attack starts during the plant operation and does not stop for a long period of time, and (b) when the attack starts before the plant operation and stops after a small period of time. In the first scenario, the plant starts to converge before the attack starts, but once the attack starts the plant state becomes highly unstable since several feedback messages are lost. This scenario is shown in the Figure 5 with the attack starting at 1.4 seconds. In the second scenario, the attack starts before the plant operation, we observe similar performance, where the plant does not stabilize, but as soon as the attack stops, the plant rapidly converges to a stable condition. This scenario is shown in the Figure 5 with the attack ending at 13.3 seconds.

These results indicate that it is important to account for attacker start and stop dynamics when modeling cyber security scenarios.

4.4 Interarrival time

We study the impact of the attack packets on the interarrival time

of the plant and controller output. The size of the attack packet can have a significant impact on time-sensitive NCS. The packet size determines the transmission time, that is, large attack packets cause longer delays as compared to small attack packets. In the presence of an attack, when there are several such packets flooding the network and interleaving with the control packets, they can cause instability in the convergence of the NCS.

For the analysis in this section, we measured network packets at the plant and controller using tcpdump [21], and then calculated the time difference between consecutive plant state output packets. In Figure 6, the y-axis plots the interarrival time of plant #4 against with the packet counts. Figure 7 shows the interarrival time as a cumulative distribution function.

We first discuss the no attack condition. Plant #4 is two hops away from the controller and the transmission time of the plant state packet of size 52 bytes, from the plant to the controller is 0.200832s. Additionally, there is a 3ms processing delay at the plant in the current implementation. The interarrival time is bimodal with a difference of 300μs between the two modes which we believe is due to the interleaving of cross traffic.

Next we investigate two attack scenarios; (a) when an attacker, generating small packets of 40 byte,s starts before the plant operation, (b) when an attacker, generating large packets of 1040 bytes, starts before the plant operation. Both scenarios have a multi-modal interarrival time distribution due to the interleaving of attack and control packets.

The results in this section indicate that depending on how the attack packets, plant state packets, and background traffic interleave, there is a significantly impact on the interarrival times between the plant output. .

5. CONCLUSION

In this paper discussed an experimentation framework for the evaluation of NCS on the DETERLab facilities. Our experimentation framework has three main components: physical dynamics, a physical-to-cyber interface, and a cyber network model. The physical system dynamics are implemented in simulation and are modeled as a scalar linear system. The physical-to-cyber interface is designed for sending and receiving data across the emulated network and allows the implementation of event-based semantics. The cyber network is modeled on the DETERLab experimentation facilities with realistic topology and traffic parameters. This modular approach provides an environment in which experiments can be rapidly configured, and can evolve to keep pace with the cyber-physical security challenges in the emerging smart infrastructures.

Our contribution complements other ongoing projects on NCS experimentation, in particular, we leverage cyber security experimentation tools and methodologies to evaluate multiple scalar linear systems under a distributed denial of service attack. While the plant dynamics are simple, the key contributions are in the simultaneous experimentation of multiple plants under a wide range of network conditions. Our results indicate that experimentation evaluation provides unique insights into the plant dynamics that are not apparent in analytical or simulation studies. We plan to expand our analyses and compare these experimental observations with theoretical performance bounds, for example, block attacks and strategic jamming attacks [2, 11] as future work.

Acknowledgements

The authors are grateful to Anthony Joseph (Berkeley), Gabor Karsai (Vanderbilt), Blaine Nelson (Berkeley), Suzanna Schmeelk (Rutgers), Galina Schwartz (Berkeley), Terry Benzel (USC/ISI), Bob

Braden (USC/ISI), and John Wroclawski (USC/ISI) for numerous discussions on NCS security. We are especially grateful to Darrel Brower for closely working with us on this project. This material is based on work partially supported by the United States Department of Homeland Security and Space and Naval Warfare Systems Center under the contract number N66001-10-C-2018 and the MIT faculty start-up grant. All findings and conclusions expressed in this material are those of the authors and do not reflect the views on the funding agencies.

6. REFERENCES

[1] A. T. Al-Hammouri, M. S. Branicky, and V. Liberatore. Co-simulation tools for networked control systems. In *Proceedings of the 11th international workshop on Hybrid Systems: Computation and Control*, HSCC '08, pages 16–29, Berlin, Heidelberg, 2008. Springer-Verlag.

[2] S. Amin, A. A. Cárdenas, and S. Sastry. Safe and secure networked control systems under denial-of-service attacks. In R. Majumdar and P. Tabuada, editors, *HSCC*, volume 5469 of *Lecture Notes in Computer Science*, pages 31–45. Springer, 2009.

[3] T. Benzel. The science of cyber security experimentation: The DETER project. *Annual Computer Security Applications Conference*, December 2011.

[4] D. C. Bergman. Power grid simulation, evaluation, and test framework. Master's thesis, University of Illinois at Urbana-Champaign, Urbana, Illinois, May 2010.

[5] A. Davis. Developing SCADA simulations with c2windtunnel. Master's thesis, Vanderbilt University, Nashville, Tennessee, May 2011.

[6] The DETERLab Facilities. http://www.deter-project.org.

[7] DETER Resources. https://trac.deterlab.net/wiki/DeterResources.

[8] S. East, J. Butts, M. Papa, and S. Shenoi. A taxonomy of attacks on the DNP3 protocol. *IFIP International Federation for Information Processing*, pages 67–81, 2009.

[9] S. Floyd and E. Kohler. Internet research needs better models. *SIGCOMM Comput. Commun. Rev.*, 33:29–34, January 2003.

[10] A. Giani, G. Karsai, T. Roosta, A. Shah, B. Sinopoli, and J. Wiley. A testbed for secure and robust scada systems. *SIGBED Rev.*, 5:4:1–4:4, July 2008.

[11] A. Gupta, C. Langbort, and T. Basar. Optimal control in the presence of an intelligent jammer with limited actions. In *CDC*, pages 1096–1101. IEEE, 2010.

[12] A. Hahn, B. Kregel, M. Govindarasu, J. Fitzpatrick, R. Adnan, S. Sridhar, and M. Higdon. Development of the powercyber scada security testbed. In *Proceedings of the Sixth Annual Workshop on Cyber Security and Information Intelligence Research*, CSIIRW '10, pages 21:1–21:4, New York, NY, USA, 2010. ACM.

[13] G. Hemingway, H. Neema, H. Nine, J. Sztipanovits, and G. Karsai. Rapid synthesis of high-level architecture-based heterogeneous simulation: A model-based integration approach. *SIMULATION*, page 16, 03 2011.

[14] A. Hussain, J. Heidemann, and C. Papadopoulos. A Framework For Classifying Denial of Service Attacks. *Proc. of the Conf. on Applications, Technologies, Architectures, and Protocols for Comp. Comm. - SIGCOMM*, page 99, 2003.

[15] A. Hussain, S. Schwab, R. Thomas, S. Fahmy, and J. Mirkovic. DDOS experiment methodology. *DETER Workshop Proceedings*, 2006.

[16] T. S. Khirwadkar. Defense against network attacks using game theory. Master's thesis, University of Illinois at Urbana-Champaign, Urbana, Illinois, May 2011.

[17] Idaho national lab SCADA testbed program. http://www.inl.gov/scada.

[18] M. Liljenstam, J. Liu, D. M. Nicol, Y. Yuan, G. Yan, and C. Grier. Rinse: The real-time immersive network simulation environment for network security exercises (extended version). *Simulation*, 82:43–59, January 2006.

[19] Xforce Attack Repository. SCADA modbus restart denial of service. http://xforce.iss.net/xforce/xfdb/20739.

[20] L. Schenato, B. Sinopoli, M. Franceschetti, K. Poolla, and S. S. Sastry. Foundations of control and estimation over lossy networks. *Proceedings of the IEEE*, 95:163–187, 2007.

[21] Wireshark Website. http://www.wireshark.org/.

Integrated Simulation and Emulation Platform for Cyber-Physical System Security Experimentation

Wei Yan[†], Yuan Xue[†], Xiaowei Li[†], Jiannian Weng[†], Timothy Busch[‡],
and Janos Sztipanovits[†]

[†]Institute for Software Integrated Systems and EECS Department, Vanderbilt University, Nashville, TN, USA

[‡]The State University of New York Institute of Technology, Utica, NY, USA

wei.yan@vanderbilt.edu, yuan.xue@vanderbilt.edu, xiaowei.li@vanderbilt.edu, jiannian.weng@vanderbilt.edu, timothy.busch@sunyit.edu, janos.sztipanovits@vanderbilt.edu

ABSTRACT

There is a pressing need to evaluate both cyber- and physical systems together and holistically for a rapidly growing number of applications using simulation and emulation in a realistic environment, which brings realistic attacks against the defensive capabilities of CPS (Cyber-Physical System). Without the support from appropriate tools and run-time environments, this assessment process can be extremely time-consuming and error-prone, if possible at all. In this paper, we present iSEE - integrated Simulation and Emulation platform for security Experimentation, as a "software supporting research infrastructure used for cyber security research and development". iSEE allows for the concurrent modeling, experimentation and evaluation of CPS that range from a fully simulated to a fully implemented system. iSEE has two major components: 1) modeling environment for system specification and experiment configuration and 2) run-time environment that supports experiment execution. iSEE employs the Model-Integrated-Computing (MIC) approach, which explicitly uses models throughout the experiment environments and integrates them at the domain-specific model level. The run-time environment of iSEE integrates Matlab and the DETERlab testbed to support realistic assessment of CPS on real distributed networking environments in its early design phase, before a fully implemented system is available. At run time, iSEE provides time synchronization and data communication and coordinates the execution of the security experiment across simulation and emulation platforms.

Categories and Subject Descriptors

I.6.7 [**Simlation and Modeling**]: Simulation Support Systems—*environments*

General Terms

Experimentation, Security

Keywords

Cyber-Physical Systems, Simulation, Emulation, Security Experiment Platform

1. INTRODUCTION

Cyber-Physical Systems (CPS) are characterized by the tight coupling and coordination among sensing, communications, computational and physical components. As CPS become increasingly complex in terms of distributed architectures and expanded capability, it becomes extremely challenging to formally analyze their security properties. Currently, many CPS are designed without considering the effects of the network operating environment (e.g., time-varying delays and packet losses). Such inadequacies during the system design can lead to catastrophic consequences after the actual systems are deployed, as these systems are interconnected to open networks and exposed to network dynamics and uncertainties. Thus, there is a pressing need to evaluate both cyber and physical systems together holistically for a rapidly growing number of applications using both simulation and emulation in a realistic environment. Without support from appropriate tools and experimental environments, this evaluation process can be extremely time-consuming and error-prone, even impossible at all.

Building such an experiment environment is a challenging task, especially if one wants to test the security properties of CPS under real security attack scenarios. Currently, the DETERlab testbed [2] is the only available emulation environment accessible by researchers to perform realistic security experiments. Yet using the DETERlab testbed alone for CPS evaluation has a number of limitations. First, experiments on the DETERlab testbed require a fully implemented software system. This prevents early evaluation of CPS when they are partially implemented. In a CPS design, a "virtual prototype" of a system can be a suite of simulation models and prototypes, each element representing a system (hardware and software) and its environment with a different fidelity. Many CPS design aspects (such as control algorithms) need to be evaluated on this "virtual prototype" in the early design phase, instead of on a fully implemented system. Second, experiment setup in the DETERlab testbed requires the user to perform significant amount of configuration work and have sufficient background knowledge in networking and security. Though SEER [1] provides a tool to facilitate this procedure, domain experts, who are not familiar with networking systems, may create inconsistent experiment setups (e.g., mismatching host IDs in the system configuration and in the attack generation) and find it very time-consuming for large-scale experiments. This creates a huge barrier for CPS security assessment. On the other hand, Matlab/Simulink [3] has been a very popular tool to model and evaluate the performance of CPS systems via simulation. Though network simulation is provided in Matlab/Simulink via Truetime toolbox [9], the accuracy of its simulation depends on the level of abstraction of the network protocol models. The operating system details, such as buffer operations, which are essential to evaluate security attack behaviors, cannot be simulated in these control simulators.

In this paper, we present iSEE - integrated Simulation and Emulation platform for cyber-physical system Security Experimentation [1]. iSEE allows for the concurrent modeling, experimentation and evaluation of CPS that range from a fully simulated to a fully implemented system. iSEE has two major components: 1) a modeling environment for system specification and experiment configuration and 2) a run-time environment that supports experiment execution. iSEE employs the Model-Integrated-Computing (MIC) [16] approach, which explicitly uses models throughout the experiment environments and integrates them at the domain-specific model level. Using the model-integrated approach enables the experiment to be rapidly reconfigured and maintains the consistency among multiple simulation models and the real software components. The run-time environment integrates the Matlab/Simulink simulation tool with the DETERlab testbed. It provides time synchronization and data communication services and coordinates the execution of the security experiment across the simulation and emulation platforms.

The rest of the paper is organized as follows. Section II presents the related work. Section III provides an overview of the system architecture. Section IV presents the model-based design and integration of CPS using the MIC technique. Section V describes the Run-Time components. The evaluations of iSEE is presented in section VI. Finally, section VII concludes this work.

2. RELATED WORK

There have been some efforts that simulate and assess CPS using a variety of tools. These efforts can be categorized into several classes, as summarized in Table 2. Most of these tools have limited capability in simulating and evaluating CPS in different ways. Matlab/Simulink [3] has been widely used for modeling and simulating control systems and provides a Truetime toolbox [9] for approximating link layer network simulation. However, the network simulation accuracy, which depends on the abstraction level of the network protocol models, is greatly limited in the Truetime toolbox, due to its inability of supporting higher level protocols (e.g., TCP or UDP). In addition, Truetime toolbox cannot simu-

late operating system level issues, such as buffer operations, which are essential for detecting security attacks. Similar tools include Modelica [4] and Ptolemy [7], which allow for the simulation of CPS under various continuous and discrete dynamics. These tools still suffer from the similar challenges as Truetime in Matlab/Simulink in terms of network simulation.

Packet-level network simulators, such as ns-2 [5] and OM-Net++ [6], provide a detailed implementation of network protocol stack. However, using ns-2 alone for NCS evaluation requires the control algorithm to be fully implemented in a high-level language such as C++. This becomes very difficult as the complexity of the control system increases.

Thus, several efforts have been made towards integrating multiple simulators in order to more effectively and accurately model and evaluate CPS. A tool chain PiccSIM [17] allows for the integration of Matlab/Simulink models with ns-2. It also provides a graphical user interface for the design of control systems and the automatic code generation of ns-2 and Matlab/Simulink models. Another work [13] couples several simulators, including ModelSim, Matlab/Simulink and ns-2, though establishing the communication between them. NCSWT [11] also integrates Matlab/Simulink and ns-2 for simulating networked control system and, in particular, uses MIC techniques to define behavior models for the control and networking systems respectively, which facilitate the code generation. Other similar works include [14, 8, 12].

Although the above integrated simulators can achieve better performances than individual simulators, the simulation accuracy is still bounded by the capability of network modeling provided by tools, such as ns-2 and OMNet++. Instead, DETERLab [2] is a realistic network emulation environment, where CPS security experiments can be carried out with better network accuracy and operating system level details. Therefore, our work iSEE, which integrates both control modeling environment (i.e., Matlab/Simulink) and network emulation environment (i.e., DETERLab), has evident benefits over the existing tools for simulating and evaluating CPS.

3. OVERVIEW ARCHITECTURE

Figure 1 presents the overall system architecture of iSEE. It has two major components: (1) the modeling environment for system specification and experiment configuration and (2) run-time environment that supports experiment execution. iSEE employs a model-integrated approach, which explicitly uses models throughout the experiment environments and integrates them at the domain-specific model level. The modeling environment of iSEE allows the user to specify (1) the system model of CPS and (2) security experiment scenario configuration. Currently, the modeling language of iSEE focuses on the modeling of networked control systems (NCS). iSEE provides an overarching modeling environment that integrates the operational semantics of Matlab simulation platform and the DETERlab emulation platform. The model interpreter generates the configuration files and necessary interface code to manage the interactions among the simulation and emulation platforms and configures the experiment scenario in the run-time environment. The model-integrated approach enables the experiment to be rapidly reconfigured and maintains the consistency among multiple simulation models and the real software components.

---

[1]Source code and demonstration video of iSEE can be found at http://vanets.vuse.vanderbilt.edu/dokuwiki/doku.php?id=research:isee.

Tool	Type	Capacity	Limitation
Truetime [9] in Mat-lab/Simulink, Modelica [4], Ptolemy [7]	control system modeling and simulation environment	model complex control algorithms	limited support for network simulation
ns-2 [5], OM-Net++ [6]	network simulation environment	packet-level simulation of network protocol stack	limited in control system modeling and design
PiccSIM [17], ModelSim [13], NCSWT [11]	integrated modeling and simulation environment of both control and network systems	model control system dynamics and simulate network behavior simultaneously	lack of realistic network accuracy and operating system level details

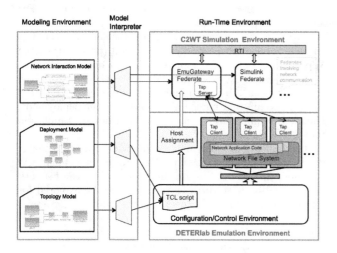

Figure 1: Overall Framework

The run-time environment integrates the Matlab/SimuLink simulation tool with the DETERlab platform. It provides time synchronization and data communication service and coordinates the execution of the security experiment across these two platforms. In our current design, the integrated system runs at the same pace as the physical clock time. A novel virtual-time-based time skew adjustment mechanism is presented to compensate the time shift between the simulation and the emulation environment. A detailed description of the design-time modeling framework and the run-time execution framework are presented in Section IV and Section V respectively.

4. MODELING ENVIRONMENT

In order to facilitate the rapid security experiment of CPS with minimal effort, we employ the model integrated computing (MIC) techniques [16]. In iSEE, we focus on the support for NCS systems and define meta-models for three domain-specific modeling languages (DSMLs), for modeling and evaluating the NCS. The DSMLs are: (1) NCS HLA Simulation Language; (2) Control Subsystem Modeling Language; (3) Networking Emulation Modeling Language. The NCS HLA simulation language in iSEE is an extension of the DSML used in the Command and Control WindTunnel system [15]. The C2WT DSML provides all of the modeling primitives required to specify the integration, deployment, and execution of a federated simulation based on HLA. The

Control subsystem modeling language in iSEE is based on the DSML used in the Networked Control System Wind-Tunnel system [11], which defines the modeling elements for describing the dynamic behavior of the system components of the NCS.

We enhance the meta-models of these two systems with the network emulation meta-models to model (1) the networking emulation configuration, (2) the relationship between the control system and the networking system, and (3) the interaction between the simulation and the emulation platforms. In particular, our extension includes three aspects: (1) Network Topology Model, which specifies network topology configuration; (2) Application Process Deployment and Communication Model, which specifies the application deployment and communication configuration; (3) Network Emulation Interaction Model, which specifies the major attributes of the information exchanged between simulation and emulation environments. The CPS experiment configuration can specify the communication semantics through network modeling, which can in turn customize the communication protocol between the simulation and emulation environment to achieve the best tradeoff between experiment realism and performance. We will illustrate the above three aspects in the following sections.

4.1 Network Topology Model

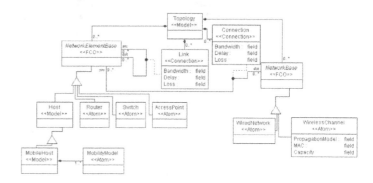

Figure 2: Network Topology Metamodel

The network topology model specifies the communication network topology. This model is particularly useful when DETERlab is used as the emulation platform. It will be used to generate the Tcl (Tool Command Language) script that configures the DETERlab network topology. If the experiment network is manually setup, this model will also provide a blueprint for the setup. The meta-model of the network topology is shown in Figure 2, which includes four types of objects:

(1) *NetworkElementBase*, which includes *Host* (end host), *Router*, and *Switch*.

(2) *Link*, which connects the *NetworkElementBase*. A link has three attributes: *Bandwidth*, *Delay* and *Loss*.

(3) *NetworkBase*, which models the network as a whole. For wired networks, the object *WiredNetwork* can be used to approximate a network whose topology is simplified.

(4) *Connection*, which connects the *NetworkBase* and *NetworkElementBase*. When connecting to a *WiredNetwork*, the *Connection* approximates a network path, where its bandwidth is the bottleneck of the path.

Figure 3 shows an example network topology model. In this example, there are two unmanned aerial vehicles (UAVs) communicating with a *ControlStation* through wired links.

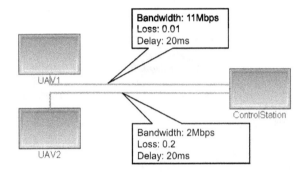

Figure 3: An example network topology model

4.2 Application Process Deployment and Communication Model

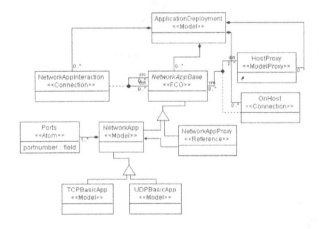

Figure 4: Application Deployment Metamodel

This model specifies the deployment of application processes on the emulation hosts and the transport-layer communication model that will be used. This model includes the following objects.

(1) *NetworkApp*, which models the network application process that is running on the emulation host. It has at least one port. The *TCPBasicApp* and *UDPBasicApp* can be prebuilt as two basic forms of network application processes to

facilitate network experiments (e.g., for background/attack traffic generation).

(2) *OnHost*, which models the deployment of a network application on an end host (i.e., *Host* in the topology model). Note the host defined in the network topology model is a virtual host. When DETERlab is used, the virtual host will be mapped to a real host where the IP address is assigned. In this case, the emulation gateway needs to keep track of the IP address and performs host mapping.

(3) *NetworkAppInteraction*, which models the communication connection between network applications. There are two types of communication models between application processes: connection-oriented and connectionless. TCP protocol is connection-oriented, while UDP protocol can work in both connection-oriented and connectionless manners. For connection-oriented communication, two application processes need to establish a connection. The information of the destination application process is predefined (prewired) in the Application Deployment model, so that it does not need to be carried in the Network Emulation model (detailed in the next subsection). In the connectionless model, the destination process information is unknown during the deployment. Thus it is required to be carried in the Network Emulation model.

The application deployment model will be used to generate Tcl files that initialize the DETERlab deployment. At run time, this model can also help to validate the network communication pattern (a feature that can be explored for security purpose in the future.). Figure 5 shows an example of application deployment model over the network as shown in Figure 3. In this example, there are two network applications. The UAVs will transfer images to the ControlStation using UDP in the connection-oriented mode; the ControlStation will send commands to the UAVs via TCP. For each UAV, there are two application processes *SendImage* and *RecvCommand* deployed. The ControlStation also has two application processes: *RecvImage* and *SendCommand* deployed.

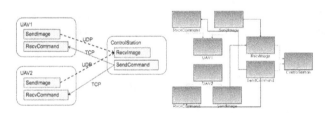

Figure 5: Application Deployment Model Example

4.3 Network Emulation Interaction Model

This model specifies how the network application processes in the CPS communicate through the network and, in particular, what information needs to be exchanged between the simulated elements and the real network applications through *EmuGateway* in the experiment. In our design, this function is enabled through *NetworkInteraction*, a special type of HLA Interaction.

As shown in Figure 6, each *NetworkInteraction* needs to have three attributes in order to be processed by the *EmuGateway*. These three parameters specify *NetworkInteraction* to be processed by which application (*ProcName*) lo-

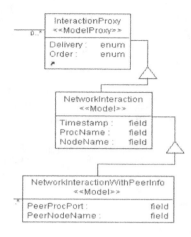

Figure 6: Network Interaction Metamodel

cated at which node (*NodeName*) and at what time (*Timestamp*).

(1) *Timestamp*, the time when this interaction should be processed by the network application process. Note that this is not the timestamp of the *NetworkInteraction* itself. The *NetworkInteraction* needs to be sent at an earlier time before this Timestamp through RTI for the sake of time synchronization.

(2) *ProcName*, the name of the network application process that will handle this *NetworkInteraction*. This name should be exactly the same as the process name used at the emulation host, as it will be passed directly by the *EmuGateway* to the *TapClient*.

(3) *NodeName*, the name of the node that hosts the network application process which handles this *NetworkInteraction*. Note that the deployment of the application process onto emulation hosts may not be known at the modeling time and the *EmuGateway* will convert this name to the real hostname/IP address at runtime.

Figure 7 shows an example of the Interaction Model for the network scenario outlined in Figure 3 and 5. In this example, the *UAVFederate* represents two simulated UAVs. The *UAVFederate* publishes NetworkInteraction *SendImageToNetwork*, which is subscribed by the *EmuGateway* federate. This interaction specifies UAV1 as the NodeName (the node which sends the image, could be other UAVs since UAV federate is responsible for multiple UAV simulations here) and *SendImage* as the ProcName (application process name). This NetworkInteraction has one parameter *ImageURL*, which is the information carried in this interaction. This implies that in this simulation experiment, only *ImageURL* is passed from the simulation environment to the emulation environment. The network application process *SendImage* needs to be responsible for retrieving the image data from this *ImageURL*. The *EmuGateway* federate publishes NetworkInteraction *RecvImageFromNetwork*, which is subscribed by the *ControlStation* federate. This interaction specifies *ControlStation* as the NodeName (the node which receives the image) and *RecvImage* as the ProcName. This NetworkInteraction has one Parameter *PacketDelay*. This shows that in this experiment, only packet delay will be sent from the network emulation environment to the simulation environment. In order for ControlStation to know

which node (UAV) is the sender, this NetworkInteraction also carries PeerNodeName (e.g., UAV1). For NetworkInteraction *SendCommandToNetwork* and *RecvCommandFromNetwork*, their parameter attribute carries *Command* as a string.

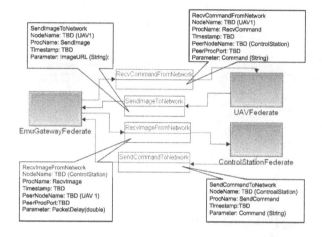

Figure 7: Example Network Interaction Model

This modeling framework is flexible to handle a variety of communication semantics. In the example shown in Figure 7, the UDP traffic resulting from the application process *SendImage* is triggered by the *SendImageToNetwork* interaction, which specifies the location of the image. Real image data will be communicated within the emulated/real network. This experiment setup allows us to evaluate the impact of data corruption (e.g., by malicious attacks) on the CPS performance. If the experiment is only interested in the transmission delay of the data (the traffic load it incurs), instead of its actual content, we can set up another interaction model with lower communication overhead between the simulation and the emulation environment. In this case, no real data is exchanged for image transfer applications. Instead, dummy data is sent with the specified sending rate and packet size to generate the appropriate traffic load. Using the *SendImageToNetwork* NetworkInteraction, the simulated UAVs (*UAVFederate*) notify the network application process *SendImage* about two parameters: *FrameInterval* and *FrameSize*.

5. RUN-TIME ENVIRONMENT

Figure 8 shows the run-time environment of iSEE. The run-time environment is built on High-Level Architecture (HLA) [10], which is a standard framework for distributed computer simulation systems. Based on this standard, communications between different simulation tools are managed by Run-Time Infrastructure (RTI), which provides a set of services such as time management and data distribution. To integrate the simulation and the emulation platforms, HLA-compliant reusable components are developed as the interface between the simulation tool, the emulation platform and RTI, so that the simulation and emulation platforms become federates of RTI. The time synchronization and data communication between the simulation and the emulation environments is the key challenge in the development of iSEE. In our current design, the emulation gateway federate will handle the data communication between the simulation environment and the DETERlab. RTI operates under the real-time mode to enforce the time advance of Matlab simulation to be at the same pace of the physical clock time.

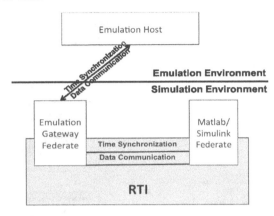

Figure 8: Run-Time components

Figure 9 shows the details of the run-time system. Here we use an example NCS system with a *Plant* (a UAV) and a *Controller*. The *Controller* sends control commands to *Plant* and the *Plant* replies with images it captures. Four networking instances are involved: *SendCommand*, *RecvCommand*, *SendImage*, and *RecvImage*.

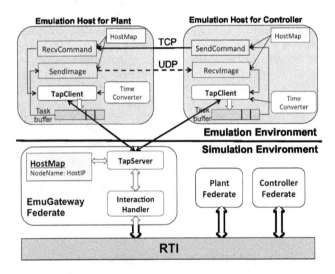

Figure 9: Implentation Architecture

5.1 System Initialization

When the integrated experiment starts, the *TapClient* will initialize the network application processes and register itself to the *TapServer* (the *TapClient* needs to know the address of the *TapServer* as *a priori*) by sending its address (real hostname or IP address), its virtual host name and its current OS time. Based on the above information, the *TapServer* will build its own *HostMap*, which keeps the mapping between the *NodeName* and the host IP addresses.

5.2 Time Synchronization

CPS simulation is required to be run in the real-time mode, which means that the simulation will run at the same pace as the physical clock. Let t_s denote the simulation time, t_e the emulation time, and t_r the real (physical) time.

We propose a novel time synchronization mechanism, where the simulation runs under a virtual time that is separated from real time, but still keeps close pace with real time. In particular, the operating system time is synchronized with real time ($t_e=t_r$), while the simulation time is separated from real time. Figure 10 illustrates our proposed scheme. Assume that the communication delay from simulation environment to emulation environment is δ_1 and δ_2 is the delay from emulation to simulation. Also assume the simulation environment has a lag of L from real time ($t_s=t_r-L$). Simulation clock advances at the same pace as the real physical clock. All outgoing traffic events with time stamp t from the simulation environment will be actually scheduled/tunneled to the emulation environment at simulation time $t-\delta_1-L$ to compensate the above lag so that it could arrive at the emulation host at real time t. For incoming traffic with timestamp $(t+\tau)$, it will arrive at the simulation environment at simulation time $t_s = t - L + \tau + \delta_2$. By making $L \geq \delta_2$, we can make sure that the event can be scheduled at time $t_s = t + \tau$.

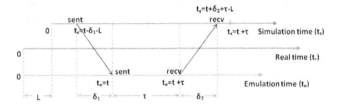

Figure 10: Time Convert Scheme

To implement this scheme, we have a time converter at each emulation host which converts the *timestamp* on each event. The time converter keeps the difference between the simulation time the emulation host OS time, which is initialized when the system starts. We use the following notations to illustrate the *timestamp* calculation:

Tos_client_start: the OS time (real time) when the *TapClient* registers itself to the *TapServer*.

Tos_server_start: the OS time at the *TapServer* when the client registration message is received.

Ts_start: the value of the simulation time when the client registration message is received.

The difference between the simulation time and the OS time at the *TapServer* is ($Tos\_server\_start - Ts\_start$). We assume that the system clocks of the emulation hosts and the simulation host are synchronized via Network Time Protocol. Thus, this difference ($Tos\_server\_start - Ts\_start$) is also the difference between the simulation time and the real time at the *TapClient*. At the *TapClient*, each incoming event with *timestamp* for scheduling will be converted from the simulation time to its emulation time with respect to the *TapClient* OS time according to the following relation.

$Timestamp\_emu = Timestamp + (Tos\_server\_start - Ts\_start) - L$.

For outgoing event, the converter will convert its *Timestamp_emu* with respect to the emulation time to the simulation time *Timestamp* as follows.

$$Timestamp = Timestamp\_emu - (Tos\_server\_start - Ts\_start) + L.$$

Here, L is the lag of the simulation time compared to the emulation time. As we have discussed earlier, L needs to be larger than δ_2, the delay from the *TapClient* to the *TapServer*, which can be calculated as $\delta_2 = Tos\_server\_start - Tos\_client\_start$. In our experiments, the value of δ_2 is around 30ms, and we use $L = k\delta_2$ ($k = 2$) considering the delay variation.

5.3 Data Communication

In the simulation environment, RTI handles the data communication, where the simulation federates and emulation gateways communicate with each other using publish/subscribe technology. The communication between the emulation gateways and the emulation environment is implemented via TCP connections to the control interfaces of the DETERlab nodes to avoid the interference to the data communication. In the DETERlab, the data communication are emulated between the data interfaces of the DETERlab nodes. In the example shown, for the traffic from *Plant* to *Controller*, the experiment data path is *Plant→EmuGateway→Plant Emulation Host→Controller Emulation Host→EmuGateway→Controller*. This routing path is reversed when the *Controller* sends traffic to the *Plant*.

6. EXPERIMENT

We design several experiments to evaluate iSEE system design and implementation. The CPS system used in the experiment is composed of an unmanned aerial vehicle (UAV), which is controlled over a network using a digital controller. The networked digital controller is designed to enable the UAV to track a desired reference trajectory. In these experiments, the simulation model *Controller* sends out reference signals, and the *Plant* will follow these signals. We record the signals received at the *Plant* side to evaluate the control performance.

6.1 Setup

Figure 11 shows the system topology and the related Tcl file. The *PlantEmuHost* represents the *Plant* emulation host, and *ControllerEmuHost* is *Controller* emulation host. All simulation environment, including RTI, Matlab federates, and *EmuGateway* federate are deployed in host named *EmuGatewayHost*.

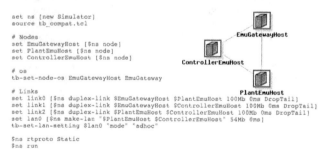

Figure 11: Topology and Tcl file

6.2 Accuracy

In this experiment, we demonstrate the accuracy of iSEE experiments. In particular, we use the NCSWT [11] system as a benchmark. The NCSWT system is an integrated simulation platform for networked control system experiment, which uses ns-2 as the network simulator and Matlab as the control system simulator. The experiment is designed to compare the result produced by iSEE with the result produced by NCSWT.

In this experiment, the sampling period of the controller signal is 0.1 seconds. The network bandwidth is 100MB with no packet loss. Figure 12 plots the UAV positions as well as the reference trajectory. We can see from the figures that the experiment results produced from iSEE - the integrated Matlab and DETERLab environment are exactly the same as the results produced from NCSWT - the integrated Matlab and ns-2 environment.

6.3 Impact of Security Attacks

Now we demonstrate the usage of iSEE in evaluating the impact of security attacks. In this experiment, attack traffic is generated in the DETERlab to disrupt the communication between the UAV and the controller. The packet loss rate varies from 10% to 30%, and the results are shown in Figure 13. We can observe from the figure that as the loss rate increases, the UAV trajectory strays further from the reference trajectories.

7. CONCLUSION

The design and analysis of CPS is a critical task due to its distributed architectures and expanded mission capability. Network emulation environment can help realistically analyze the impact of network phenomena on the overall system performance. By integrating emulation environment with the simulation environment, we present iSEE, an integrated platform to evaluate CPS with greater realism in the network experiments. We present a case study using iSEE to evaluate our system performance. The results show that iSEE is capable of modeling and evaluating CPS accurately and performing security experiments. Currently, iSEE design only supports real-time experiment execution. In the future, we will enhance it with the support for fully virtualized time execution.

8. ACKNOWLEDGMENTS

We would like to thank Himanshu Neema, Gabor Karsai for helpful inputs and discussions on this work and anonymous reviewers for their feedback to improve the readability of the paper. This research is supported in part by the U.S. Army Research Office (ARO W911NF-10-1-0005), Lockheed Martin, NSF TRUST Science and Technology Center (CCF-0424422), NSF Grant OCI-1127396, the Air Force Research Lab Visiting Faculty Research Program and the Air Force Research lab Summer Faculty Extension Grant. The views and conclusions contained in this document are those of the authors and should not be interpreted as representing the official policies, either expressed or implied, of the U.S. Government.

9. REFERENCES

[1] Deter seer. http://seer.deterlab.net/.
[2] Deterlab. http://isi.deterlab.net/.
[3] Matlab. http://www.mathworks.com.
[4] Modelica and modelica association. http://www.modelica.org.

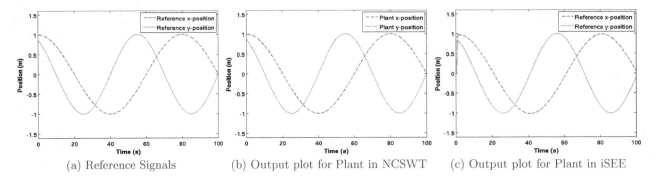

(a) Reference Signals   (b) Output plot for Plant in NCSWT   (c) Output plot for Plant in iSEE

Figure 12: Output plots for reference, and plants in NCSWT and iSEE

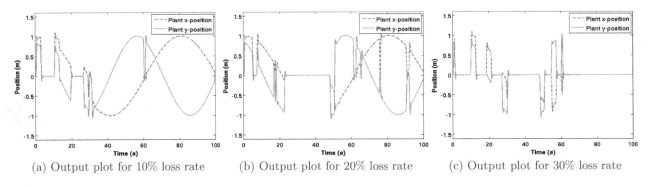

(a) Output plot for 10% loss rate   (b) Output plot for 20% loss rate   (c) Output plot for 30% loss rate

Figure 13: Plots of UAV trajectory for packet loss rates

[5] The network simulator ns-2. http://isi.edu.nsnam/ns.

[6] Omnet++. http://www.omnetpp.org.

[7] The ptolemy project.
http://ptolemy.eecs.berkeley.edu.

[8] A. T. Al-Hammouri, M. S. Branicky, and V. Liberatore. Co-simulation tools for networked control systems. In *Proceedings of the 11th international workshop on Hybrid Systems: Computation and Control*, HSCC '08, pages 16–29, Berlin, Heidelberg, 2008. Springer-Verlag.

[9] A. Cervin, M. Ohlin, and D. Henriksson. Simulation of networked control systems using truetime. In *Proceedings of the 3rd International Workshop on Networked Control Systems: Tolerant to Faults*, Nancy, France, 2007.

[10] J. S. Dahmann, R. M. Fujimoto, and R. M. Weatherly. The department of defense high level architecture. In *Proceedings of the 29th conference on Winter simulation*, WSC '97, pages 142–149, Washington, DC, USA, 1997. IEEE Computer Society.

[11] E. Eyisi, J. Bai, D. Riley, J. Weng, W. Yan, Y. Xue, X. Koutsoukos, and J. Sztipanovits. Ncswt: An integrated modeling and simulation tool for networked control systems. Technical report, Institute for Software and Integrated Systems, Vanderbilt University, 2011.

[12] M. Hasan, H. Yu, A. Carrington, and T. Yang. Co-simulation of wireless networked control systems over mobile ad hoc network using simulink and opnet. *Communications, IET*, 3(8):1297 –1310, august 2009.

[13] U. Hatnik and S. Altmann. Using modelsim, matlab/simulink and ns for simulation of distributed systems. In *Parallel Computing in Electrical Engineering, 2004. PARELEC 2004. International Conference on*, pages 114 – 119, sept. 2004.

[14] O. Heimlich, R. Sailer, and L. Budzisz. Nmlab: A co-simulation framework for matlab and ns-2. In *Proceedings of the 2010 Second International Conference on Advances in System Simulation*, SIMUL '10, pages 152–157, Washington, DC, USA, 2010. IEEE Computer Society.

[15] G. Hemingway, H. Neema, H. Nine, J. Sztipanovits, and G. Karsai. Rapid synthesis of high-level architecture-based heterogeneous simulation: a model-based integration approach. In *Simulation*, volume 88, March 2012.

[16] G. Karsai, J. Sztipanovits, A. Ledeczi, and T. Bapty. Model-integrated development of embedded software. *Proceedings of the IEEE*, 91(1):145 – 164, jan 2003.

[17] T. Kohtamaki, M. Pohjola, J. Brand, and L. Eriksson. Piccsim toolchain - design, simulation and automatic implementation of wireless networked control systems. In *Networking, Sensing and Control, 2009. ICNSC '09. International Conference on*, pages 49 –54, march 2009.

Author Index

Amin, Saurabh 73

Başar, Tamer 41

Busch, Timothy 81

Bushnell, Linda 31

Butler-Purry, Karen 21

Chang, Jian 11

Clark, Andrew 31

Enyioha, Chinwendu 11

Hussain, Alefiya 73

Johansson, Karl H. 55, 65

Kar, Soummya 65

Koutsoukos, Xenofon 1

Kundur, Deepa 21

LeBlanc, Heath J. 1

Lee, Insup 11

Li, Xiaowei 81

Liu, Shan 21

Mo, Yilin 47

Pappas, George J. 11

Pérez, Daniel 55

Poovendran, Radha 31

Sandberg, Henrik 55

Sinopoli, Bruno 47

Sundaram, Shreyas 1

Sundaram, Shreyas 11

Sztipanovits, Janos 81

Teixeira, André 55

Venkatasubramanian, Krishna K. ... 11

Weimer, James 65

Weng, Jiannian 81

Xue, Yuan 81

Yan, Wei 81

Zhang, Haotian 1

Zhu, Quanyan 41

Zourntos, Takis 21

www.ingramcontent.com/pod-product-compliance
Lightning Source LLC
Chambersburg PA
CBHW082111070326
40689CB00052B/4532

9781450312639